With ex[illegible] forecasts, you can chart a course to romance, adventure, good health, or career opportunities while gaining valuable insight into yourself and others. Offering a daily outlook for 18 full months, this fascinating guide shows you:

- The important dates in your life
- What to expect from an astrological reading
- How the stars can help you stay healthy and fit

  And more!

Let this sound advice guide you through a year of heavenly possibilities—for today and for every day of 2008!

SYDNEY OMARR'S® DAY-BY-DAY ASTROLOGICAL GUIDE FOR

ARIES—March 21–April 19
TAURUS—April 20–May 20
GEMINI—May 21–June 20
CANCER—June 21–July 22
LEO—July 23–August 22
VIRGO—August 23–September 22
LIBRA—September 23–October 22
SCORPIO—October 23–November 21
SAGITTARIUS—November 22–December 21
CAPRICORN—December 22–January 19
AQUARIUS—January 20–February 18
PISCES—February 19–March 20

IN 2008

SYDNEY OMARR'S®

DAY-BY-DAY ASTROLOGICAL GUIDE FOR

ARIES

MARCH 21–APRIL 19

2008

By Trish MacGregor
with Carol Tonsing

A SIGNET BOOK

SIGNET
Published by New American Library, a division of
Penguin Group (USA) Inc., 375 Hudson Street,
New York, New York 10014, USA
Penguin Group (Canada), 90 Eglinton Avenue East, Suite 700, Toronto,
Ontario M4P 2Y3, Canada (a division of Pearson Penguin Canada Inc.)
Penguin Books Ltd., 80 Strand, London WC2R 0RL, England
Penguin Ireland, 25 St. Stephen's Green, Dublin 2,
Ireland (a division of Penguin Books Ltd.)
Penguin Group (Australia), 250 Camberwell Road, Camberwell, Victoria 3124,
Australia (a division of Pearson Australia Group Pty. Ltd.)
Penguin Books India Pvt. Ltd., 11 Community Centre, Panchsheel Park,
New Delhi - 110 017, India
Penguin Group (NZ), 67 Apollo Drive, Rosedale, North Shore,
Auckland 1311, New Zealand (a division of Pearson New Zealand Ltd.)
Penguin Books (South Africa) (Pty.) Ltd., 24 Sturdee Avenue,
Rosebank, Johannesburg 2196, South Africa

Penguin Books Ltd., Registered Offices:
80 Strand, London WC2R 0RL, England

First published by Signet, an imprint of New American Library,
a division of Penguin Group (USA) Inc.

First Printing, June 2007
10 9 8 7 6 5 4 3 2 1

CONTENTS

INTRODUCTION

Put Astrology in Your Life

This year marks a time of transition as our personal universe opens up with possibilities we never imagined. Thanks to the Internet, we have a command-control center from which we can travel the globe at warp speed. We can meet friends and lovers in cyberspace, gather information from remote sources in moments, and manage the details of our daily lives online. But, as the saying goes, the more things change, the more they stay the same. In our personal lives, we are still searching for the same things that have always made life worth living: love, meaningful work, and fulfilling personal relationships.

Astrology is an age-old tool that can guide us in our search, one that works as well today as it has for several millennia. It can be a support system, career coach, and guide through difficult times. It can help you find your own strengths or assess your marketable talents to land the perfect job. Like links in the Internet, astrological clues can speed you from where you are now to where you'd like to be. But just like many of the newest high-tech laptops, there's a learning curve before you can use it to best advantage. It will take some practice and familiarity to operate effectively in your life. Fortunately a little knowledge can get you up and running quickly.

In this year's guide, we give you basic information to help you get hands-on with astrology. We tell you what you need to know about your sun sign and how to decipher the mysterious symbols on a horoscope chart. Then you can look up other planets in your horoscope to find out how each contributes to your total personality.

Many readers are fascinated by astrology's insights into

relationships. This leap year, find out who you're most likely to get along with and why, then how to attract the right sign. You'll see the celebrity combinations with your sign that made romantic history—and some that didn't.

Whether it's wealth-building advice, fashion tips, or help finding the perfect gift for a hard-to-please relative, astrology has something to say. Astrology can even guide you to the best place to take your vacation. For those who like to surf the Web, we recommend astrology-savvy sites where you can get your chart calculated free. Connecting with other astrology fans is a breeze with the reputable conferences, clubs, and even an accredited college that we list.

There are so many ways to put astrology into your life. Redecorating your home? Follow your sun sign's colors and styles to create the perfect environment. Share your birthday with a celebrity. Design a fitness program according to your sign's preferences.

So here are the year's picks and predictions, along with eighteen months of on-target daily horoscopes to make 2008 your best year ever.

CHAPTER 1

It's A Year of Change: What This Means for You

Astrologers judge the trends of a year by following the slow-moving planets, from Jupiter through Pluto. A change in sign indicates a new cycle, with new emphasis. The farthest planets (Uranus, Neptune, and Pluto), which stay in a sign for at least seven years, cause a very significant change in the atmosphere when they change signs. Shifts in Jupiter, which changes every year, and Saturn, which changes every two years, are more obvious in current events and daily lives. Jupiter generally brings a fortunate, expansive emphasis to its new sign, while Saturn's two-year cycle is a reality check, bringing tests of maturity, discipline, and responsibility.

Does Pluto Still Count?

At this writing, astronomers have demoted tiny Pluto from being a full-fledged planet to a dwarf planet, outranked by its celestial siblings. However, astrologers have been tracking its influence since Pluto was discovered in 1930 and have witnessed that this minuscule celestial body has a powerful effect on both a personal and a global level. So Pluto, which moves into the sign of Capricorn this year, will still be called a planet by astrologers and will be given just as much importance as before.

Capricorn Is the Sign to Watch

This year, we will be moving from a fire-sign emphasis to an earth-sign emphasis as Jupiter, Saturn, and Pluto all take up residence in earth signs. Until January 2008, Pluto had been emphasizing everything associated with Sagittarius to prepare us philosphically and spiriturally for things to come. Perhaps the most pervasive sign of Pluto in Sagittarius over the past few years has been globalization in all its forms, re-forming boundaries, creating new forms of travel, interacting with exotic cultures and religions as never before.

As it passed through truth-telling Sagittarius, Pluto shifted our emphasis away from acquiring wealth to a quest for the meaning of it all, as upward strivers discover that money and power are not enough and religious extremists assert themselves. We search the cosmos for something to believe in when many lies and scandals are exposed to public view, exposing leaders in the corporate, political, and religious domains. When ideals and idols are shattered, it becomes time to reevaluate our goals and ask ourselves what is really important in our lives.

Sagittarius is the sign of linking everything together; therefore, the trend has been to find ways to interconnect on spiritual, philosophical, and intellectual levels. The spiritual emphasis of Pluto in Sagittarius has filtered down to our home lives, as religion—and religious controversy—has entered local communities. Vast church complexes are being built to combine religious activities with sports centers, health clubs, malls, and theme parks. Religious education and book publishing have expanded as well.

Sagittarius is known for love of animals, especially horses. It's no surprise that horse racing has become popular again and that America has never been more pet happy. Look for extremes related to animal welfare, such as vegetarianism as a lifestyle. As habitats are destroyed, the care, feeding, and control of wild animals will become a larger issue, especially when deer, bears, and coyotes invade our backyard.

The Sagittarius love of the outdoors combined with

Pluto's power has already promoted extreme sports, especially those that require strong legs, like rock climbing, trekking, or snowboarding. Expect the trend toward more adventurous travel to continue, as well as fitness or sports-oriented vacations. Exotic hiking trips to unexplored territories, mountain-climbing expeditions, spa vacations, and sports-associated resorts are part of this trend.

Publishing, which is associated with Sagittarius, has been transformed by global conglomerates and the Internet. It is fascinating that the online bookstore Amazon.com took the Sagittarius-influenced name of the fierce female tribe of archer warriors.

Capricorn Brings Us Down to Earth

This year, both Pluto and Jupiter will meet in Capricorn, which marks a major shift in emphasis to Capricorn-related themes. Until 2024, Pluto will exert its influence in this practical, building, healing earth sign. Capricorn relates to structures, institutions, order, mountains and mountain countries, mineral rights, and issues involving the elderly and growing older—all of which will be emphasized in the coming years. It is the sign of established order, corporations, big business—all of which will be accented. Possibly, it will fall to business structures to create a new sense of order in the world.

Starting this year, you should feel the rumblings of change in the Capricorn area of your horoscope and in the world at large. The last time Pluto was in Capricorn was the years up to and during the American Revolutionary War. Therefore this should be an important time on the United States political scene, as well as a reflection of the aging and maturing of American society in general. Both the rise and fall of the Ottoman Empire happened under Pluto in Capricorn.

Jupiter in Capricorn

During the year that Jupiter remains in a sign, the fields associated with that sign are the ones that arouse excitement and enthusiasm, usually providing excellent opportunities for expansion, fame, and fortune.

One place we notice the Jupiter influence is in fashion, which should veer away from the flamboyance and sexuality of recent years to a more conservative look. Capricorn is concerned with quality, status, and prestige, and should elevate our collective taste level.

Those born under Capricorn should have many opportunities during the year. However, the key is to keep your feet on the ground. The flip side of Jupiter is that there are no limits. You can expand off the planet under a Jupiter transit, which is why the planet is often called the Gateway to Heaven. If something is going to burst (such as an artery) or overextend or go over the top in some way, it could happen under a supposedly lucky Jupiter transit. So beware.

Those born under Cancer may find their best opportunities working with partners this year, as Jupiter will be transiting their seventh house of relationships.

Saturn in Virgo: The Maturing of the Baby Boomers, Reforms in Care and Maintenance

Saturn, the planet of limitation, testing, and restriction, is now transiting Virgo. This is a time when Virgo issues—health care and maintenance and moral standards and controls—will come to the fore. For the next two years, we will be adjusting the structures of our lives, making changes so that we can function at an optimal efficient level. We'll be challenged with a reality check in areas where we have been too optimistic or expansive.

Continuing Trends

Uranus and Neptune continue to do a kind of astrological dance called a mutual reception. This is a supportive relationship where Uranus is in Pisces, the sign ruled by Neptune, while Neptune is in Aquarius, the sign ruled by Uranus. When this dance is over in 2011, it is likely that we will be living under very different political and social circumstances.

Uranus in Pisces

Uranus, known as the Great Awakener, tends to cause both upheaval and innovation in the sign it transits. During previous episodes of Uranus in Pisces, great religions and spiritual movements have come into being, most recently Mormonism and Christian Fundamentalism. In its most positive mode, Pisces promotes imagination and creativity, the art of illusion in theater and film, the inspiration of great artists. A water sign, Pisces is naturally associated with all things liquid—oceans, oil, alcohol—and with those creatures that live in the water—fish, the fishing industry, fish habitats, and fish farming. Currently there is a great debate going on about overfishing, contamination of fish, and fish farming. The underdog, the enslaved, and the disenfranchised should also benefit from Uranus in Pisces.

Since Uranus is a disruptive influence that aims to challenge the status quo, the forces of nature that manifest will most likely be in the Pisces area: oceans, seas, and rivers. We have seen unprecedented rainy seasons, floods, mud slides, and disastrous hurricanes. Note that 2005's devastating Hurricane Katrina hit an area known for both the oil and fishing industries.

Pisces is associated with the prenatal phase of life, which is related to regenerative medicine. The controversy over embryonic stem cell research should continue to be debated. Petroleum issues, both in the oil-producing countries and offshore oil drilling, will come to a head. Uranus in

Pisces suggests that development of new hydroelectric sources may provide the power we need to continue our current power-thirsty lifestyle.

As in previous eras, there should continue to be a flourishing of the arts. We are seeing many new artistic forms developing now, such as computer-created actors and special effects. The sky's the limit on this influence.

Those who have problems with Uranus are those who resist change, so the key is to embrace the future.

Neptune in Aquarius

Neptune is a planet of imagination and creativity, but also of deception and illusion. Neptune is associated with hospitals, which have been the subject of much controversy. On the positive side, hospitals are acquiring cutting-edge technology. The atmosphere of many hospitals is already changing from the intimidating and sterile environment of the past to that of a health-promoting spa. Alternative therapies, such as massage, diet counseling, and aromatherapy, are becoming commonplace, which expresses this Neptune trend. New procedures in plastic surgery, also a Neptune glamour field, and anti-aging therapies are restoring the illusion of youth.

However, issues involving the expense and quality of health care and the evolving relationship between doctors, drug companies, and HMOs reflect a darker side of this trend.

What About the New Planets?

Our solar system is very crowded; astronomers continue to discover new objects circling the sun. In addition to the familiar planets, there are dwarf planets, comets, cometoids, asteroids, and strange icy bodies in the Kuiper Belt beyond Neptune. The newest object at this writing is a planetlike orb slightly larger than Pluto, discovered in 2005, which was tentatively named Xena, after the TV series heroine. Recently this dwarf planet was christened with a permanent name by its dicoverer, Dr. Michael E. Brown of the California Institute of Technology. He dubbed the new planet Eris, after a goddess of discord and strife. In mythology, Eris was a troublemaker who made men think their opinions were right and others wrong. What an appropriate name for a planet discovered during a time of discord in the Middle East and elsewhere! Eris has a companion moon named Dysnomia for her daughter, described as a demon spirit of lawlessness. With mythological associations like these, we wonder what the effect of this mother-daughter duo will be. Once Eris's orbit is established, astrologers will track the impact of this planet on our horoscopes. Eris takes about 560 years to orbit the sun, which means its emphasis in a given astrological sign will affect several generations.

CHAPTER 2

Put Time on Your Side

"Do not squander time, for that is the stuff that life is made of," said Benjamin Franklin, our practical Founding Father. Yet many times your best-laid plans run amuck, your schedule is upset by sudden events, or your projects stall. On the other hand, there are days when projects get done effortlessly, people respond to you favorably, and perhaps you have some extra sex appeal.

Astrology offers many explanations why this might happen. For instance, when mischievous Mercury creates havoc with communications, it's time to back up your vital computer files, read between the lines of contracts, and be extra patient with coworkers. When Venus passes through your sign you've got extra sex appeal, time to try a knockout new outfit or hairstyle, and the nerve to ask someone you'd like to know better to dinner. Venus timing can also help you charm clients with a stunning sales pitch or make an offer they won't refuse.

In this chapter, you will learn how to manage your time by working with natural astrological cycles. You can find your best times to do specific projects as well as which times to avoid them. You will also learn how to read the moods of the moon and make them work for you. Use the information in this chapter and the planet tables in this book and also use the moon sign listings in your daily forecasts.

Here are the happenings to note on your agenda:

- Dates of your sun sign (high-energy period)
- The month previous to your sun sign (low-energy period)

- Dates of planets in your sign this year
- Full and new moons (Pay special attention when these fall in your sun sign!)
- Eclipses
- Moon in your sun sign every month, as well as moon in the opposite sign (listed in daily forecast)
- Mercury retrogrades
- Other retrograde periods

Your High-Power Time

Every birthday starts off a new cycle of solar energy for you. You should feel a new surge of vitality as the powerful sun enters your sign. This is the time when predominant energies are most favorable to you. So go for it! Start new projects, make your big moves (especially when the new moon is in your sign, doubling your charisma). You'll get the recognition you deserve now, when everyone is attuned to your sun sign. Look in the tables in this book to see if other planets will also be passing through your sun sign at this time. Venus (love, beauty), Mars (energy, drive), and Mercury (communication, mental sharpness) reinforce the sun and give an extra boost to your life in the areas they affect. Venus will rev up your social and love life, making you seem especially attractive. Mars amplifies your energy and drive. Mercury fuels your brainpower and helps you communicate. Jupiter signals an especially lucky period of expansion.

There are two downtimes related to the sun. During the month before your birthday period, when you are winding up your annual cycle, you could be feeling especially vulnerable and depleted. So at that time get extra rest, watch your diet, and take it easy. Don't overstress yourself. Use this time to gear up for a big "push" when the sun enters your sign.

Another downtime is when the sun is in a sign opposite your sun sign (six months from your birthday). That's when the prevailing energies are very different from yours. You may feel at odds with the world. You'll have to work harder for recognition because people are not on your wavelength. However, this could be a good time to work on a team, in cooperation with others, or behind the scenes.

Plan Your Day with the Moon

The moon is a powerful tool to divine the mood of the moment. You can work with the moon in two ways. Plan by the *sign* the moon is in; plan by the *phase* of the moon. The sign will tell you the kind of activities that suit the moon's mood. The phase will tell you the best time to start or finish a certain activity.

Working with the phases of the moon is as easy as looking up at the night sky. During the new moon, when both the sun and moon are in the same sign, begin new ventures—especially activities that are favored by that sign. Then you'll utilize the powerful energies pulling you in the same direction. You'll be focused outward, toward action, and in a doing mode. Postpone breaking off, terminating, deliberating, or reflecting—activities that require introspection and passive work. These are better suited to a later moon phase.

Get your project under way during the first quarter. Then go public at the full moon, a time of high intensity, when feelings come out into the open. This is your time to shine—to express yourself. Be aware, however, that because pressures are being released, other people will also be letting off steam. Since confrontations are possible, take advantage of this time either to air grievances or to avoid arguments.

About three days after the full moon comes the disseminating phase, a time when the energy of the cycle begins to wind down. From the last quarter of the moon to the next new moon, it's a time to cut off unproductive relationships, do serious thinking, and focus on inward-directed activities.

You'll feel some new and full moons more strongly than others, especially those new moons that fall in your sun sign and full moons in your opposite sign. Because that full moon happens at your low-energy time of year, it is likely to be an especially stressful time in a relationship, when any hidden problems or unexpressed emotions could surface.

Full and New Moons in 2008

All dates are calculated for eastern standard time and eastern daylight time.

New Moon—January 8 in Capricorn
Full Moon—January 22 in Leo

New Moon—February 6 in Aquarius (solar eclipse)
Full Moon—February 20 in Virgo (lunar eclipse)

New Moon—March 7 in Pisces
Full Moon—March 21 in Libra

New Moon—April 5 in Aries
Full Moon—April 20 in Scorpio

New Moon—May 5 in Taurus
Full Moon—May 19 in Scorpio (second full moon in Scorpio)

New Moon—June 3 in Gemini
Full Moon—June 18 in Sagittarius

New Moon—July 2 in Cancer
Full Moon—July 18 in Capricorn

New Moon—August 1 in Leo (solar eclipse)
Full Moon—August 16 in Aquarius (lunar eclipse)
New Moon—August 30 in Virgo

Full Moon—September 15 in Pisces
New Moon—September 29 in Libra

Full Moon—October 14 in Aries

New Moon—October 28 in Scorpio

Full Moon—November 13 in Taurus
New Moon—November 27 in Sagittarius

New Moon—December 12 in Gemini
Full Moon—December 27 in Capricorn

How to Schedule Activities by the Moon Sign

To forecast the daily emotional "weather," to determine your monthly high and low days, or to synchronize your activities with the cycles of the moon, take note of the moon sign under your daily forecast at the end of the book. Here are some of the activities favored and the moods you are likely to encounter under each moon sign.

Moon in Aries: Get Moving!

The new moon in Aries is an ideal time to start new projects. Everyone is pushy, raring to go, rather impatient, and short-tempered. Leave details and follow-up for later. Competitive sports or martial arts are great ways to let off steam. Quiet types could use some assertiveness, but it's a great day for dynamos. Be careful not to step on too many toes.

Moon in Taurus: Lay the Foundations for Success

Do solid, methodical tasks like follow-through or backup work. Make investments, buy real estate, do appraisals, do some hard bargaining. Attend to your property. Get out in the country or spend some time in your garden. Enjoy creature comforts, music, a good dinner, sensual lovemaking. Forget starting a diet—this is a day when you'll feel self-indulgent.

Moon in Gemini: Communicate

Talk means action today. Telephone, write letters, fax! Make new contacts, stay in touch with steady customers. You can juggle lots of tasks today. It's a great time for mental activity of any kind. Don't try to pin people down—they, too, are feeling restless. Keep it light. Flirtations and socializing are good. Watch gossip—and don't give away secrets.

Moon in Cancer: Pay Attention to Loved Ones

This is a moody, sensitive, emotional time. People respond to personal attention, to mothering. Stay at home, have a family dinner, call your mother. Nostalgia, memories, and psychic powers are heightened. You'll want to hang on to people and things (don't clean out your closets now). You could have shrewd insights into what others really need and want. Pay attention to dreams, intuition, and gut reactions.

Moon in Leo: Be Confident

Everybody is in a much more confident, warm, generous mood. It's a good day to ask for a raise, show what you can do, dress like a star. People will respond to flattery, enjoy a bit of drama and theater. You may be extravagant, treat yourself royally, and show off a bit—but don't break the bank! Be careful you don't promise more than you can deliver.

Moon in Virgo: Be Practical

Do practical down-to-earth chores. Review your budget, make repairs, be an efficiency expert. Not a day to ask for a raise. Tend to personal care and maintenance. Have a health checkup, go on a diet, buy vitamins or health food. Make your home spotless. Take care of details and piled-up chores. Reorganize your work and life so they run more smoothly and efficiently. Save money. Be prepared for others to be in a critical, faultfinding mood.

Moon in Libra: Be Diplomatic

Attend to legal matters. Negotiate contracts. Arbitrate. Do things with your favorite partner. Socialize. Be romantic. Buy a special gift, a beautiful object. Decorate yourself or your surroundings. Buy new clothes. Throw a party. Have an elegant, romantic evening. Smooth over any ruffled feathers. Avoid confrontations. Stick to civilized discussions.

Moon in Scorpio: Solve Problems

This is a day to do things with passion. You'll have excellent concentration and focus. Try not to get too intense emotionally. Avoid sharp exchanges with loved ones. Others may tend to go to extremes, get jealous, overreact. Great for troubleshooting, problem solving, research, scientific work—and making love. Pay attention to those psychic vibes.

Moon in Sagittarius: Sell and Motivate

A great time for travel, philosophical discussions, setting long-range career goals. Work out, do sports, buy athletic equipment. Others will be feeling upbeat, exuberant, and adventurous. Risk taking is favored. You may feel like taking a gamble, betting on the horses, visiting a local casino, buying a lottery ticket. Teaching, writing, and spiritual activities also get the green light. Relax outdoors. Take care of animals.

Moon in Capricorn: Get Organized

You can accomplish a lot now, so get on the ball! Attend to business. Issues concerning your basic responsibilities, duties, family, and elderly parents could crop up. You'll be expected to deliver on promises. Weed out the deadwood from your life. Get a dental checkup. Not a good day for gambling or taking risks.

Moon in Aquarius: Join the Group

A great day for doing things with groups—clubs, meetings, outings, politics, parties. Campaign for your candidate. Work for a worthy cause. Deal with larger issues that affect humanity—the environment and metaphysical questions. Buy a computer or electronic gadget. Watch TV. Wear something outrageous. Try something you've never done before. Present an original idea. Don't stick to a rigid schedule—go with the flow. Take a class in meditation, mind control, yoga.

Moon in Pisces: Be Creative

This can be a very creative day, so let your imagination work overtime. Film, theater, music, ballet could inspire you. Spend some time alone, resting and reflecting, reading or writing poetry. Daydreams can also be profitable. Help those less fortunate. Lend a listening ear to someone who may be feeling blue. Don't overindulge in self-pity or escapism, however. People are especially vulnerable to substance abuse now. Turn your thoughts to romance and someone special.

Retrogrades: When the Planets Seem to Backstep

All the planets, except for the sun and moon, have times when they appear to move backward—or retrograde—as it seems from our point of view on earth. At these times, planets do not work as they normally do. So it's best to "take a break" from that planet's energies in our life and to do some work on an inner level.

Mercury Retrograde: The Key Is in "Re"

Mercury goes retrograde most often, and its effects can be especially irritating. When it reaches a short distance ahead of the sun several times a year, it seems to move backward from our point of view. Astrologers often compare retrograde motion to the optical illusion that occurs when we ride on a train that passes another train traveling at a different speed—the second train appears to be moving in reverse.

What this means to you is that the Mercury-ruled areas of your life—analytical thought processes, communications, scheduling—are subject to all kinds of confusion. Be prepared. Communications equipment can break down. Schedules may be changed on short notice. People are late for appointments or don't show up at all. Traffic is terrible. Major purchases malfunction, don't work out, or get delivered in the wrong color. Letters don't arrive or are delivered to the wrong address. Employees will make errors that have to be corrected later. Contracts don't work out or must be renegotiated.

Since most of us can't put our lives on "hold" during Mercury retrogrades, we should learn to tame the trickster and make it work for us. The key is in the prefix *re-*. This is the time to go back over things in your life, *re*flect on what you've done during the previous months. Now you can get deeper insights, spot errors you've missed. So take time to *re*view and *re*evaluate what has happened. *Re*st and *re*ward yourself—it's a good time to take a vacation, especially if you *re*visit a favorite place. *Re*organize your work and finish up projects that are backed up. Clean out your desk and closets. Throw away what you can't *re*cycle. If you must sign contracts or agreements, do so with a contingency clause that lets you *re*evaluate the terms later.

Postpone major purchases or commitments for the time being. Don't get married (unless you're *re*marrying the same person). Try not to *re*ly on other people keeping appointments, contracts, or agreements to the letter; have several alternatives. Double-check and *re*ad between the lines.

Don't buy anything connected with communications or transportation (if you must, be sure to cover yourself).

Mercury retrograding through your sun sign will intensify its effect on your life.

If Mercury was retrograde when you were born, you may be one of the lucky people who don't suffer the frustrations of this period. If so, your mind probably works in a very intuitive, insightful way.

The sign in which Mercury is retrograding can give you an idea of what's in store—as well as the sun signs that will be especially challenged.

Mercury Retrogrades in 2008

Mercury has three retrograde periods, which fall in the air signs (Aquarius, Gemini, Libra) this year. This means it will be especially important to watch all activities which involve mental processes and communication.

January 28 to February 18 in Aquarius
May 26 to June 19 in Gemini
September 24 to October 15 in Libra

Venus Retrograde: Relationships Move Backward

Retrograding Venus can cause your relationships to take a backward step, or it can make you extravagant and impractical. Shopping till you drop and buying what you cannot afford are problems at this time. It's *not* a good time to redecorate—you'll hate the color of the walls later. Postpone getting a new hairstyle. Try not to fall in love either. But if you wish to make amends in an already troubled relationship, make peaceful overtures at this time.

Venus Retrogrades in 2008

There are no Venus retrograde periods in 2008.

Use the Go Power of Mars

Mars shows how and when to get where you want to go. Timing your moves with Mars on your side can give you a big push. On the other hand, pushing Mars the wrong way can guarantee that you'll run into frustrations in every corner. Your best times to forge ahead are during the weeks when Mars is traveling through your sun sign or your Mars sign (look these up in the tables in this book). Also consider times when Mars is in a compatible sign (fire with air signs, or earth with water signs). You'll be sure to have planetary power on your side.

Mars Retrogrades in 2008

Mars is retrograde in Gemini until January 30, 2008.

When Other Planets Retrograde

The slower-moving planets stay retrograde for months at a time (Jupiter, Saturn, Neptune, Uranus, and Pluto).

When Saturn is retrograde, it's an uphill battle with self-discipline. You may not be in the mood for work. You may feel more like hanging out at the beach than getting things done.

Neptune retrograde promotes a dreamy escapism from reality, when you may feel you're in a fog (Pisces will feel this, especially).

Uranus retrograde may mean setbacks in areas where there have been sudden changes, when you may be forced to regroup or reevaluate the situation.

Pluto retrograde is a time to work on establishing proportion and balance in areas where there have been recent dramatic transformations.

When the planets move forward again, there's a shift in the atmosphere. Activities connected with each planet start moving ahead, plans that were stalled get rolling. Make a special note of those days on your calendar and proceed accordingly.

Other Retrogrades in 2008

The five slower-moving planets all go retrograde in 2008.

Jupiter retrogrades from May 9 to September 7 in Capricorn.

Saturn retrogrades from December 19, 2007, until May 2, 2008, in Virgo. It turns retrograde again on December 31.

Uranus retrogrades from June 26 to November 27 in Pisces.

Neptune retrogrades from May 26 to November 1 in Aquarius.

Pluto turns retrograde from April 2 in Capricorn, then returns to Sagittarius on June 13. It turns direct in Sagittarius on September 8 and reenters Capricorn on November 26.

CHAPTER 3

Planetary Shake-Ups This Year

When the planetary weather is stormy, it's best to be prepared. Fortunately we can predict certain times when there are more likely to be shake-ups in your world, such as eclipses and Saturn transits, two events that could slow you down or make you change direction. With some basic astrological knowledge, you can find out where these events are likely to impact your life and what to expect when they happen.

Eclipses Clear the Air

Eclipses can bring on milestones in your life, if they aspect a key point in your horoscope. In general, they shake up the status quo, bringing hidden areas out into the open. During this time, problems you've been avoiding or have brushed aside can surface to demand your attention. A good coping strategy is to accept whatever comes up as a challenge that could make a positive difference in your life. And don't forget the power of your sense of humor. If you can laugh at something, you'll never be afraid of it.

What Is the Best Thing to Do During an Eclipse?

When the natural rhythms of the sun and moon are disturbed, it's best to postpone important activities. Be sure to mark eclipse days on your calendar, especially if the eclipse falls in your birth sign. This year, those born under Aquarius, Leo, and Virgo should take special note of the feelings that arise. With lunar eclipses, some possibilities could be a break from attachments or the healing of an illness or substance abuse, which had been triggered by the subconscious. The temporary event could be a healing time, when you gain perspective. During solar eclipses, when you might be in a highly subjective state, pay attention to the hidden subconscious patterns that surface, the emotional truth that is revealed at this time.

The effect of the eclipse can reverberate for some time, often months after the event. But it is especially important to stay cool and make no major moves during the period known as the shadow of the eclipse, which begins about a week before and lasts until at least three days after the eclipse. After three days, the daily rhythms should return to normal, and you can proceed with business as usual.

This Year's Eclipse Dates

February 6: Solar eclipse in Aquarius
February 20: Lunar eclipse in Virgo
August 1: Solar eclipse in Leo
August 16: Lunar eclipse in Aquarius

Saturn Gives You a Reality Check

When Saturn hits a critical point in your horoscope, you can count on an experience that will make you slow up, pull back, and reexamine your life. It is a call to eliminate what is not working, to shape up, to set priorities, to examine the boundaries and structures in your life (or lack of them) and set new ones. During this process, you may feel restricted, frustrated, or inhibited—not a fun time, but one that will serve you well in the long run. You may need to take on more responsibilities that will test your limits.

By the end of its twenty-eight-year trip around the zodiac, Saturn will have tested you in all areas of your life. The major tests happen in seven-year cycles, when Saturn passes over the angles of your chart, which means your rising sign, the top of your chart or midheaven, your descendant, and the nadir or bottom of your chart. This is when the real life-changing experiences happen. But you are also in for a testing period whenever Saturn passes a planet in your chart or stresses that planet from a distance. It is useful to check your planetary positions with the timetable of Saturn or prepare in advance, or at least to brace yourself.

When Saturn returns to its location at the time of your birth, at approximately age twenty-eight, you'll have your first Saturn return. At this time, a person usually takes stock or settles down to find his mission in life and assume full adult duties and responsibilities.

Another way Saturn helps us is to reveal the karmic lessons from previous lives and give us the chance to overcome them. So look at Saturn's challenges as much-needed opportunities for self-improvement.

Outwitting the Planets

Second-guessing Saturn and the eclipses this year is easy if you have a copy of your horoscope calculated by a computer. This enables you to pinpoint the area of your life that will be affected. However, you can make an educated guess, by setting up a rough diagram on your own. If you'd like to find out which area of your life this year's Saturn change is most likely to affect, follow these easy steps.

First, you must know the time of day you were born and look up your rising sign listed on the tables in this book (see chapter 7). Set up an estimated horoscope by drawing a circle, then dividing it into four parts by making a cross directly through the center. Continue to divide each of the parts into thirds, as if you were dividing a cake, until you have twelve slices. Write your rising sign on the middle left-hand slice, which would be the nine o'clock point, if you were looking at your watch. Then write the following signs on the dividing line of each slice, working counterclockwise, until you have listed all twelve signs of the zodiac.

You should now have a basic diagram of your horoscope

chart (minus the planets, of course). Starting with your rising-sign slice, number each portion consecutively, again working counterclockwise.

Since this year's eclipses will fall in Aquarius, Leo, and Virgo, find the number of these slices, or houses, on the chart and read the following descriptions for the kinds of issues that are likely to be emphasized. Saturn is now traveling through Virgo, so check this house in your chart for Saturn-related events.

If an eclipse or Saturn falls in your FIRST HOUSE:

Events cause you to examine the ways you are acting independently and push you to become more visible, to assert yourself. This is a time when you feel compelled to make your own decisions. You may want to change your physical appearance, body image, or style of dress in some way. Under affliction, there might be illness or physical harm.

If an eclipse or Saturn falls in your SECOND HOUSE:

This is the place where you consider all matters of security. You consolidate your resources, earn money, acquire property, and decide what you value and what you want to own. On a deeper level, this house reveals your sense of self-worth.

If an eclipse or Saturn falls in your THIRD HOUSE:

Here you reach out to others, express your ideas, and explore different courses of action. You may feel especially restless or have confrontations with neighbors or siblings. In your search for more knowledge, you may decide to improve your skills, get more education, or sign up for a course that interests you. Local transportation, especially your car, might be affected by an eclipse here.

If an eclipse or Saturn falls in your FOURTH HOUSE:

Here is where you put down roots and establish a base. You'll consider what home really means to you. Issues involving parents, the physical setup or location of your home, and your immediate family demand your attention. You may be especially concerned with parenting or relationships with your own mother. You may consider moving your home to a new location or leaving home.

If an eclipse or Saturn falls in your FIFTH HOUSE:

Here is where you express yourself, either through your personal talents or through procreating children. You are interested in making your special talents visible. This is also the house of love affairs and the romantic aspect of life, where you flirt, have fun, and enjoy the excitement of love. Hobbies and crafts fall in this area.

If an eclipse or Saturn falls in your SIXTH HOUSE:

How well are you doing your job? This is your maintenance department, where you take care of your health, organize your life, and set up a daily routine. It is also the place where you perfect your skills and add polish to your life. The chores you do every day, the skills you learn, and the techniques you use fall here. If something doesn't work in your life, an eclipse is sure to bring this to light. If you've been neglecting your health, diet, and fitness, you'll probably pay the consequences during an eclipse. Or you may be faced with work that requires much routine organization and steady effort, rather than creative ability. Or you may be required to perform services for others.

If an eclipse or Saturn falls in your SEVENTH HOUSE:

This is the area of committed relationships, of those which involve legal agreements, of working in a close relationship with another. Here you'll be dealing with how you relate, what you'll be willing to give up for the sake of a marriage or partnership. Eclipses here can put extra pressure on a relationship and, if it's not working, precipitate a breakup. Lawsuits and open enemies also reside here.

If an eclipse or Saturn falls in your EIGHTH HOUSE:

This area is concerned with power and control. Consider what you are willing to give up in order that something might happen. Power struggles, intense relationships, and desires to penetrate deeper mysteries belong here. Debts, loans, financial matters that involve another party, and wheeling and dealing also come into focus. So does sex, where you surrender your individual power to create a new life together. Matters involving birth and death are also involved here.

If an eclipse or Saturn falls in your NINTH HOUSE:
Here is where you look at the big picture. You'll seek information that helps you find meaning in life: higher education, religion, travel, global issues. Eclipses here can push you to get out of your rut, to explore something you've never done before, and to expand your horizons.

If an eclipse or Saturn falls in your TENTH HOUSE:
This is the high-profile point in your chart. Here is where you consider how society looks at you and your position in the outside world. You'll be concerned about whether you receive proper credit for your work and if you're recognized by higher-ups. Promotions, raises, and other forms of recognition can be given or denied. If you have worked hard, Saturn can give you well-deserved rewards here. Either your standing in your career or in your community can be challenged, or you'll be publicly acknowledged for achieving a goal. An eclipse here can make you famous or burst your balloon if you've been too ambitious or neglecting other areas of your life.

If an eclipse or Saturn falls in your ELEVENTH HOUSE:
Your relationship with groups of people comes under scrutiny during an eclipse: whom you are identified with, whom you socialize with, and how well you are accepted by other members of your team. Activities of clubs and political parties, networking, and other social interactions become important. You'll be concerned about what other people think.

If an eclipse or Saturn falls in your TWELFTH HOUSE:
This is the time when the focus turns to your inner life. An especially favorable eclipse here might bring you great insight and inspiration. On the other hand, events may happen that cause you to retreat from public life. Here is where we go to be alone or to work in retreats, hospitals, or religious institutions, or to explore psychotherapy. Here is where you deliver selfless service, through charitable acts. Good aspects from an eclipse could promote an ability to go with the flow or to rise above the competition to find an inner, almost mystical strength that enables you to connect with the deepest needs of others.

CHAPTER 4

Blame It on Moon Glow: The Moon's Effect on Emotions

In some astrological systems, the moon sign is considered just as important as the sun sign. It adds many levels of meaning to a horoscope, because it reveals how a person reacts to life's problems, what makes the person feel comfortable, secure, romantic. The moon reveals secrets like what you really care about. It's the emotional factor in the horoscope, representing the receptive, reflective, female, nurturing self. It also reflects who you were nurtured by—the mother or mother figure in your chart. In a man's chart, the moon position describes his receptive, emotional, yin side, as well as the woman in his life who will have the deepest effect, usually his mother. (Venus reveals the kind of woman who will attract him physically.)

The moon is more at home in some signs than others. It rules maternal Cancer and is exalted in Taurus—both comforting, home-loving signs where the natural emotional energies of the moon are easily and productively expressed. But when the moon is in the opposite signs—Capricorn and Scorpio—it leaves the comfortable nest and deals with emotional issues of power and achievement in the outside world. Those of you with the moon in these signs are likely to find your emotional role more challenging in life.

Since detailed moon tables are too extensive for this book, check through the following listing to find the moon sign that feels most familiar.

Moon in Aries

This placement makes you both independent and ardent. An idealist, you tend to fall in and out of love easily. You love a challenge but could cool once your quarry is captured. Your emotional reactions are fast and fiery, quickly expressed and quickly forgotten. You may not think before expressing your feelings. It's not easy to hide how you feel. Channeling all your emotional energy could be one of your big challenges.

Moon in Taurus

A sentimental soul, you are very fond of the good life, and you gravitate toward solid, secure relationships. You like displays of affection and creature comforts—all the tangible trappings of a cozy, safe, calm atmosphere. You are sensual and steady emotionally, but very stubborn, possessive, and determined. You can't be pushed, and you tend to dislike changes. You should make an effort to broaden your horizons and to take a risk sometimes. You may become very attached to your home turf. You may also be a collector of objects that are meaningful to you.

Moon in Gemini

You crave mental stimulation and variety in life, which you usually get through either an ever-varied social life, the excitement of flirtation and/or multiple professional involvements. You may marry more than once and have a rather chaotic emotional life due to your difficulty with commitment and settling down, as well as your need to be constantly on the go. (Be sure to find a partner who is as outgoing as you are.) You will have to learn at some point to focus your energies because you tend to be somewhat fragmented—to do two things at once, to have two homes or even two lovers. If you can find a creative way to express your many-faceted nature, you'll be ahead of the game.

Moon in Cancer

This is the most powerful lunar position, which is sure to make a deep imprint on your character. Your needs are very much associated with your reaction to the needs of others. You are very sensitive, caring, and self-protective, though some of you may mask this with a hard shell, like the moon-sensitive crab. This placement also gives an excellent memory, keen intuition, and an uncanny ability to perceive the needs of others. All of the lunar phases will affect you, especially full moons and eclipses, so you would do well to mark them on your calendar. Because you're happiest at home, you may work at home or turn your office into a second home, where you can nurture and comfort people. (You may tend to mother the world.) With natural psychic, intuitive ability, you might be drawn to occult work in some way. Or you may get professionally involved with providing food and shelter to others.

Moon in Leo

This warm, passionate moon takes everything to heart. You are attracted to all that is noble, generous, and aristocratic in life (and may be a bit of a snob). You have an innate ability to take command emotionally, but you do need strong support, loyalty, and loud applause from those you love. You are possessive of your loved ones and your turf and will roar if anyone threatens to take over your territory.

Moon in Virgo

You are rather cool until you decide if others measure up. But once someone or something meets your ideal standards, you hold up your end of the arrangement perfectly. You may, in fact, drive yourself too hard to attain some notion of perfection. Try to be a bit easier on yourself and others. Don't always act the censor! You love to be the teacher and are drawn to situations where you can change others for the better, but sometimes you must learn to accept others for what they are—enjoy what you have!

Moon in Libra

Like other air-sign moons, you think before you feel. Therefore, you may not immediately recognize the emotional needs of others. However, you are relationship oriented and may find it difficult to be alone or to do things alone. After you have learned emotional balance by leaning on yourself first, you can have excellent partnerships. It is best for you to avoid extremes, which set your scales swinging and can make your love life precarious. You thrive in a rather conservative, traditional, romantic relationship, where you receive attention and flattery—but not possessiveness—from your partner. You'll be your most charming in an elegant, harmonious atmosphere.

Moon in Scorpio

This is a moon that enjoys and responds to intense, passionate feelings. You may go to extremes and have a very dramatic emotional life, full of ardor, suspicion, jealousy, and obsession. It would be much healthier to channel your need for power and control into meaningful work. This is a good position for anyone in the fields of medicine, police work, research, the occult, psychoanalysis, or intuitive work, because life-and-death situations don't faze you. However, you do take personal disappointments very hard.

Moon in Sagittarius

You take life's ups and downs with good humor and the proverbial grain of salt. You'll love 'em and leave 'em—take off on a great adventure at a moment's notice. Born free could be your slogan. Attracted by the exotic, you have wanderlust mentally and physically. You may be too much in search of new mental and spiritual stimulation to ever settle down.

Moon in Capricorn

Are you ever accused of being too cool and calculating? You have an earthy side, but you take prestige and position very seriously. Your strong drive to succeed extends to your romantic life, where you will be devoted to improving your lifestyle, rising to the top. A structured situation where you can advance methodically makes you feel wonderfully secure. You may be attracted to someone older or very much younger or from a different social world. It may be difficult to look at the lighter side of emotional relationships. Though this moon is placed in the sign of its detriment, the good news is that you tend to be very dutiful and responsible to those you care for.

Moon in Aquarius

You are a people collector with many friends of all backgrounds. You are happiest surrounded by people and may feel uneasy when left alone. Though you usually stay friends with lovers, intense emotions and demanding one-on-one relationships turn you off. You don't like anything to be too rigid or scheduled. Though tolerant and understanding, you can be emotionally unpredictable and may opt for an unconventional love life. With plenty of space, you will be able to sustain relationships with liberal, freedom-loving types.

Moon in Pisces

You are very responsive and empathetic to others, especially if they have problems or are the underdog. (Be on guard against attracting too many people with sob stories.) You'll be happiest if you can express your creative imagination in the arts or in the spiritual or healing professions. Because you may tend to escape in fantasies or overreact to the moods of others, you need an emotional anchor to help you keep a firm foothold in reality. Steer clear of too much escapism (especially in alcohol) or reclusiveness. Places near water soothe your moods. Working in a field that gives you emotional variety will also help you be productive.

CHAPTER 5

Hands-On Astrology for Beginners

After you learn all about your zodiac sign (and those of your friends), you may be ready to delve more deeply into astrology. This chapter can get you up and running. It's a quick owner's manual, your fast track to getting hands-on with astrology. You'll learn the difference between a sign and a constellation (they're not the same). And what happens in a house. You'll be able to define a sign and figure out why astrologers say what they do about each one. When you look at your astrological chart, you'll have a good idea of what's going on in each portion of the horoscope. Here's your key to understanding the basic principles of this fascinating, but often confusing subject.

Signs and Constellations: What's the Difference?

Most readers know their signs, but many often confuse them with constellations. Signs are actually a type of celestial real estate, located on the zodiac, an imaginary 360-degree belt circling the earth. This belt is divided into twelve equal thirty-degree portions, which are the signs. There's a lot of confusion about the difference between the signs and the constellations of the zodiac. The latter are patterns of stars that originally marked the twelve divisions, like signposts. Though a sign is named after the constellation that once marked the same area, the constellations are no longer in the same place relative to the earth that they were many centuries ago. Over hundreds of years, the earth's orbit has shifted, so that from our point of view here on earth, the constellations seem to have moved. However, the signs remain in place. (Most Western astrology uses the twelve-equal-part division of the zodiac, though there are some other methods of astrology that still use the constellations instead of the signs.)

Most people think of themselves in terms of their sun sign. A sun sign refers to the sign the sun is orbiting through at a given moment (from our point of view here on earth). For instance, "I'm an Aries" means that the sun was passing through Aries when that person was born. However, there are nine other planets (plus asteroids, fixed stars, and sensitive points) that also form our total astrological personality, and some or many of these will be located in other signs. No one is completely Aries, with all astrological components in one sign! (Please note that, in astrology, the sun and moon are usually referred to as planets, though of course they're not.) Pluto is also still called a planet by astrologers.

As we mentioned before, the sun signs are places on the zodiac. They do not do anything (the planets are the doers). However, they are associated with many things, depending on their location.

How We Define the Signs

The definitions of the signs evolved systematically from four components that interrelate. These four different criteria are a sign's element: its quality, its polarity or sex, and its order in the progression of the zodiac. All these factors work together to tell us what the sign is like.

The system is magically mathematical. The number 12—as in the twelve signs of the zodiac—is divisible by 4, by 3, and by 2. There are four elements, three qualities, and two polarities, which follow each other in sequence around the zodiac.

The four elements (earth, air, fire, and water) are the building blocks of astrology. The use of an element to describe a sign probably dates from man's first attempts to categorize what he saw. Ancient sages believed that all things were composed of combinations of these basic elements—earth, air, fire, and water. This included the human character, which was fiery/choleric, earthy/melancholy, airy/sanguine, or watery/phlegmatic. The elements also correspond to our emotional (water), physical (earth), mental (air) and spiritual (fire) natures. The energies of each of the elements were then observed to be related to the time of year when the sun was passing through a certain segment of the zodiac.

Those born with the sun in fire signs—Aries, Leo, Sagittarius—embody the characteristic of that element. Optimism, warmth, hot tempers, enthusiasm, and spirit are typical of these signs. Taurus, Virgo, and Capricorn are earthy—more grounded, physical, materialistic, organized and deliberate than fire-sign people. Air-sign people—Gemini, Libra, and Aquarius—are mentally oriented communicators. Water signs—Cancer, Scorpio, and Pisces—are emotional, sensitive, and creative.

Think of what each element does to the others. Water puts out fire or evaporates under heat. Air fans the flames or blows them out. Earth smothers fire, drifts and erodes with too much wind, becomes mud or fertile soil with water. Those are often perfect analogies for the relationships between people of different sun-sign elements. This astrochemistry was one of the first ways man described his relationships. Fortunately, no one is entirely air or fire. We all have a bit, or a lot, of each element in our horoscopes. It is this unique mix that defines each astrological personality.

Within each element, there are three qualities that describe types of behavior associated with the sign. Those of cardinal signs are activists, go-getters. These four signs—Aries, Cancer, Libra, and Capricorn—begin each season. Fixed signs, which happen in the middle of the season, are associated with builders, stabilizers. You'll find that sun signs Taurus, Leo, Scorpio, and Aquarius are usually gifted with concentration, stamina, and focus. Mutable signs—Gemini, Virgo, Sagittarius, and Pisces—fall at the end of each season and thus are considered catalysts for change. People born under mutable signs are flexible, adaptable.

The polarity of a sign is either its positive or negative charge. It can be masculine, active, positive, and yang like air or fire signs. Or feminine, reactive, negative, and yin like the water and earth signs.

Finally, we consider the sign's place in the order of the zodiac. This is vital to the balance of all the forces and the transmission of energy moving through the signs. You may have noticed that your sign is quite different from your neighboring sign on either side. Yet each seems to grow out of its predecessor like links in a chain and transmits a synthesis of energy gathered along the chain to the following sign, beginning with the fire-powered, active, positive charge of Aries.

How the Signs Add Up

SIGN	ELEMENT	QUALITY	POLARITY	PLACE
Aries	fire	cardinal	masculine	first
Taurus	earth	fixed	feminine	second
Gemini	air	mutable	masculine	third
Cancer	water	cardinal	feminine	fourth
Leo	fire	fixed	masculine	fifth
Virgo	earth	mutable	feminine	sixth
Libra	air	cardinal	masculine	seventh
Scorpio	water	fixed	feminine	eighth
Sagittarius	fire	mutable	masculine	ninth
Capricorn	earth	cardinal	feminine	tenth
Aquarius	air	fixed	masculine	eleventh
Pisces	water	mutable	feminine	twelfth

Your Sign's Special Planet

Each sign has a ruling planet that is most compatible with its energies. Mars adds its fiery assertive characteristics to Aries. The sensual beauty and comfort-loving side of Venus rules Taurus, whereas the idealistic side of Venus rules Libra. Quick-moving Mercury rules two mutable signs, Gemini and Virgo. Its mental agility belongs to Gemini while its analytical, critical side is best expressed in Virgo. The changeable emotional moon is associated with Cancer, while the outgoing Leo personality is ruled by the sun. Scorpio originally shared Mars, but when Pluto was discovered in this century, its powerful magnetic energies were deemed more suitable to the intense vibrations of the fixed water sign Scorpio. Though Pluto has, as of this writing, been downgraded, it is still considered by astrologers to be a powerful force in the horoscope. Disciplined Capricorn is ruled by Saturn, and expansive Sagittarius by Jupiter. Unpredictable Aquarius is ruled by Uranus and creative, imaginative Pisces by Neptune. In a horoscope, if a planet is placed in the sign it rules, it is sure to be especially powerful.

The Layout of a Horoscope Chart

A horoscope chart is a map of the heavens at a given moment in time. It looks like a wheel divided with twelve spokes. In between each of the spokes is a section called a house.

Each house deals with a different area of life and is influenced by a special sign and a planet. Astrologers look at the house to tell in what area of life an event is happening or about to happen.

The house is governed by the sign passing over the spoke (or cusp of the house) at that particular moment. Though the first house is naturally associated with Aries and Mars, it would also have an additional Capricorn influence if that sign was passing over the house cusp at the time the chart was cast. The sequence of the houses starts with the first house located at the left center spoke (or the number 9 position, if you were reading a clock). The houses are then read counterclockwise around the chart, with the fourth house at the bottom of the chart, and the tenth house at the top or twelve o'clock position.

Where do the planets belong? Around the horoscope, planets are placed within the houses according to their location at the time of the chart. That is why it is so important to have an accurate time; with no specific time, the planets have no specific location in the houses and one cannot determine which area of life they will apply to. Since the signs move across the houses as the earth turns, planets in a house will naturally intensify the importance of that house. The house that contains the sun is naturally one of the most prominent.

The First House: Home of Aries and Mars

The sign passing over the first house at the time of your birth is known as your *ascendant,* or *rising sign*. The first house is the house of "firsts"—the first impression you make, how you initiate matters, the image you choose to project. This is where you advertise yourself, where you project your personality. Planets that fall here will intensify the way you come across to others.

The Second House: Home of Taurus and Venus

This house is where you experience the material world—what you value. Here are your attitudes about money, possessions, finances, whatever belongs to you, and what you own, as well as your earning and spending capacity. On a deeper level, this house reveals your sense of self-worth, the inner values that draw wealth in various forms.

The Third House: Home of Gemini and Mercury

This house describes how you communicate with others, how you reach out to others nearby, and how you interact with the immediate environment. It shows how your thinking process works and the way you express your thoughts. Are you articulate or tongue-tied? Can you think on your feet? This house also shows your first relationships, your experiences with brothers and sisters, and how you deal with people close to you such as your neighbors or pals. It's where you take short trips, write letters, or use the telephone. It shows how your mind works in terms of left-brain logical and analytical functions.

The Fourth House: Home of Cancer and the Moon

The fourth house shows the foundation of life, the psychological underpinnings. At the bottom of the chart, this house shows how you are nurtured and made to feel secure—your roots! It shows your early home environment and the circumstances at the end of your life (your final "home") as well as the place you call home now. Astrologers look here for information about the parental nurturers in your life.

The Fifth House: Home of Leo and the Sun

The fifth house is where the creative potential develops. Here you express yourself and procreate in the sense that children are outgrowths of your creative ability. But this house most represents your inner childlike self who delights in play. If your inner security has been established by the time you reach this house, you are now free to have fun, romance, and love affairs and to give of yourself. This is also the place astrologers look for playful love affairs, flirtations, and brief romantic encounters (rather than long-term commitments).

The Sixth House: Home of Virgo and Mercury

The sixth house has been called the "care and maintenance" department. This house shows how you take care of your body and organize yourself to perform efficiently in the world. Here is where you get things done, look after others, and fulfill service duties such as taking care of pets. Here is what you do to survive on a day-to-day basis. The sixth house demands order in your life; otherwise there would be chaos. This house is your "job" (as opposed to your career, which is the domain of the tenth house), your diet, and your health and fitness regimens.

The Seventh House: Home of Libra and Venus

This house shows your attitude toward partners and those with whom you enter into commitments, contracts, or agreements. Here is the way you relate to others, as well as your close, intimate, one-on-one relationships (including open enemies—those you "face off" with). Open hostilities, lawsuits, divorces, and marriages happen here. If the first house represents the "I," the seventh or opposite house is the "not-I"—the complementary partner you attract by the way you come across. If you are having trouble with partnerships, consider what you are attracting by the energies of your first and seventh houses.

The Eighth House: Home of Scorpio and Pluto (also Mars)

The eighth house refers to how you merge with something or someone, and how you handle power and control. This is one of the most mysterious and powerful houses, where your energy transforms itself from "I" to "we." As you give up power and control by uniting with something or someone, two kinds of energies merge and become something greater, leading to a regeneration of the self on a higher level. Here are your attitudes toward sex, shared resources, taxes (what you share with the government). Because this house involves what belongs to others, you face issues of control and power struggles, or undergo a deep psychological transformation as you bond with another. Here you transcend yourself with dreams, drugs, and occult or psychic experiences that reflect the collective unconscious.

The Ninth House: Home of Sagittarius and Jupiter

The ninth house shows your search for wisdom and higher knowledge—your belief system. As the third house represents the "lower mind," its opposite on the wheel, the ninth house, is the "higher mind"—the abstract, intuitive, spiritual mind that asks "big" questions like "Why are we here?" After the third house has explored what was close at hand, the ninth stretches out to broaden you mentally with higher education and travel. Here you stretch spiritually with religious activity. Since you are concerned with how everything is related, you tend to push boundaries, take risks. Here is where you express your ideas in a book or thesis, where you pontificate, philosophize, or preach.

The Tenth House: Home of Capricorn and Saturn

The tenth house is associated with your public life and high-profile activities. Located directly overhead at the "high noon" position on the horoscope wheel, this is the most "visible" house in the chart, the one where the world sees you. It deals with your career (but not your routine "job") and your reputation. Here is where you go public, take on responsibilities (as opposed to the fourth house, where you stay home). This will affect the career you choose and your "public relations." This house is also associated with your father figure or the main authority figure in your life.

The Eleventh House: Home of Aquarius and Uranus

The eleventh house is where you extend yourself to a group, a goal, or a belief system. This house is where you define what you really want, the kinds of friends you have, your political affiliations, and the kind of groups you identify with as an equal. Here is where you become concerned with "what other people think" or where you rebel against social conventions. Here is where you could become a socially conscious humanitarian or a partygoing social butterfly. It's where you look to others to stimulate you and discover your kinship to the rest of humanity. The sign on this house can help you understand what you gain and lose from friendships.

The Twelfth House: Home of Pisces and Neptune

Old-fashioned astrologers used to put a rather negative spin on this house, calling it the house of self-undoing. When we undo ourselves, we surrender control, boundaries, limits, and rules. The twelfth house is where the boundaries between yourself and others become blurred and you become selfless. But instead of being self-undoing, the twelfth house can be a place of great creativity and talent. It is the place where you can tap into the collective unconscious, where your imagination is limitless.

In your trip around the zodiac, you've gone from the I of self-assertion in the first house to the final house, which symbolizes the dissolution that happens before rebirth. The twelfth house is where accumulated experiences are processed in the unconscious. Spiritually oriented astrologers look to this house for evidence of past lives and karma. Places where we go for solitude or to do spiritual or reparatory work belong here, such as retreats, religious institutions, or hospitals. Here is also where we withdraw from society voluntarily or involuntarily or are put in prison because of antisocial activity. Selfless giving through charitable acts is part of this house, as is dependence on charity.

In your daily life, the twelfth house reveals your deepest intimacies, your best-kept secrets, especially those you hide from yourself and keep repressed deep in the unconscious. It is where we surrender a sense of a separate self to a deep feeling of wholeness, such as selfless service in religion or any activity that involves merging with the greater whole. Many sports stars have important planets in the twelfth house that enable them to play in the zone, finding an inner, almost mystical, strength that transcends their limits.

Who's Home in Your Houses?

Houses are stronger or weaker depending on how many planets are inhabiting them. If there are many planets in a given house, it follows that the activities of that house will be especially important in your life. If the planet that rules the house is also located there, this too adds power to the house.

CHAPTER 6

Getting to Know All Your Planets

When you know a person's sun sign, you already know some very useful generic qualities about that person. But when you know the placement of all ten planets, that person becomes an astrological individual, with a unique horoscope. The horoscope chart lights up with colorations from many different signs and planets. Therefore, you'll have a much more accurate profile, and with the full planetary picture of the horoscope, you'll be more capable of predicting how that individual will act in a given situation.

The planets are the actors of the chart, each representing a basic force in life. The sign and house where the planet is located represent how and where this force will manifest. The importance of a planet in your horoscope depends on its position. A planet that's close to your rising sign will be highlighted in your chart. If two or more planets are grouped together in one sign, they usually operate like a team, playing off each other rather than expressing their energy singularly. A lone planet that stands far away from the others is usually outstanding and often calls the shots.

The sign of each planet also has a powerful influence. In some signs, the planetary energies are very much at home and can easily express themselves. In others, the planet has to work harder and is slightly out of sorts. The sign that most corresponds to the energies of a planet is said to be ruled by that planet and obviously is the best place for it to be. The next best place is in a sign where it is exalted, or especially harmonious. On the other hand, there are places in the horoscope where a planet has to work harder to play its role, such as the sign opposite a planet's rulership, which embodies the opposite area of life, and the sign opposite its exaltation. However, a planet that must work harder can actually be more complete, because it must stretch itself to meet the challenges of living in a more difficult sign. Like world leaders who've had to struggle for greatness, this planet may actually develop great strength and character.

Here's a list of the best places for each planet to be. Note that, as new planets were discovered, they replaced the traditional rulers of signs which best complemented their energies.

ARIES—Mars
TAURUS—Venus, in its most sensual form
GEMINI—Mercury, in its communicative role
CANCER—the moon
LEO—the sun
VIRGO—also Mercury, this time in its more critical capacity
LIBRA—also Venus, in its more aesthetic, judgmental form
SCORPIO—Pluto, replacing Mars, the sign's original ruler
SAGITTARIUS—Jupiter
CAPRICORN—Saturn
AQUARIUS—Uranus, replacing Saturn, its original ruler
PISCES—Neptune, replacing Jupiter, its original ruler

A person who has many planets in exalted signs is lucky indeed, for here is where the planet can accomplish the most and be its most influential and creative.

SUN—exalted in Aries, where its energy creates action
MOON—exalted in Taurus, where instincts and reactions operate on a highly creative level
MERCURY—exalted in Aquarius, where it can reach analytical heights
VENUS—exalted in Pisces, a sign whose sensitivity encourages love and creativity
MARS—exalted in Capricorn, a sign that puts energy to work productively
JUPITER—exalted in Cancer, where it encourages nurturing and growth

SATURN—at home in Libra, where it steadies the scales of justice and promotes balanced, responsible judgment

URANUS—powerful in Scorpio, where it promotes transformation

NEPTUNE—especially favored in Cancer, where it gains the security to transcend to a higher state

PLUTO—exalted in Pisces, where it dissolves the old cycle to make way for transition to the new

The Personal Planets: Mercury, Venus, and Mars

These planets work in your immediate personal life.

Mercury affects how you communicate and how your mental processes work. Are you a quick study who grasps information rapidly? Or do you learn more slowly and thoroughly? How is your concentration? Can you express yourself easily? Are you a good writer? All these questions can be answered by your Mercury placement.

Venus shows what you react to. What turns you on? What appeals to you aesthetically? Are you charming to others? Are you attractive to look at? Your taste, your refinement, your sense of balance and proportion are all Venus-ruled.

Mars is your outgoing energy, your drive and ambition. Do you reach out for new adventures? Are you assertive? Are you motivated? Self-confident? Hot-tempered? How you channel your energy and drive is revealed by your Mars placement.

Mercury Shows How Your Mind Works

Mercury shows how you think and speak, how logical you are. Since it stays close to the sun, read the description for Mercury in your sun sign, then the sign preceding and following it. Then decide which reflects the way you think.

Mercury in Aries

Your mind is very active and assertive. It approaches a plan aggressively. You never hesitate to say what you think, never shy away from a battle. In fact, you may relish a verbal confrontation. Tact is not your strong point, so you may have to learn not to trip over your tongue.

Mercury in Taurus

This is a cautious Mercury. Though you may be a slow learner, you have good concentration and mental stamina. You want to make your ideas really happen. You'll attack a problem methodically and consider every angle thoroughly, never jumping to conclusions. You'll stick with a subject until you master it.

Mercury in Gemini

You are a wonderful communicator with great facility for expressing yourself both verbally and in writing. You love gathering all kinds of information. You probably finish other people's sentences, and express yourself with eloquent hand gestures. You can talk to anybody anytime . . . and probably have phone and e-mail bills to prove it. You read anything from sci-fi to Shakespeare, and might need an extra room just for your book collection. Though you learn fast, you may lack focus and discipline. Watch a tendency to jump from subject to subject.

Mercury in Cancer

You rely on intuition more than logic. Your mental processes are usually colored by your emotions, so you may seem shy or hesitant to voice your opinions. However, this placement gives you the advantage of great imagination and empathy in the way you communicate with others.

Mercury in Leo

You are enthusiastic and very dramatic in the way you express yourself. You like to hold the attention of groups, and could be a great public speaker. Your mind thinks big, so you prefer to deal with the overall picture rather than with the details.

Mercury in Virgo

This is one of the best places for Mercury. It should give you critical ability, attention to details, and thorough analysis. Your mind focuses on the practical side of things. This type of thinking is very well suited to being a teacher or editor.

Mercury in Libra

You're either a born diplomat who smoothes over ruffled feathers or a talented debater. Many lawyers have this placement. However, since you're forever weighing the pros and cons of a situation, you may vacillate when making decisions.

Mercury in Scorpio

This is an investigative mind that stops at nothing to get the answers. You may have a sarcastic, stinging wit or a gift for the cutting remark. There's always a grain of truth to your verbal sallies, thanks to your penetrating insight.

Mercury in Sagittarius

You are a supersalesman with a tendency to expound. Though you are very broad-minded, you can be dogmatic when it comes to telling others what's good for them. You won't hesitate to tell the truth as you see it, so watch a tendency toward tactlessness. On the plus side, you have a great sense of humor. This position of Mercury is often considered by astrologers to be at a disadvantage because

Sagittarius opposes Gemini, the sign Mercury rules, and squares off with Virgo, another Mercury-ruled sign. What often happens is that Mercury in Sagittarius oversteps its bounds and loses sight of the facts in a situation. Do a reality check before making promises you may not be able to deliver.

Mercury in Capricorn

This placement endows good mental discipline. You have a love of learning and a very orderly approach to your subjects. You will patiently plod through the facts and figures until you have mastered the tasks. You grasp structured situations easily, but may be short on creativity.

Mercury in Aquarius

An independent, original thinker, you'll have more cutting-edge ideas than the average person. You will be quick to check out any unusual opportunities. Your opinions are so well-researched and grounded that once your mind is made up, it is difficult to change.

Mercury in Pisces

You have the psychic and intuitive mind of a natural poet. Learn to make use of your creative imagination. You may think in terms of helping others, but check a tendency to be vague and forgetful of details.

Venus Relates

Venus shows where you receive pleasure, what you love to do. Find your Venus placement from the charts at the end of this chapter by looking for the year of your birth in the left-hand column. Then follow the line of that year across the page until you reach the time period of your birthday. The sign heading that column will be your Venus. If you were born on a day when Venus was changing signs, check the signs preceding or following that day to determine if that sign feels more like your Venus nature.

Venus in Aries

You can't stand to be bored, confined, or ordered around. But a good challenge, maybe even a rousing row, turns you on. Confess—don't you pick a fight now and then just to get someone stirred up? You're attracted by the chase, not the catch, which could cause some problems in your love life if the object of your affection becomes too attainable. You like to wear red, and you can spot a trend before anyone else.

Venus in Taurus

All your senses work in high gear. You love to be surrounded by glorious tastes, smells, textures, sounds, and visuals. Austerity is not for you! Neither is being rushed. You like time to enjoy your pleasures. Soothing surroundings with plenty of creature comforts are your cup of tea. You like to feel secure in your nest, with no sudden jolts or surprises. You like familiar objects—in fact, you may hate to let anything or anyone go.

Venus in Gemini

You are a lively, sparkling personality who thrives in a situation that affords a constant variety and a frequent change of scenery. A varied social life is important to you, with plenty of stimulation and a chance to engage in some light flirtation. Commitment may be difficult, because playing the field is so much fun.

Venus in Cancer

An atmosphere where you feel protected, coddled, and mothered is best for you. You love to be surrounded by children in a cozy, homelike situation. You are attracted to those who are tender and nurturing, who make you feel secure and well provided for. You may be quite secretive about your emotional life, or attracted to clandestine relationships.

Venus in Leo

First-class attention in large doses turns you on, and so does the glitter of real gold and the flash of mirrors. You like to feel like a star at all times, surrounded by your admiring audience. The side effect is that you may be attracted to flatterers and tinsel, while the real gold requires some digging.

Venus in Virgo

Everything neatly in its place? On the surface, you are attracted to an atmosphere where everything is in perfect order, but underneath are some basic, earthy urges. You are attracted to those who appeal to your need to teach, to be of service, or to play out a Pygmalion fantasy. You are at your best when you are busy doing something useful.

Venus in Libra

Elegance and harmony are your key words. You can't abide an atmosphere of contention. Your taste tends toward the classic, with light harmonies of color—nothing clashing, trendy, or outrageous. You love doing things with a partner, and should be careful to pick one who is decisive but patient enough to let you weigh the pros and cons. And steer clear of argumentative types!

Venus in Scorpio

Hidden mysteries intrigue you. In fact, anything that is too open and aboveboard is a bit of a bore. You surely have a stack of whodunits by the bed, along with an erotic magazine or two. You like to solve puzzles, and may also be fascinated with the occult, crime, or scientific research. Intense, all-or-nothing situations add spice to your life, and you love to ferret out the secrets of others. But you could get burned by your flair for living dangerously. The color black, spicy food, dark wood furniture, and heady perfume all get you in the right mood.

Venus in Sagittarius

If you are not actually a world traveler, your surroundings are sure to reflect your love of faraway places. You like a casual outdoor atmosphere and a dog or two to pet. There should be plenty of room for athletic equipment and suitcases. You're attracted to kindred souls who love to travel and who share your freedom-loving philosophy of life. Athletics and spiritual or New Age pursuits could be other interests.

Venus in Capricorn

No fly-by-night relationships for you! You want substance in life, and you are attracted to whatever will help you get where you are going. Status objects turn you on. And so do those who have a serious, responsible, businesslike approach as well as those who remind you of a beloved parent. It is characteristic of this placement to be attracted to someone of a different generation. Antiques, traditional clothing, and dignified behavior are becoming to you.

Venus in Aquarius

This Venus wants to make friends, to be "cool." You like to be in a group, particularly one pushing a worthy cause. You feel quite at home surrounded by people, and could even court fame. Yet all the while you remain detached from any intense commitment. Original ideas and unpredictable people fascinate you. You don't like everything to be planned out in advance, preferring spontaneity and delightful surprises.

Venus in Pisces

This Venus loves to give of yourself, and you find plenty of takers. Stray animals and people appeal to your heart and your pocketbook, but be careful to look at their motives realistically once in a while. You are extremely vulnerable to sob stories of all kinds. Fantasy, the arts (especially film, dance, and theater), and psychic or spiritual activities also speak to you.

Mars Creates Action

Mars is the mover and shaker in your life. It shows how you pursue your goals, whether you have energy to burn or proceed at a slow, steady pace. It will also show how you get angry. Do you explode or do a slow burn or hold everything inside, then get revenge later?

To find your Mars, turn to the charts on pages 88–97. Then find your birth year in the left-hand column and trace the line across horizontally until you come to the column headed by the month of your birth. There you will find an abbreviation of your Mars sign. If the description of your Mars sign doesn't ring true, read the description of the signs preceding and following it. You may have been born on a day when Mars was changing signs, in which case your Mars might be in the adjacent sign.

Mars in Aries

In the sign it rules, Mars shows its brilliant fiery nature. You have an explosive temper and can be quite impatient. On the other hand, you have tremendous courage, energy, and drive. You'll let nothing stand in your way as you race to be first! Obstacles are met head-on and broken through by force. However, those that require patience and persistence can have you exploding in rage. You're a great starter, but not necessarily around for the finish.

Mars in Taurus

Slow, steady, concentrated energy gives you staying power to last until the finish line. You have great stamina, and you never give up. Your tactic is to wear away obstacles with your persistence. Often you come out a winner because you've had the patience to hang in there. When angered, you do a slow burn.

Mars in Gemini

You can't sit still for long. This Mars craves variety. You often have two or more things going on at once—it's all an amusing game to you. Your life can get very complicated, but that only adds spice and stimulation. What drives you into a nervous, hyper state? Boredom, sameness, routine, and confinement. You can do wonderful things with your hands, and you have a way with words.

Mars in Cancer

You rarely attack head-on. Instead, you'll keep things to yourself, make plans in secret, and always cover your actions. This might be interpreted by some as manipulative, but you are only being self-protective. You get furious when anyone knows too much about you. But you do like to know all about others. Your mothering and feeding instincts can be put to good use if you work in the food, hotel, or child-care business. You may have to overcome your fragile sense of security, which prompts you not to take risks and to get physically upset when criticized. Don't take things so personally!

Mars in Leo

You have a very dominant personality that takes center stage. Modesty is not one of your traits, nor is taking a backseat. You prefer giving the orders, and have been known to make a dramatic scene if they are not obeyed.

Properly used, this Mars confers leadership ability, endurance, and courage.

Mars in Virgo

You are the faultfinder of the zodiac. You notice every detail. Mistakes of any kind make you very nervous. You may worry, even if everything is going smoothly. You may not express your anger directly, but you sure can nag. You have definite likes and dislikes, and you are sure you can do the job better than anyone else. You are certainly more industrious and detail-oriented than other signs. Your Mars energy is often most positively expressed in some kind of teaching role.

Mars in Libra

This Mars will have a passion for beauty, justice, and art. Generally, you will avoid confrontations at all costs. You prefer to spend your energy finding diplomatic solutions or weighing pros and cons. Your other techniques are passive aggression or exercising your well-known charm to get people to do what you want.

Mars in Scorpio

This is a powerful placement, so intense that it demands careful channeling into worthwhile activities. Otherwise, you could become obsessed with your sexuality or might use your need for power and control to manipulate others. You are strong-willed, shrewd, and very private about your affairs, and you'll usually have a secret agenda behind your actions. Your great stamina, focus, and discipline would be excellent assets for careers in the military or medical fields, especially research or surgery. When angry, you don't get mad—you get even!

Mars in Sagittarius

This expansive Mars often propels people into sales, travel, athletics, or philosophy. Your energies function well when you are on the move. You have a hot temper, and are inclined to say what you think before you consider the consequences. You shoot for high goals—and talk endlessly about them—but you may be weak on groundwork. This Mars needs a solid foundation. Watch a tendency to take unnecessary risks.

Mars in Capricorn

This is an ambitious Mars with an excellent sense of timing. You have an eye for those who can be of use to you, and you may dismiss people ruthlessly when you're angry, but you drive yourself hard and deliver full value. This is a good placement for an executive. You'll aim for status and a high material position in life, and you'll keep climbing despite the odds. A great Mars to have!

Mars in Aquarius

This is the most rebellious Mars. You seem to have a drive to assert yourself against the status quo. You may enjoy provoking people, shocking them out of traditional views. Or this placement could express itself in an offbeat sex life. Somehow you often find yourself in unconventional situations. You enjoy being a leader of an active group, which pursues forward-looking studies, politics, or goals.

Mars in Pisces

This Mars is a good actor who knows just how to appeal to the sympathies of others. You create and project wonderful fantasies, or you use your sensitive antennae to crusade for those less fortunate. You get what you want through creating a veil of illusion and glamour. This is a good Mars for someone in the creative and imaginative fields—a dancer, performer, photographer, actor. Many famous film stars have this placement. Watch a tendency to manipulate by making others feel sorry for you.

Jupiter Expands Your Life

This big, bright, swirling mass of gases is associated with abundance, prosperity, and the kind of windfall you get without too much hard work. You're optimistic under Jupiter's influence, when anything seems possible. You'll travel, expand your mind with higher education, and publish to share your knowledge widely. On the other hand, Jupiter's influence is neither discriminating nor disciplined. It represents the principle of growth without judgment, and therefore could result in extravagance, weight gain, laziness, and carelessness, if not kept in check.

Be sure to look up your Jupiter in the tables in this book. When the current position of Jupiter is favorable, you may get that lucky break. This is a great time to try new things, take risks, travel, or get more education. Opportunities seem to open up easily, so take advantage of them.

Once a year, Jupiter changes signs. That means you are due for an expansive time every twelve years, when Jupiter travels through your sun sign. You'll also have up periods every four years, when Jupiter is in the same element as your sun sign.

Jupiter in Aries

You are the soul of enthusiasm and optimism. Your luckiest times are when you are getting started on an exciting project or selling an idea that you really believe in. You may have to watch a tendency to be arrogant with those who do not share your enthusiasm. You follow your impulses, often ignoring budget or other commonsense limitations. To produce real, solid benefits, you'll need patience and follow-through wherever this Jupiter falls in your horoscope.

Jupiter in Taurus

You'll spend on beautiful material things, especially those that come from nature—items made of rare woods, natural fabrics, or precious gems, for instance. You can't have too much comfort or too many sensual pleasures. Watch a tendency to overindulge in good food, or to overpamper yourself with nothing but the best. Spartan living is not for you! You may be especially lucky in matters of real estate.

Jupiter in Gemini

You are the great talker of the zodiac, and you may be a great writer, too. But restlessness could be your weak point. You jump around, talk too much, and could be a jack-of-all-trades. Keeping a secret is especially difficult, so you'll have to watch a tendency to spill the beans. Since you love to be at the center of a beehive of activity, you'll have a vibrant social life. Your best opportunities will come through your talent for language—speaking, writing, communicating, and selling.

Jupiter in Cancer

You are luckiest in situations where you can find emotional closeness or deal with basic security needs such as food, nurturing, or shelter. You may be a great collector. Or you may simply love to accumulate things—you are the one who stashes things away for a rainy day. You probably have a very good memory and love children. In fact, you may have many children to care for. The food, hotel, child-care, and shipping businesses hold good opportunities for you.

Jupiter in Leo

You are a natural showman who loves to live in a larger-than-life way. Yours is a personality full of color that always finds its way into the limelight. You can't have too much attention or applause. Showbiz is a natural place for you, and so is any area where you can play to a crowd.

Exercising your flair for drama, your natural playfulness, and your romantic nature brings you good fortune. But watch a tendency to be overly extravagant or to monopolize center stage.

Jupiter in Virgo

You actually love those minute details others find boring. To you, they make all the difference between the perfect and the ordinary. You are the fine craftsman who spots every flaw. You expand your awareness by finding the most efficient methods and by being of service to others. Many of you will be drawn to medical or teaching fields. You'll also have luck in publishing, crafts, nutrition, and service professions. Watch out for a tendency to overwork.

Jupiter in Libra

This is an other-directed Jupiter that develops best with a partner. The stimulation of others helps you grow. You are also most comfortable in harmonious, beautiful situations and you work well with artistic people. You have a great sense of fair play and an ability to evaluate the pros and cons of a situation. You usually prefer to play the role of diplomat rather than adversary.

Jupiter in Scorpio

You love the feeling of power and control, of taking things to their limit. You can't resist a mystery. Your shrewd, penetrating mind sees right through to the heart of most situations and people. You have luck in work that provides for solutions to matters of life and death. You may be drawn to undercover work, behind-the-scenes intrigue, psychotherapy, the occult, and sex-related ventures. Your challenge will be to develop a sense of moderation and tolerance for other beliefs. You may have luck in handling other people's money—insurance, taxes, and inheritance can bring you a windfall.

Jupiter in Sagittarius

Independent, outgoing, and idealistic, you'll shoot for the stars. This Jupiter compels you to travel far and wide, both physically and mentally, via higher education. You may have luck while traveling in an exotic place. You also have luck with outdoor ventures, exercise, and animals, particularly horses. Since you tend to be very open about your opinions, watch a tendency to be tactless and to exaggerate. Instead, use your wonderful sense of humor to make your point.

Jupiter in Capricorn

Jupiter is much more restrained in Capricorn, the sign of rules and authority. Here, Jupiter can make you overwork and heighten any ambition or sense of duty you may have. You'll expand in areas that advance your position, putting you farther up the social or corporate ladder. You are lucky working within the establishment in a very structured situation where you can show off your ability to organize and reap rewards for your hard work.

Jupiter in Aquarius

This is another freedom-loving Jupiter, with great tolerance and originality. You are at your best when you are working for a humanitarian cause and in the company of many supporters. This is a good Jupiter for a political career. You'll relate to all kinds of people on all social levels. You have an abundance of original ideas, but you are best off away from routine and any situation that imposes rigid rules. You need mental stimulation!

Jupiter in Pisces

You are a giver whose feelings and pocketbook are easily touched by others, so choose your companions with care. You could be the original sucker for a hard-luck story. Better find a worthy hospital or a charity that will appreciate your selfless support. You have a great creative imagination. You may attract good fortune in fields related to oil, perfume, pharmaceuticals, petroleum, dance, footwear, and alcohol. But beware of overindulgence in alcohol—focus on a creative outlet instead.

Saturn Puts on the Brakes

Jupiter speeds you up with *lucky breaks* and quick energy. Then along comes Saturn to slow you down with the *disciplinary brakes*. Saturn has unfairly been called a malefic planet, one of the bad guys of the zodiac. On the contrary, Saturn is one of our best friends, the kind who tells you what you need to hear even if it's not good news. Under a Saturn transit, we grow up, take responsibility for our lives, and emerge from whatever test this planet has in store as far wiser, more capable and mature human beings. It is when we are under pressure that we grow stronger.

When Saturn hits a critical point in your horoscope, you can count on an experience that will make you slow up, pull back, and reexamine your life. It is a call to eliminate what is not working and to shape up. By the end of its twenty-eight-year trip around the zodiac, Saturn will have tested you in all areas of your life. The major tests happen in seven-year cycles, when Saturn passes over the angles of your chart—your rising sign, the top of your chart or midheaven, your descendant, and the nadir, or bottom, of your chart. This is when the real life-changing experiences happen. But you are also in for a testing period whenever Saturn passes a planet in your chart or stresses that planet from a distance. Therefore, it is useful to check your planetary positions with the timetable of Saturn to prepare in advance, or at least to brace yourself.

When Saturn returns to its location at the time of your birth, at approximately age twenty-eight, you'll have your first Saturn return. At this time, a person usually takes stock or settles down to find his mission in life and assumes full adult duties and responsibilities.

Another way Saturn helps us is to reveal the karmic lessons from previous lives and give us the chance to overcome them. So look at Saturn's challenges as much-needed opportunities for self-improvement. Under a Jupiter influence, you'll have more fun, but Saturn gives you solid, long-lasting results.

Look up your natal Saturn in the tables in this book for clues on where you need work.

Saturn in Aries

Saturn here puts the brakes on Aries' natural drive and enthusiasm. There is often an angry side to this placement. You don't let anyone push you around, and you know what's best for yourself. Following orders is not your strong point, and neither is diplomacy. You tend to be quick to go on the offensive in relationships, attacking first, before anyone attacks you. Because no one quite lives up to your standards, you often wind up doing everything yourself. You'll have to learn to cooperate and tone down self-centeredness. Both Pat Buchanan and Saddam Hussein have this Saturn.

Saturn in Taurus

A big issue is getting control of the cash flow. There will be lean periods that can be frightening, but you have the patience and endurance to stick them out and the methodical drive to prosper in the end. Learn to take a philosophical attitude, like Ben Franklin, who also had this placement and who said, "A penny saved is a penny earned."

Saturn in Gemini

You are a serious student of life, but you may have difficulty communicating or sharing your knowledge. You may be shy, speak slowly, or have fears about communicating, like Eleanor Roosevelt. You dwell in the realms of science, theory, or abstract analysis—even when you are dealing with the emotions, like Sigmund Freud, who also had this placement.

Saturn in Cancer

Your tests come with establishing a secure emotional base. In doing so, you may have to deal with some very basic fears centering on your early home environment. Most of your Saturn tests will have emotional roots in those early childhood experiences. You may have difficulty remaining objective in terms of what you try to achieve. So it will be especially important for you to deal with negative feelings such as guilt, paranoia, jealousy, resentment, and suspicion. Galileo and Michelangelo also navigated these murky waters.

Saturn in Leo

This is an authoritarian Saturn—a strict, demanding parent who may deny the pleasure principle in your zeal to see that rules are followed. Though you may feel guilty about taking the spotlight, you are very ambitious and loyal. You have to watch a tendency toward rigidity, also toward overwork and holding back affection. Joseph Kennedy and Billy Graham share this placement.

Saturn in Virgo

This is a cautious, exacting Saturn. You are intensely hard on yourself. Most of all, you give yourself the roughest time with your constant worries about every little detail, often making yourself sick. You may have difficulties setting priorities and getting the job done. Your tests will come in learning tolerance and understanding of others. Charles de Gaulle, Mae West, and Nathaniel Hawthorne had this meticulous Saturn.

Saturn in Libra

Saturn is exalted here, which makes this planet an ally. You may choose very serious, older partners in life, perhaps stemming from a fear of dependency. You need to learn to stand solidly on your own before you commit to another.

You are extremely cautious as you deliberate every involvement—with good reason. It is best that you find an occupation that makes good use of your sense of duty and honor. Steer clear of fly-by-night situations. Both Khruschev and Mao Tse-tung had this placement.

Saturn in Scorpio

You have great staying power. This Saturn tests you in situations involving the control of others. You may feel drawn to some kind of intrigue or undercover work, like J. Edgar Hoover. Or there may be an air of mystery surrounding your life and death, like Marilyn Monroe and Robert Kennedy, who both had this placement. There are lessons to be learned from your sexual involvements. Often sex is used for manipulation or is somehow out of the ordinary. The Roman emperor Caligula and the transsexual Christine Jorgensen are extreme cases.

Saturn in Sagittarius

Your challenges and lessons will come from tests of your spiritual and philosophical values, as happened to Martin Luther King and Gandhi. You are high-minded and sincere with this reflective, moral placement. Uncompromising in your ethical standards, you could become a benevolent despot.

Saturn in Capricorn

With the help of Saturn at maximum strength, your judgment will improve with age. And like Spencer Tracy's screen image, you'll be the gray-haired hero with a strong sense of responsibility. You advance in life slowly but steadily, always with a strong hand at the helm and an eye for the advantageous situation. Like Pat Robertson, you're likely to stand for conservative values. Negatively, you may be a loner, prone to periods of melancholy.

Saturn in Aquarius

Your tests come from relationships with groups. Do you care too much about what others think? Do you feel like an outsider, like Greta Garbo? You may fear being different from others and therefore slight your own unique, forward-looking gifts. Or like Lord Byron and Howard Hughes, you may take the opposite tack and rebel in the extreme. You can apply discipline to accomplish great humanitarian goals, as Albert Schweitzer did.

Saturn in Pisces

Your fear of the unknown and the irrational may lead you to the safety and protection of an institution. You may go on the run like Jesse James, who had this placement, to avoid looking too deeply inside. Or you might go in the opposite, more positive direction and develop a disciplined psychoanalytic approach, which puts you more in control of your feelings. Some of you will take refuge in work with hospitals, charities, or religious institutions. Queen Victoria, who had this placement, symbolized an era when institutions of all kinds were sustained. Discipline applied to artistic work, especially poetry and dance, or to spiritual work, such as yoga or meditation, might be helpful.

How Uranus, Neptune, and Pluto Influence a Whole Generation

These three planets remain in signs such a long time that a whole generation bears the imprint of the sign. Mass movements, great sweeping changes, fads that characterize a generation, even the issues of the conflicts and wars of the time are influenced by these "outer three" planets. When one of those distant planets changes signs, there is a definite shift in the atmosphere, the feeling of the end of an era.

Since these planets are so far away from the sun—too distant to be seen by the naked eye—they pick up signals from the universe at large. These planetary receivers literally link the sun with distant energies, and then perform a similar function in your horoscope by linking your central character with intuitive, spiritual, transformative forces from the cosmos. Each planet has a special domain, and will reflect this in the area of your chart where it falls.

Uranus Is the Surprise Ingredient

Uranus is the unexpected ingredient that sets you and your generation apart. There is nothing ordinary about this quirky green planet that seems to be traveling on its side, surrounded by a swarm of moons. Is it any wonder that astrologers assigned it to Aquarius, the most eccentric and gregarious sign? Uranus seems to wend its way around the sun, marching to its own tune.

Significantly, Uranus follows Saturn, the planet of limitations and structures. Often we get caught up in the structures we have created to give ourselves a sense of security. However, if we lose contact with our spiritual roots, then Uranus is likely to jolt us out of our comfortable rut and wake us up.

Uranus energy is electrical, happening in sudden flashes. It is not influenced by karma or past events, nor does it regard tradition, sex, or sentiment. The Uranus key words are surprise and awakening. Suddenly, there's that flash of inspiration, that bright idea, that totally new approach to revolutionize whatever scheme you were undertaking. A Uranus event takes you by surprise; it happens from out of the blue, for better or for worse. The Uranus place in your life is where you awaken and become your own person, leaving the structures of Saturn behind. And it is probably the most unconventional place in your chart.

Look up the sign of Uranus at the time of your birth and see where you follow your own tune.

Uranus in Aries

Birth Dates:

March 31, 1927–November 4, 1927

January 13, 1928–June 6, 1934
October 10, 1934–March 28, 1935

Your generation is original, creative, pioneering. It developed the computer, the airplane, and the cyclotron. You let nothing hold you back from exploring the unknown, and you have a powerful mixture of fire and electricity behind you. Women of your generation were among the first to be liberated. You were the unforgettable style setters. You have a surprise in store for everyone. Like Yoko Ono, Grace Kelly, and Jacqueline Onassis, your life may be jolted by sudden and violent changes.

Uranus in Taurus

Birth Dates:

June 6, 1934–October 10, 1934
March 28, 1935–August 7, 1941
October 5, 1941–May 15, 1942

The great territorial shake-ups of World War II began during your generation. You are independent, probably self-employed or would like to be. You have original ideas about making money, and you brace yourself for sudden changes of fortune. This Uranus can cause shake-ups, particularly in finances, but it can also make you a born entrepreneur, like Martha Stewart.

Uranus in Gemini

Birth Dates:

August 7, 1941–October 5, 1941
May 15, 1942–August 30, 1948
November 12, 1948–June 10, 1949

You were the first children to be influenced by television. Now, in your adult years, your generation stocks up on answering machines, cell phones, computers, and fax machines—any new way you can communicate. You have an inquiring mind, but your interests may be rather short-lived. This Uranus can be easily fragmented if there is no structure and focus.

Uranus in Cancer

Birth Dates:

August 30, 1948–November 12, 1948
June 10, 1949–August 24, 1955
January 28, 1956–June 10, 1956

This generation came at a time when divorce was becoming commonplace, so your home image is unconventional. You may have an unusual relationship with your parents; you may have come from a broken home or an unconventional one. You'll have unorthodox ideas about parenting, intimacy, food, and shelter. You may also be interested in dreams, psychic phenomena, and memory work.

Uranus in Leo

Birth Dates:

August 24, 1955–January 28, 1956
June 10, 1956–November 1, 1961
January 10, 1962–August 10, 1962

This generation understood how to use electronic media. Many of your group are now leaders in the high-tech industries, and you also understand how to use the new media to promote yourself. Like Isadora Duncan, you may have a very eccentric kind of charisma and a life that is sparked by unusual love affairs. Your children, too, may have traits that are out of the ordinary. Where this planet falls in your chart, you'll have a love of freedom, be a bit of an egomaniac, and show the full force of your personality in a unique way, like tennis great Martina Navratilova.

Uranus in Virgo

Birth Dates:

November 1, 1961–January 10, 1962
August 10, 1962–September 28, 1968
May 20, 1969–June 24, 1969

You'll have highly individual work methods. Many of you will be finding newer, more practical ways to use computers. Like Einstein, who had this placement, you'll break the rules brilliantly. Your generation came at a time of student rebellions, the civil rights movement, and the general acceptance of health foods. Chances are, you're concerned about pollution and cleaning up the environment. You may also be involved with nontraditional healing methods.

Uranus in Libra

Birth Dates:
September 28, 1968–May 20, 1969
June 24, 1969–November 21, 1974
May 1, 1975–September 8, 1975

Your generation will be always changing partners. Born during the era of women's liberation, you may have come from a broken home and may have no clear image of what a marriage entails. There will be many sudden splits and experiments before you settle down. Your generation will be much involved in legal and political reforms and in changing artistic and fashion looks.

Uranus in Scorpio

Birth Dates:
November 21, 1974–May 1, 1975
September 8, 1975–February 17, 1981
March 20, 1981–November 16, 1981

Interest in transformation, meditation, and life after death signaled the beginning of New Age consciousness. Your generation recognizes no boundaries, no limits, and no external controls. You'll have new attitudes toward death and dying, psychic phenomena, and the occult. Like Mae West and Casanova, you'll shock 'em sexually, too.

Uranus in Sagittarius

Birth Dates:
February 17, 1981–March 20, 1981
November 16, 1981–February 15, 1988
May 27, 1988–December 2, 1988

Could this generation be the first to travel in outer

space? An earlier generation with this placement included Charles Lindbergh and a time when the first zeppelins and the Wright Brothers were conquering the skies. Uranus here forecasts great discoveries, mind expansion, and long-distance travel. Like Galileo and Martin Luther, those born in these years will generate new theories about the cosmos and mankind's relation to it.

Uranus in Capricorn

Birth Dates:

December 20, 1904–January 30, 1912
September 4, 1912–November 12, 1912
February 15, 1988–May 27, 1988
December 2, 1988–April 1, 1995
June 9, 1995–January 12, 1996

This generation, now growing up, will challenge traditions with the help of electronic gadgets. In these years, we got organized with the help of technology put to practical use. The Internet was born following the great economic boom of the 1990s. Great leaders who were movers and shakers of history, like Julius Caesar and Henry VIII, were born under this placement.

Uranus in Aquarius

Birth Dates:

January 30, 1912–September 4, 1912
November 12, 1912–April 1, 1919
August 16, 1919–January 22, 1920
April 1, 1995–June 9, 1995
January 12, 1996–March 10, 2003
September 15, 2003–December 30, 2003

Uranus in Aquarius is the strongest placement for this planet. Recently we've had the opportunity to witness the full force of its power of innovation, as well as its sudden wake-up calls and insistence on humanitarian values. This was a time of high-tech development, when home computers became as ubiquitous as television. It was a time of globalization, of surprise attacks (9/11), and underdeveloped countries demanding attention. The last generation with this placement produced great innovative minds such as Leonard Bernstein and Orson Welles. The next will become another radical breakthrough generation, much concerned with global issues that involve all humanity.

Uranus in Pisces

Birth Dates:

April 1, 1919–August 16, 1919
January 22, 1920–March 31, 1927
November 4, 1927–January 12, 1928
March 10, 2003–September 15, 2003
December 20, 2003–May 28, 2010

Uranus is now in Pisces, ushering in a new generation. In the past century, Uranus in Pisces focused attention on the rise of electronic entertainment—radio and the cinema—and the secretiveness of Prohibition. This produced a generation of idealists exemplified by Judy Garland's theme "Somewhere over the Rainbow." Uranus in Pisces also hints at stealth activities, at hospital and prison reform, at high-tech drugs and medical experiments, at shake-ups and reforms in the Pisces-ruled petroleum industry, offshore drilling in new and unusual locations. Issues regarding the water and oil supply, water-related storm damage (Hurricane Katrina), sudden hurricanes, and floods demand our attention.

Neptune Is the Magic Solvent

Neptune is often maligned as the planet of illusions that dissolves reality, enabling you to escape the material world. Under Neptune's influence, you see what you want to see. But Neptune also encourages you to create. It embodies glamour, subtlety, mystery, and mysticism, and it governs anything that takes you beyond the mundane world, including out-of-body experiences.

Neptune acts to transcend your ordinary perceptions to take you to another level, where you experience either confusion or ecstasy. Its force can pull you off course only if you allow this to happen. Those who use Neptune wisely can translate their daydreams into poetry, theater, design, or inspired moves in the business world, avoiding the tricky "con artist" side of this planet.

Find your Neptune listed below.

Neptune in Cancer

Birth Dates:

July 19, 1901–December 25, 1901
May 21, 1902–September 23, 1914
December 14, 1914–July 19, 1915
March 19, 1916–May 2, 1916

Dreams of the homeland, idealistic patriotism, and glamorization of the nurturing assets of women characterized this time. You who were born here have unusual psychic ability and deep insights into basic needs of others.

Neptune in Leo

Birth Dates:

September 23, 1914–December 14, 1914
July 19, 1915–March 19, 1916
May 2, 1916–September 21, 1928
February 19, 1929–July 24, 1929

Neptune in Leo brought us the glamour and high living of the 1920s and the big spenders of that time. The Neptune temptations of gambling, seduction, theater, and lavish entertaining distracted from the realities of the age. Those born in that generation also made great advances in the arts.

Neptune in Virgo

Birth Dates:

September 21, 1928–February 19, 1929
July 24, 1929–October 3, 1942
April 17, 1943–August 2, 1943

Neptune in Virgo encompassed the 1930s, the Great Depression, and the beginning of World War II, when a new order was born. There was a time of facing "what doesn't work." Many were unemployed and found solace at the movies, watching the great Virgo star Greta Garbo or the escapist dance films of Busby Berkeley. New public services were born. Those with Neptune in Virgo later spread the gospel of health and fitness. This generation's devotion to spending hours at the office inspired the term *workaholic*.

Neptune in Libra

Birth Dates:

October 3, 1942–April 17, 1943
August 2, 1943–December 24, 1955
March 12, 1956–October 19, 1956
June 15, 1957–August 6, 1957

This was the time of World War II and the postwar period, when the world regained balance and returned to relative stability. Neptune in Libra was the romantic generation who would later be concerned with relating. As this generation matured, there was a new trend toward marriage and commitment. Racial and sexual equality became important issues, as they redesigned traditional roles to suit modern times.

Neptune in Scorpio

Birth Dates:

December 24, 1955–March 12, 1956
October 19, 1956–June 15, 1957
August 6, 1957–January 4, 1970
May 3, 1970–November 6, 1970

Neptune in Scorpio brought in a generation that would become interested in transformative power. Born in an era that glamorized sex, drugs, rock and roll, and Eastern religion, they matured in a more sobering time of AIDS, cocaine abuse, and New Age spirituality. As they evolve, they will become active in healing the planet from the results of the abuse of power.

Neptune in Sagittarius

Birth Dates:

January 4, 1970–May 3, 1970
November 6, 1970–January 19, 1984
June 23, 1984–November 21, 1984

Neptune in Sagittarius was the time when space and astronaut travel became a reality. The Neptune influence glamorized new approaches to mysticism, religion, and mind expansion. This generation will take a new approach to spiritual life, with emphasis on visions, mysticism, and clairvoyance.

Neptune in Capricorn

Birth Dates:

January 19, 1984–June 23, 1984
November 21, 1984–January 29, 1998

Neptune in Capricorn brought a time when delusions about material power were glamorized in the mid-1980s and 1990s. There was a boom in the stock market, and the Internet era spawned young tycoons who later lost it all. It was also a time when the psychic and occult worlds spawned a new category of business enterprise, and sold services on television.

Neptune in Aquarius

Birth Dates:

January 29, 1998–April 4, 2011

This should continue to be a time of breakthroughs. Here the creative influence of Neptune reaches a universal audience. This is a time of dissolving barriers, of globalization—when we truly become one world. During this transit of high-tech Aquarius, new kinds of entertainment media reach across cultural differences. However, the transit of Neptune has also raised boundary issues between cultures, especially in Middle Eastern countries with Neptune-ruled oil fields. As Neptune raises issues of social and political structures not being as solid as they seem, this could continue to produce rebellion and chaos in the environment. However, by using imagination (Neptune) in partnership with a global view (Aquarius) we could reach creative solutions.

Those born with this placement should be true citizens of the world with a remarkable creative ability to transcend social and cultural barriers.

Pluto Can Transform You

Though Pluto is a tiny, mysterious body in space, its influence is great. When Pluto zaps a strategic point in your horoscope, your life changes dramatically.

Little Pluto is the power behind the scenes; it affects you at deep levels of consciousness, causing events to come to the surface that will transform you and your generation. Nothing escapes, or is sacred, with this probing planet. Its purpose is to wipe out the past so something new can happen.

The Pluto place in your horoscope is where you have invisible power (Mars governs the visible power), where you can transform, heal, and affect the unconscious needs of the masses. Pluto tells lots about how your generation projects power, what makes it seem cool to others. And when Pluto changes signs, there is a whole new concept of what's cool. Pluto's strange elliptical orbit occasionally runs inside the orbit of neighboring Neptune. Because of its eccentric path, the length of time Pluto stays in any given sign can vary from thirteen to thirty-two years. It covered only seven signs in the last century.

Pluto in Gemini

Birth Dates:

Late 1800s–May 26, 1914

This was a time of mass suggestion and breakthroughs in communications, a time when many brilliant writers such as Ernest Hemingway and F. Scott Fitzgerald were born. Henry Miller, D. H. Lawrence, and James Joyce scandalized society by using explicit sexual images and language in their literature. "Muckraking" journalists exposed corruption. Pluto-ruled Scorpio President Theodore Roosevelt said, "Speak softly, but carry a big stick." This generation had an intense need to communicate and made major breakthroughs in knowledge. A compulsive restlessness and a thirst for a variety of experiences characterized many of this generation.

Pluto in Cancer

Birth Dates:
May 26, 1914–June 14, 1939

Dictators and mass media arose to wield emotional power over the masses. Women's rights was a popular issue. Deep sentimental feelings, acquisitiveness, and possessiveness characterized these times and people. Most of the great stars of the Hollywood era that embodied the American image were born during this period: Grace Kelly, Esther Williams, Frank Sinatra, Lana Turner, to name a few.

Pluto in Leo

Birth Dates:
June 14, 1939–August, 19, 1957

The performing arts played on the emotions of the masses. Mick Jagger, John Lennon, and rock and roll were born at this time. So were "baby boomers" like Bill and Hillary Clinton. Those born here tend to be self-centered, powerful, and boisterous. This generation does its own thing, for better or for worse.

Pluto in Virgo

Birth Dates:
August 19, 1957–October 5, 1971
April 17, 1972–July 30, 1972

This is the "yuppie" generation that sparked a mass movement toward fitness, health, and career. It is a much more sober, serious, driven generation than the fun-loving Pluto in Leo. During this time, machines were invented to process detail work efficiently. Inventions took a practical turn with answering machines, fax machines, car phones, and home office equipment—all making the workplace far more efficient.

Pluto in Libra

Birth Dates:

October 5, 1971–April 17, 1972
July 30, 1972–November 5, 1983
May 18, 1984–August 27, 1984

A mellower generation, people born at this time are concerned with partnerships, working together, and finding diplomatic solutions to problems. Marriage is important to this generation, and they will define it by combining traditional values with equal partnership. This was a time of women's liberation, gay rights, ERA, and legal battles over abortion, all of which transformed our ideas about relationships.

Pluto in Scorpio

Birth Dates:

November 5, 1983–May 18, 1984
August 27, 1984–January 17, 1995

Pluto was in the sign it rules for a comparatively short period of time. However, this was a time of record achievements, destructive sexually transmitted diseases, nuclear power controversies, and explosive political issues. Pluto destroys in order to create new understanding—the phoenix rising from the ashes—which should be some consolation for those of you who felt Pluto's force before 1995. Sexual shockers were par for the course during these intense years when black clothing, transvestites, body piercing, tattoos, and sexually explicit advertising pushed the boundaries of good taste.

Pluto in Sagittarius

Birth Dates:

January 17, 1995–April 20, 1995

November 10, 1995–January 26, 2008

During the most recent Pluto transit, we were pushed to expand our horizons, to find deeper spiritual meaning in life. Pluto's opposition with Saturn in 2001 brought an enormous conflict between traditional societies and the forces of change. It signals a time when religious convictions exerted more power in our political life as well.

Since Sagittarius is associated with travel, Pluto, the planet of extremes, made space travel a reality for some wealthy adventurers, who paid for the privilege of travel on space shuttles.

New dimensions in electronic publishing, concern with animal rights and the environment, and an increasing emphasis on extreme forms of religion are other signs of these times. Charismatic religious leaders asserted themselves and questions of the boundaries between church and state arose. There were also sexual scandals associated with the church. Because this period ends this year, hopefully we will have developed far-reaching philosphies to elevate our lives with a new sense of purpose.

Pluto in Capricorn

Birth Dates:

January 25, 2008–June 13, 2008

November 26, 2008–January 20, 2024

Since Pluto in Jupiter-ruled Sagittarius signaled a time of expansion and globalization, Pluto's entry into Saturn-ruled Capricorn this year will signal a time of adjustment, of facing reality and limitations, then finding pragmatic solutions. It will be a time when a new structure is imposed, when we become concerned with what actually works. Because Capricorn is associated with corporations and also with responsibility and duty, look for dramatic changes in business practices, hopefully with more attention paid to ethical and social responsibility as well as the bottom line. Big business will have enormous power during this transit, perhaps handling what governments have been unable to accomplish. There will be an emphasis on trimming down, perhaps a new belt-tightening regime. And since Capricorn is the sign of Father Time, there will be a new emphasis on the aging of the population. The generation born now is sure to be a more practical and realistic one than that of their older Pluto-in-Sagittarius siblings.

VENUS SIGNS 1901–2008

	Aries	Taurus	Gemini	Cancer	Leo	Virgo
1901	3/29–4/22	4/22–5/17	5/17–6/10	6/10–7/5	7/5–7/29	7/29–8/23
1902	5/7–6/3	6/3–6/30	6/30–7/25	7/25–8/19	8/19–9/13	9/13–10/7
1903	2/28–3/24	3/24–4/18	4/18–5/13	5/13–6/9	6/9–7/7	7/7–8/17 9/6–11/8
1904	3/13–5/7	5/7–6/1	6/1–6/25	6/25–7/19	7/19–8/13	8/13–9/6
1905	2/3–3/6 4/9–5/28	3/6–4/9 5/28–7/8	7/8–8/6	8/6–9/1	9/1–9/27	9/27–10/21
1906	3/1–4/7	4/7–5/2	5/2–5/26	5/26–6/20	6/20–7/16	7/16–8/11
1907	4/27–5/22	5/22–6/16	6/16–7/11	7/11–8/4	8/4–8/29	8/29–9/22
1908	2/14–3/10	3/10–4/5	4/5–5/5	5/5–9/8	9/8–10/8	10/8–11/3
1909	3/29–4/22	4/22–5/16	5/16–6/10	6/10–7/4	7/4–7/29	7/29–8/23
1910	5/7–6/3	6/4–6/29	6/30–7/24	7/25–8/18	8/19–9/12	9/13–10/6
1911	2/28–3/23	3/24–4/17	4/18–5/12	5/13–6/8	6/9–7/7	7/8–11/18
1912	4/13–5/6	5/7–5/31	6/1–6/24	6/24–7/18	7/19–8/12	8/13–9/5
1913	2/3–3/6 5/2–5/30	3/7–5/1 5/31–7/7	7/8–8/5	8/6–8/31	9/1–9/26	9/27–10/20
1914	3/14–4/6	4/7–5/1	5/2–5/25	5/26–6/19	6/20–7/15	7/16–8/10
1915	4/27–5/21	5/22–6/15	6/16–7/10	7/11–8/3	8/4–8/28	8/29–9/21
1916	2/14–3/9	3/10–4/5	4/6–5/5	5/6–9/8	9/9–10/7	10/8–11/2
1917	3/29–4/21	4/22–5/15	5/16–6/9	6/10–7/3	7/4–7/28	7/29–8/21
1918	5/7–6/2	6/3–6/28	6/29–7/24	7/25–8/18	8/19–9/11	9/12–10/5
1919	2/27–3/22	3/23–4/16	4/17–5/12	5/13–6/7	6/8–7/7	7/8–11/8
1920	4/12–5/6	5/7–5/30	5/31–6/23	6/24–7/18	7/19–8/11	8/12–9/4
1921	2/3–3/6 4/26–6/1	3/7–4/25 6/2–7/7	7/8–8/5	8/6–8/31	9/1–9/25	9/26–10/20
1922	3/13–4/6	4/7–4/30	5/1–5/25	5/26–6/19	6/20–7/14	7/15–8/9
1923	4/27–5/21	5/22–6/14	6/15–7/9	7/10–8/3	8/4–8/27	8/28–9/20
1924	2/13–3/8	3/9–4/4	4/5–5/5	5/6–9/8	9/9–10/7	10/8–11/12
1925	3/28–4/20	4/21–5/15	5/16–6/8	6/9–7/3	7/4–7/27	7/28–8/21

Libra	Scorpio	Sagittarius	Capricorn	Aquarius	Pisces
8/23–9/17	9/17–10/12	10/12–1/16	1/16–2/9	2/9–3/5	3/5–3/29
			11/7–12/5	12/5–1/11	
10/7–10/31	10/31–11/24	11/24–12/18	12/18–1/11	2/6–4/4	1/11–2/6
					4/4–5/7
8/17–9/6	12/9–1/5			1/11–2/4	2/4–2/28
11/8–12/9					
9/6–9/30	9/30–10/25	1/5–1/30	1/30–2/24	2/24–3/19	3/19–4/13
		10/25–11/18	11/18–12/13	12/13–1/7	
10/21–11/14	11/14–12/8	12/8–1/1/06			1/7–2/3
8/11–9/7	9/7–10/9	10/9–12/15	1/1–1/25	1/25–2/18	2/18–3/14
	12/15–12/25	12/25–2/6			
9/22–10/16	10/16–11/9	11/9–12/3	2/6–3/6	3/6–4/2	4/2–4/27
			12/3–12/27	12/27–1/20	
11/3–11/28	11/28–12/22	12/22–1/15			1/20–2/4
8/23–9/17	9/17–10/12	10/12–11/17	1/15–2/9	2/9–3/5	3/5–3/29
			11/17–12/5	12/5–1/15	
10/7–10/30	10/31–11/23	11/24–12/17	12/18–12/31	1/1–1/15	1/16–1/28
				1/29–4/4	4/5–5/6
11/19–12/8	12/9–12/31		1/1–1/10	1/11–2/2	2/3–2/27
9/6–9/30	1/1–1/4	1/5–1/29	1/30–2/23	2/24–3/18	3/19–4/12
	10/1–10/24	10/25–11/17	11/18–12/12	12/13–12/31	
10/21–11/13	11/14–12/7	12/8–12/31		1/1–1/6	1/7–2/2
8/11–9/6	9/7–10/9	10/10–12/5	1/1–1/24	1/25–2/17	2/18–3/13
	12/6–12/30	12/31			
9/22–10/15	10/16–11/8	1/1–2/6	2/7–3/6	3/7–4/1	4/2–4/26
		11/9–12/2	12/3–12/26	12/27–12/31	
11/3–11/27	11/28–12/21	12/22–12/31		1/1–1/19	1/20–2/13
8/22–9/16	9/17–10/11	1/1–1/14	1/15–2/7	2/8–3/4	3/5–3/28
		10/12–11/6	11/7–12/5	12/6–12/31	
10/6–10/29	10/30–11/22	11/23–12/16	12/17–12/31	1/1–4/5	4/6–5/6
11/9–12/8	12/9–12/31		1/1–1/9	1/10–2/2	2/3–2/26
9/5–9/30	1/1–1/3	1/4–1/28	1/29–2/22	2/23–3/18	3/19–4/11
	9/31–10/23	10/24–11/17	11/18–12/11	12/12–12/31	
10/21–11/13	11/14–12/7	12/8–12/31		1/1–1/6	1/7–2/2
8/10–9/6	9/7–10/10	10/11–11/28	1/1–1/24	1/25–2/16	2/17–3/12
	11/29–12/31				
9/21–10/14	1/1	1/2–2/6	2/7–3/5	3/6–3/31	4/1–4/26
	10/15–11/7	11/8–12/1	12/2–12/25	12/26–12/31	
11/13–11/26	11/27–12/21	12/22–12/31		1/1–1/19	1/20–2/12
8/22–9/15	9/16–10/11	1/1–1/14	1/15–2/7	2/8–3/3	3/4–3/27
		10/12–11/6	11/7–12/5	12/6–12/31	

VENUS SIGNS 1901–2008

	Aries	Taurus	Gemini	Cancer	Leo	Virgo
1926	5/7–6/2	6/3–6/28	6/29–7/23	7/24–8/17	8/18–9/11	9/12–10/5
1927	2/27–3/22	3/23–4/16	4/17–5/11	5/12–6/7	6/8–7/7	7/8–11/9
1928	4/12–5/5	5/6–5/29	5/30–6/23	6/24–7/17	7/18–8/11	8/12–9/4
1929	2/3–3/7 4/20–6/2	3/8–4/19 6/3–7/7	7/8–8/4	8/5–8/30	8/31–9/25	9/26–10/19
1930	3/13–4/5	4/6–4/30	5/1–5/24	5/25–6/18	6/19–7/14	7/15–8/9
1931	4/26–5/20	5/21–6/13	6/14–7/8	7/9–8/2	8/3–8/26	8/27–9/19
1932	2/12–3/8	3/9–4/3	4/4–5/5 7/13–7/27	5/6–7/12 7/28–9/8	9/9–10/6	10/7–11/1
1933	3/27–4/19	4/20–5/28	5/29–6/8	6/9–7/2	7/3–7/26	7/27–8/20
1934	5/6–6/1	6/2–6/27	6/28–7/22	7/23–8/16	8/17–9/10	9/11–10/4
1935	2/26–3/21	3/22–4/15	4/16–5/10	5/11–6/6	6/7–7/6	7/7–11/8
1936	4/11–5/4	5/5–5/28	5/29–6/22	6/23–7/16	7/17–8/10	8/11–9/4
1937	2/2–3/8 4/14–6/3	3/9–4/13 6/4–7/6	7/7–8/3	8/4–8/29	8/30–9/24	9/25–10/18
1938	3/12–4/4	4/5–4/28	4/29–5/23	5/24–6/18	6/19–7/13	7/14–8/8
1939	4/25–5/19	5/20–6/13	6/14–7/8	7/9–8/1	8/2–8/25	8/26–9/19
1940	2/12–3/7	3/8–4/3	4/4–5/5 7/5–7/31	5/6–7/4 8/1–9/8	9/9–10/5	10/6–10/31
1941	3/27–4/19	4/20–5/13	5/14–6/6	6/7–7/1	7/2–7/26	7/27–8/20
1942	5/6–6/1	6/2–6/26	6/27–7/22	7/23–8/16	8/17–9/9	9/10–10/3
1943	2/25–3/20	3/21–4/14	4/15–5/10	5/11–6/6	6/7–7/6	7/7–11/8
1944	4/10–5/3	5/4–5/28	5/29–6/21	6/22–7/16	7/17–8/9	8/10–9/2
1945	2/2–3/10 4/7–6/3	3/11–4/6 6/4–7/6	7/7–8/3	8/4–8/29	8/30–9/23	9/24–10/18
1946	3/11–4/4	4/5–4/28	4/29–5/23	5/24–6/17	6/18–7/12	7/13–8/8
1947	4/25–5/19	5/20–6/12	6/13–7/7	7/8–8/1	8/2–8/25	8/26–9/18
1948	2/11–3/7	3/8–4/3	4/4–5/6 6/29–8/2	5/7–6/28 8/3–9/7	9/8–10/5	10/6–10/31
1949	3/26–4/19	4/20–5/13	5/14–6/6	6/7–6/30	7/1–7/25	7/26–8/19
1950	5/5–5/31	6/1–6/26	6/27–7/21	7/22–8/15	8/16–9/9	9/10–10/3
1951	2/25–3/21	3/22–4/15	4/16–5/10	5/11–6/6	6/7–7/7	7/8–11/9

Libra	Scorpio	Sagittarius	Capricorn	Aquarius	Pisces
10/6–10/29	10/30–11/22	11/23–12/16	12/17–12/31	1/1–4/5	4/6–5/6
11/10–12/8	12/9–12/31	1/1–1/7	1/8	1/9–2/1	2/2–2/26
9/5–9/28	1/1–1/3	1/4–1/28	1/29–2/22	2/23–3/17	3/18–4/11
	9/29–10/23	10/24–11/16	11/17–12/11	12/12–12/31	
10/20–11/12	11/13–12/6	12/7–12/30	12/31	1/1–1/5	1/6–2/2
8/10–9/6	9/7–10/11	10/12–11/21	1/1–1/23	1/24–2/16	2/17–3/12
	11/22–12/31				
9/20–10/13	1/1–1/3	1/4–2/6	2/7–3/4	3/5–3/31	4/1–4/25
	10/14–11/6	11/7–11/30	12/1–12/24	12/25–12/31	
11/2–11/25	11/26–12/20	12/21–12/31		1/1–1/18	1/19–2/11
8/21–9/14	9/15–10/10	1/1–1/13	1/14–2/6	2/7–3/2	3/3–3/26
		10/11–11/5	11/6–12/4	12/5–12/31	
10/5–10/28	10/29–11/21	11/22–12/15	12/16–12/31	1/1–4/5	4/6–5/5
11/9–12/7	12/8–12/31		1/1–1/7	1/8–1/31	2/1–2/25
9/5–9/27	1/1–1/2	1/3–1/27	1/28–2/21	2/22–3/16	3/17–4/10
	9/28–10/22	10/23–11/15	11/16–12/10	12/11–12/31	
10/19–11/11	11/12–12/5	12/6–12/29	12/30–12/31	1/1–1/5	1/6–2/1
8/9–9/6	9/7–10/13	10/14–11/14	1/1–1/22	1/23–2/15	2/16–3/11
	11/15–12/31				
9/20–10/13	1/1–1/3	1/4–2/5	2/6–3/4	3/5–3/30	3/31–4/24
	10/14–11/6	11/7–11/30	12/1–12/24	12/25–12/31	
11/1–11/25	11/26–12/19	12/20–12/31		1/1–1/18	1/19–2/11
8/21–9/14	9/15–10/9	1/1–1/12	1/13–2/5	2/6–3/1	3/2–3/26
		10/10–11/5	11/6–12/4	12/5–12/31	
10/4–10/27	10/28–11/20	11/21–12/14	12/15–12/31	1/1–4/5	4/6–5/5
11/9–12/7	12/8–12/31		1/1–1/7	1/8–1/31	2/1–2/24
9/3–9/27	1/1–1/2	1/3–1/27	1/28–2/20	2/21–3/16	3/17–4/9
	9/28–10/21	10/22–11/15	11/16–12/10	12/11–12/31	
10/19–11/11	11/12–12/5	12/6–12/29	12/30–12/31	1/1–1/4	1/5–2/1
8/9–9/6	9/7–10/15	10/16–11/7	1/1–1/21	1/22–2/14	2/15–3/10
	11/8–12/31				
9/19–10/12	1/1–1/4	1/5–2/5	2/6–3/4	3/5–3/29	3/30–4/24
	10/13–11/5	11/6–11/29	11/30–12/23	12/24–12/31	
11/1–11/25	11/26–12/19	12/20–12/31		1/1–1/17	1/18–2/10
8/20–9/14	9/15–10/9	1/1–1/12	1/13–2/5	2/6–3/1	3/2–3/25
		10/10–11/5	11/6–12/5	12/6–12/31	
10/4–10/27	10/28–11/20	11/21–12/13	12/14–12/31	1/1–4/5	4/6–5/4
11/10–12/7	12/8–12/31		1/1–1/7	1/8–1/31	2/1–2/24

VENUS SIGNS 1901–2008

	Aries	Taurus	Gemini	Cancer	Leo	Virgo
1952	4/10–5/4	5/5–5/28	5/29–6/21	6/22–7/16	7/17–8/9	8/10–9/3
1953	2/2–3/3	3/4–3/31	7/8–8/3	8/4–8/29	8/30–9/24	9/25–10/18
	4/1–6/5	6/6–7/7				
1954	3/12–4/4	4/5–4/28	4/29–5/23	5/24–6/17	6/18–7/13	7/14–8/8
1955	4/25–5/19	5/20–6/13	6/14–7/7	7/8–8/1	8/2–8/25	8/26–9/18
1956	2/12–3/7	3/8–4/4	4/5–5/7	5/8–6/23	9/9–10/5	10/6–10/31
			6/24–8/4	8/5–9/8		
1957	3/26–4/19	4/20–5/13	5/14–6/6	6/7–7/1	7/2–7/26	7/27–8/19
1958	5/6–5/31	6/1–6/26	6/27–7/22	7/23–8/15	8/16–9/9	9/10–10/3
1959	2/25–3/20	3/21–4/14	4/15–5/10	5/11–6/6	6/7–7/8	7/9–9/20
					9/21–9/24	9/25–11/9
1960	4/10–5/3	5/4–5/28	5/29–6/21	6/22–7/15	7/16–8/9	8/10–9/2
1961	2/3–6/5	6/6–7/7	7/8–8/3	8/4–8/29	8/30–9/23	9/24–10/17
1962	3/11–4/3	4/4–4/28	4/29–5/22	5/23–6/17	6/18–7/12	7/13–8/8
1963	4/24–5/18	5/19–6/12	6/13–7/7	7/8–7/31	8/1–8/25	8/26–9/18
1964	2/11–3/7	3/8–4/4	4/5–5/9	5/10–6/17	9/9–10/5	10/6–10/31
			6/18–8/5	8/6–9/8		
1965	3/26–4/18	4/19–5/12	5/13–6/6	6/7–6/30	7/1–7/25	7/26–8/19
1966	5/6–5/31	6/1–6/26	6/27–7/21	7/22–8/15	8/16–9/8	9/9–10/2
1967	2/24–3/20	3/21–4/14	4/15–5/10	5/11–6/6	6/7–7/8	7/9–9/9
					9/10–10/1	10/2–11/9
1968	4/9–5/3	5/4–5/27	5/28–6/20	6/21–7/15	7/16–8/8	8/9–9/2
1969	2/3–6/6	6/7–7/6	7/7–8/3	8/4–8/28	8/29–9/22	9/23–10/17
1970	3/11–4/3	4/4–4/27	4/28–5/22	5/23–6/16	6/17–7/12	7/13–8/8
1971	4/24–5/18	5/19–6/12	6/13–7/6	7/7–7/31	8/1–8/24	8/25–9/17
1972	2/11–3/7	3/8–4/3	4/4–5/10	5/11–6/11		
			6/12–8/6	8/7–9/8	9/9–10/5	10/6–10/30
1973	3/25–4/18	4/18–5/12	5/13–6/5	6/6–6/29	7/1–7/25	7/26–8/19
1974	5/5–5/31	6/1–6/25	6/26–7/21	7/22–8/14	8/15–9/8	9/9–10/2
1975	2/24–3/20	3/21–4/13	4/14–5/9	5/10–6/6	6/7–7/9	7/10–9/2
					9/3–10/4	10/5–11/9

Libra	Scorpio	Sagittarius	Capricorn	Aquarius	Pisces
9/4–9/27	1/1–1/2	1/3–1/27	1/28–2/20	2/21–3/16	3/17–4/9
	9/28–10/21	10/22–11/15	11/16–12/10	12/11–12/31	
10/19–11/11	11/12–12/5	12/6–12/29	12/30–12/31	1/1–1/5	1/6–2/1
8/9–9/6	9/7–10/22	10/23–10/27	1/1–1/22	1/23–2/15	2/16–3/11
	10/28–12/31				
9/19–10/13	1/1–1/6	1/7–2/5	2/6–3/4	3/5–3/30	3/31–4/24
	10/14–11/5	11/6–11/30	12/1–12/24	12/25–12/31	
11/1–11/25	11/26–12/19	12/20–12/31		1/1–1/17	1/18–2/11
8/20–9/14	9/15–10/9	1/1–1/12	1/13–2/5	2/6–3/1	3/2–3/25
		10/10–11/5	11/6–12/6	12/7–12/31	
10/4–10/27	10/28–11/20	11/21–12/14	12/15–12/31	1/1–4/6	4/7–5/5
11/10–12/7	12/8–12/31		1/1–1/7	1/8–1/31	2/1–2/24
9/3–9/26	1/1–1/2	1/3–1/27	1/28–2/20	2/21–3/15	3/16–4/9
	9/27–10/21	10/22–11/15	11/16–12/10	12/11–12/31	
10/18–11/11	11/12–12/4	12/5–12/28	12/29–12/31	1/1–1/5	1/6–2/2
8/9–9/6	9/7–12/31		1/1–1/21	1/22–2/14	2/15–3/10
9/19–10/12	1/1–1/6	1/7–2/5	2/6–3/4	3/5–3/29	3/30–4/23
	10/13–11/5	11/6–11/29	11/30–12/23	12/24–12/31	
11/1–11/24	11/25–12/19	12/20–12/31		1/1–1/16	1/17–2/10
8/20–9/13	9/14–10/9	1/1–1/12	1/13–2/5	2/6–3/1	3/2–3/25
		10/10–11/5	11/6–12/7	12/8–12/31	
10/3–10/26	10/27–11/19	11/20–12/13	2/7–2/25	1/1–2/6	4/7–5/5
			12/14–12/31	2/26–4/6	
11/10–12/7	12/8–12/31		1/1–1/6	1/7–1/30	1/31–2/23
9/3–9/26	1/1	1/2–1/26	1/27–2/20	2/21–3/15	3/16–4/8
	9/27–10/21	10/22–11/14	11/15–12/9	12/10–12/31	
10/18–11/10	11/11–12/4	12/5–12/28	12/29–12/31	1/1–1/4	1/5–2/2
8/9–9/7	9/8–12/31		1/1–1/21	1/22–2/14	2/15–3/10
9/18–10/11	1/1–1/7	1/8–2/5	2/6–3/4	3/5–3/29	3/30–4/23
	10/12–11/5	11/6–11/29	11/30–12/23	12/24–12/31	
10/31–11/24	11/25–12/18	12/19–12/31		1/1–1/16	1/17–2/10
8/20–9/13	9/14–10/8	1/1–1/12	1/13–2/4	2/5–2/28	3/1–3/24
		10/9–11/5	11/6–12/7	12/8–12/31	
10/3–10/26	10/27–11/19	11/20–12/13	12/14–12/31	3/1–4/6	4/7–5/4
			1/30–2/28	1/1–1/29	
11/10–12/7	12/8–12/31		1/1–1/6	1/7–1/30	1/31–2/23

VENUS SIGNS 1901–2008

	Aries	Taurus	Gemini	Cancer	Leo	Virgo
1976	4/8–5/2	5/2–5/27	5/27–6/20	6/20–7/14	7/14–8/8	8/8–9/1
1977	2/2–6/6	6/6–7/6	7/6–8/2	8/2–8/28	8/28–9/22	9/22–10/17
1978	3/9–4/2	4/2–4/27	4/27–5/22	5/22–6/16	6/16–7/12	7/12–8/6
1979	4/23–5/18	5/18–6/11	6/11–7/6	7/6–7/30	7/30–8/24	8/24–9/17
1980	2/9–3/6	3/6–4/3	4/3–5/12	5/12–6/5	9/7–10/4	10/4–10/30
			6/5–8/6	8/6–9/7		
1981	3/24–4/17	4/17–5/11	5/11–6/5	6/5–6/29	6/29–7/24	7/24–8/18
1982	5/4–5/30	5/30–6/25	6/25–7/20	7/20–8/14	8/14–9/7	9/7–10/2
1983	2/22–3/19	3/19–4/13	4/13–5/9	5/9–6/6	6/6–7/10	7/10–8/27
					8/27–10/5	10/5–11/9
1984	4/7–5/2	5/2–5/26	5/26–6/20	6/20–7/14	7/14–8/7	8/7–9/1
1985	2/2–6/6	6/7–7/6	7/6–8/2	8/2–8/28	8/28–9/22	9/22–10/16
1986	3/9–4/2	4/2–4/26	4/26–5/21	5/21–6/15	6/15–7/11	7/11–8/7
1987	4/22–5/17	5/17–6/11	6/11–7/5	7/5–7/30	7/30–8/23	8/23–9/16
1988	2/9–3/6	3/6–4/3	4/3–5/17	5/17–5/27	9/7–10/4	10/4–10/29
			5/27–8/6	8/28–9/22	9/22–10/16	
1989	3/23–4/16	4/16–5/11	5/11–6/4	6/4–6/29	6/29–7/24	7/24–8/18
1990	5/4–5/30	5/30–6/25	6/25–7/20	7/20–8/13	8/13–9/7	9/7–10/1
1991	2/22–3/18	3/18–4/13	4/13–5/9	5/9–6/6	6/6–7/11	7/11–8/21
					8/21–10/6	10/6–11/9
1992	4/7–5/1	5/1–5/26	5/26–6/19	6/19–7/13	7/13–8/7	8/7–8/31
1993	2/2–6/6	6/6–7/6	7/6–8/1	8/1–8/27	8/27–9/21	9/21–10/16
1994	3/8–4/1	4/1–4/26	4/26–5/21	5/21–6/15	6/15–7/11	7/11–8/7
1995	4/22–5/16	5/16–6/10	6/10–7/5	7/5–7/29	7/29–8/23	8/23–9/16
1996	2/9–3/6	3/6–4/3	4/3–8/7	8/7–9/7	9/7–10/4	10/4–10/29
1997	3/23–4/16	4/16–5/10	5/10–6/4	6/4–6/28	6/28–7/23	7/23–8/17
1998	5/3–5/29	5/29–6/24	6/24–7/19	7/19–8/13	8/13–9/6	9/6–9/30
1999	2/21–3/18	3/18–4/12	4/12–5/8	5/8–6/5	6/5–7/12	7/12–8/15
					8/15–10/7	10/7–11/9
2000	4/6–5/1	5/1–5/25	5/25–6/13	6/13–7/13	7/13–8/6	8/6–8/31
2001	2/2–6/6	6/6–7/5	7/5–8/1	8/1–8/26	8/26–9/20	9/20–10/15
2002	3/7–4/1	4/1–4/25	4/25–5/20	5/20–6/14	6/14–7/10	7/10–8/7
2003	4/21–5/16	5/16–6/9	6/9–7/4	7/4–7/29	7/29–8/22	8/22–9/15
2004	2/8–3/5	3/5–4/3	4/3–8/7	8/7–9/6	9/6–10/3	10/3–10/28
2005	3/22–4/15	4/15–5/10	5/10–6/3	6/3–6/28	6/28–7/23	7/23–8/17
2006	5/3–5/29	5/29–6/24	6/24–7/19	7/19–8/12	8/12–9/6	9/6–9/30
2007	2/21–3/16	3/17–4/10	4/11–5/7	5/8–6/4	6/5–7/13	7/14–8/7
					8/8–10/6	10/7–11/7
2008	4/6–4/30	5/1–5/24	5/25–6/17	6/18–7/11	7/12–8/4	8/5–8/29

Libra	Scorpio	Sagittarius	Capricorn	Aquarius	Pisces
9/1–9/26	9/26–10/20	1/1–1/26	1/26–2/19	2/19–3/15	3/15–4/8
10/17–11/10	11/10–12/4	12/4–12/27	12/27–1/20/78		1/4–2/2
8/6–9/7	9/7–1/7			1/20–2/13	2/13–3/9
9/17–10/11	10/11–11/4	1/7–2/5	2/5–3/3	3/3–3/29	3/29–4/23
		11/4–11/28	11/28–12/22	12/22–1/16/80	
10/30–11/24	11/24–12/18	12/18–1/11/81			1/16–2/9
8/18–9/12	9/12–10/9	10/9–11/5	1/11–2/4	2/4–2/28	2/28–3/24
			11/5–12/8	12/8–1/23/82	
10/2–10/26	10/26–11/18	11/18–12/12	1/23–3/2	3/2–4/6	4/6–5/4
			12/12–1/5/83		
11/9–12/6	12/6–1/1/84			1/5–1/29	1/29–2/22
9/1–9/25	9/25–10/20	1/1–1/25	1/25–2/19	2/19–3/14	3/14–4/7
		10/20–11/13	11/13–12/9	12/10–1/4	
10/16–11/9	11/9–12/3	12/3–12/27	12/28–1/19		1/4–2/2
8/7–9/7	9/7–1/7			1/20–2/13	2/13–3/9
9/16–10/10	10/10–11/3	1/7–2/5	2/5–3/3	3/3–3/28	3/28–4/22
		11/3–11/28	11/28–12/22	12/22–1/15	
10/29–11/23	11/23–12/17	12/17–1/10			1/15–2/9
8/18–9/12	9/12–10/8	10/8–11/5	1/10–2/3	2/3–2/27	2/27–3/23
			11/5–12/10	12/10–1/16/90	
10/1–10/25	10/25–11/18	11/18–12/12	1/16–3/3	3/3–4/6	4/6–5/4
			12/12–1/5		
11/9–12/6	12/6–12/31	12/31–1/25/92		1/5–1/29	1/29–2/22
8/31–9/25	9/25–10/19	10/19–11/13	1/25–2/18	2/18–3/13	3/13–4/7
			11/13–12/8	12/8–1/3/93	
10/16–11/9	11/9–12/2	12/2–12/26	12/26–1/19		1/3–2/2
8/7–9/7	9/7–1/7			1/19–2/12	2/12–3/8
9/16–10/10	10/10–11/13	1/7–2/4	2/4–3/2	3/2–3/28	3/28–4/22
		11/3–11/27	11/27–12/21	12/21–1/15	
10/29–11/23	11/23–12/17	12/17–1/10/97			1/15–2/9
8/17–9/12	9/12–10/8	10/8–11/5	1/10–2/3	2/3–2/27	2/27–3/23
			11/5–12/12	12/12–1/9	
9/30–10/24	10/24–11/17	11/17–12/11	1/9–3/4	3/4–4/6	4/6–5/3
11/9–12/5	12/5–12/31	12/31–1/24		1/4–1/28	1/28–2/21
8/31–9/24	9/24–10/19	10/19–11/13	1/24–2/18	2/18–3/12	3/13–4/6
			11/13–12/8	12/8	
10/15–11/8	11/8–12/2	12/2–12/26	12/26/01–	12/8/00–1/3/01	1/3–2/2
			1/18/02		
8/7–9/7	9/7–1/7/03		12/26/01–1/18	1/18–2/11	2/11–3/7
9/15–10/9	10/9–11/2	1/7–2/4	2/4–3/2	3/2–3/27	3/27–4/21
		11/2–11/26	11/26–12/21	12/21–1/14/04	
10/28–11/22	11/22–12/16	12/16–1/9/05		1/1–1/14	1/14–2/8
8/17–9/11	9/11–10/8	10/8–11/15	1/9–2/2	2/2–2/26	2/26–3/22
			11/5–12/15	12/15–1/1/06	
9/30–10/24	10/24–11/17	11/17–12/11	1/1–3/5	3/5–4/6	4/6–5/3
11/8–12/4	12/5–12/29	12/30–1/24/08		1/3–1/26	1/27–2/20
8/30–9/22	9/23–10/17	10/18–11/11	1/24–2/16	2/17–3/11	3/12–4/5
			11/12–12/6	12/7–1/2/09	

How to Use the Mars, Jupiter, and Saturn Tables

Find the year of your birth on the left side of each column. The dates when the planet entered each sign are listed on the right side of each column. (Signs are abbreviated to three letters.) Your birthday should fall on or between each date listed, and your planetary placement should correspond to the earlier sign of that period.

All planet changes are calculated for the Greenwich Mean Time zone.

MARS SIGNS 1901–2008

1901	MAR	1	Leo
	MAY	11	Vir
	JUL	13	Lib
	AUG	31	Scp
	OCT	14	Sag
	NOV	24	Cap
1902	JAN	1	Aqu
	FEB	8	Pic
	MAR	19	Ari
	APR	27	Tau
	JUN	7	Gem
	JUL	20	Can
	SEP	4	Leo
	OCT	23	Vir
	DEC	20	Lib
1903	APR	19	Vir
	MAY	30	Lib
	AUG	6	Scp
	SEP	22	Sag
	NOV	3	Cap
	DEC	12	Aqu
1904	JAN	19	Pic
	FEB	27	Ari
	APR	6	Tau
	MAY	18	Gem
	JUN	30	Can
	AUG	15	Leo
	OCT	1	Vir
	NOV	20	Lib
1905	JAN	13	Scp
	AUG	21	Sag
	OCT	8	Cap
	NOV	18	Aqu
	DEC	27	Pic
1906	FEB	4	Ari
	MAR	17	Tau
	APR	28	Gem
	JUN	11	Can
	JUL	27	Leo
	SEP	12	Vir
	OCT	30	Lib
	DEC	17	Scp
1907	FEB	5	Sag
	APR	1	Cap
	OCT	13	Aqu
	NOV	29	Pic
1908	JAN	11	Ari
	FEB	23	Tau
	APR	7	Gem
	MAY	22	Can
	JUL	8	Leo
	AUG	24	Vir
	OCT	10	Lib
	NOV	25	Scp

1909	JAN	10	Sag
	FEB	24	Cap
	APR	9	Aqu
	MAY	25	Pic
	JUL	21	Ari
	SEP	26	Pic
	NOV	20	Ari
1910	JAN	23	Tau
	MAR	14	Gem
	MAY	1	Can
	JUN	19	Leo
	AUG	6	Vir
	SEP	22	Lib
	NOV	6	Scp
	DEC	20	Sag
1911	JAN	31	Cap
	MAR	14	Aqu
	APR	23	Pic
	JUN	2	Ari
	JUL	15	Tau
	SEP	5	Gem
	NOV	30	Tau
1912	JAN	30	Gem
	APR	5	Can
	MAY	28	Leo
	JUL	17	Vir
	SEP	2	Lib
	OCT	18	Scp
	NOV	30	Sag
1913	JAN	10	Cap
	FEB	19	Aqu
	MAR	30	Pic
	MAY	8	Ari
	JUN	17	Tau
	JUL	29	Gem
	SEP	15	Can
1914	MAY	1	Leo
	JUN	26	Vir
	AUG	14	Lib
	SEP	29	Scp
	NOV	11	Sag
	DEC	22	Cap
1915	JAN	30	Aqu
	MAR	9	Pic
	APR	16	Ari
	MAY	26	Tau
	JUL	6	Gem
	AUG	19	Can
	OCT	7	Leo
1916	MAY	28	Vir
	JUL	23	Lib
	SEP	8	Scp
	OCT	22	Sag
	DEC	1	Cap
1917	JAN	9	Aqu
	FEB	16	Pic
	MAR	26	Ari
	MAY	4	Tau
	JUN	14	Gem
	JUL	28	Can
	SEP	12	Leo
	NOV	2	Vir
1918	JAN	11	Lib
	FEB	25	Vir
	JUN	23	Lib
	AUG	17	Scp
	OCT	1	Sag
	NOV	11	Cap
	DEC	20	Aqu
1919	JAN	27	Pic
	MAR	6	Ari
	APR	15	Tau
	MAY	26	Gem
	JUL	8	Can
	AUG	23	Leo
	OCT	10	Vir
	NOV	30	Lib
1920	JAN	31	Scp
	APR	23	Lib
	JUL	10	Scp
	SEP	4	Sag
	OCT	18	Cap
	NOV	27	Aqu
1921	JAN	5	Pic
	FEB	13	Ari
	MAR	25	Tau

Year	Month	Day	Sign
	MAY	6	Gem
	JUN	18	Can
	AUG	3	Leo
	SEP	19	Vir
	NOV	6	Lib
	DEC	26	Scp
1922	FEB	18	Sag
	SEP	13	Cap
	OCT	30	Aqu
	DEC	11	Pic
1923	JAN	21	Ari
	MAR	4	Tau
	APR	16	Gem
	MAY	30	Can
	JUL	16	Leo
	SEP	1	Vir
	OCT	18	Lib
	DEC	4	Scp
1924	JAN	19	Sag
	MAR	6	Cap
	APR	24	Aqu
	JUN	24	Pic
	AUG	24	Aqu
	OCT	19	Pic
	DEC	19	Ari
1925	FEB	5	Tau
	MAR	24	Gem
	MAY	9	Can
	JUN	26	Leo
	AUG	12	Vir
	SEP	28	Lib
	NOV	13	Scp
	DEC	28	Sag
1926	FEB	9	Cap
	MAR	23	Aqu
	MAY	3	Pic
	JUN	15	Ari
	AUG	1	Tau
1927	FEB	22	Gem
	APR	17	Can
	JUN	6	Leo
	JUL	25	Vir
	SEP	10	Lib
	OCT	26	Scp
	DEC	8	Sag
1928	JAN	19	Cap
	FEB	28	Aqu
	APR	7	Pic
	MAY	16	Ari
	JUN	26	Tau
	AUG	9	Gem
	OCT	3	Can
	DEC	20	Gem
1929	MAR	10	Can
	MAY	13	Leo
	JUL	4	Vir
	AUG	21	Lib
	OCT	6	Scp
	NOV	18	Sag
	DEC	29	Cap
1930	FEB	6	Aqu
	MAR	17	Pic
	APR	24	Ari
	JUN	3	Tau
	JUL	14	Gem
	AUG	28	Can
	OCT	20	Leo
1931	FEB	16	Can
	MAR	30	Leo
	JUN	10	Vir
	AUG	1	Lib
	SEP	17	Scp
	OCT	30	Sag
	DEC	10	Cap
1932	JAN	18	Aqu
	FEB	25	Pic
	APR	3	Ari
	MAY	12	Tau
	JUN	22	Gem
	AUG	4	Can
	SEP	20	Leo
	NOV	13	Vir
1933	JUL	6	Lib
	AUG	26	Scp
	OCT	9	Sag
	NOV	19	Cap

	DEC	28	Aqu
1934	FEB	4	Pic
	MAR	14	Ari
	APR	22	Tau
	JUN	2	Gem
	JUL	15	Can
	AUG	30	Leo
	OCT	18	Vir
	DEC	11	Lib
1935	JUL	29	Scp
	SEP	16	Sag
	OCT	28	Cap
	DEC	7	Aqu
1936	JAN	14	Pic
	FEB	22	Ari
	APR	1	Tau
	MAY	13	Gem
	JUN	25	Can
	AUG	10	Leo
	SEP	26	Vir
	NOV	14	Lib
1937	JAN	5	Scp
	MAR	13	Sag
	MAY	14	Scp
	AUG	8	Sag
	SEP	30	Cap
	NOV	11	Aqu
	DEC	21	Pic
1938	JAN	30	Ari
	MAR	12	Tau
	APR	23	Gem
	JUN	7	Can
	JUL	22	Leo
	SEP	7	Vir
	OCT	25	Lib
	DEC	11	Scp
1939	JAN	29	Sag
	MAR	21	Cap
	MAY	25	Aqu
	JUL	21	Cap
	SEP	24	Aqu
	NOV	19	Pic
1940	JAN	4	Ari
	FEB	17	Tau
	APR	1	Gem
	MAY	17	Can
	JUL	3	Leo
	AUG	19	Vir
	OCT	5	Lib
	NOV	20	Scp
1941	JAN	4	Sag
	FEB	17	Cap
	APR	2	Aqu
	MAY	16	Pic
	JUL	2	Ari
1942	JAN	11	Tau
	MAR	7	Gem
	APR	26	Can
	JUN	14	Leo
	AUG	1	Vir
	SEP	17	Lib
	NOV	1	Scp
	DEC	15	Sag
1943	JAN	26	Cap
	MAR	8	Aqu
	APR	17	Pic
	MAY	27	Ari
	JUL	7	Tau
	AUG	23	Gem
1944	MAR	28	Can
	MAY	22	Leo
	JUL	12	Vir
	AUG	29	Lib
	OCT	13	Scp
	NOV	25	Sag
1945	JAN	5	Cap
	FEB	14	Aqu
	MAR	25	Pic
	MAY	2	Ari
	JUN	11	Tau
	JUL	23	Gem
	SEP	7	Can
	NOV	11	Leo
	DEC	26	Can
1946	APR	22	Leo
	JUN	20	Vir

	AUG	9	Lib
	SEP	24	Scp
	NOV	6	Sag
	DEC	17	Cap
1947	JAN	25	Aqu
	MAR	4	Pic
	APR	11	Ari
	MAY	21	Tau
	JUL	1	Gem
	AUG	13	Can
	OCT	1	Leo
	DEC	1	Vir
1948	FEB	12	Leo
	MAY	18	Vir
	JUL	17	Lib
	SEP	3	Scp
	OCT	17	Sag
	NOV	26	Cap
1949	JAN	4	Aqu
	FEB	11	Pic
	MAR	21	Ari
	APR	30	Tau
	JUN	10	Gem
	JUL	23	Can
	SEP	7	Leo
	OCT	27	Vir
	DEC	26	Lib
1950	MAR	28	Vir
	JUN	11	Lib
	AUG	10	Scp
	SEP	25	Sag
	NOV	6	Cap
	DEC	15	Aqu
1951	JAN	22	Pic
	MAR	1	Ari
	APR	10	Tau
	MAY	21	Gem
	JUL	3	Can
	AUG	18	Leo
	OCT	5	Vir
	NOV	24	Lib
1952	JAN	20	Scp
	AUG	27	Sag
	OCT	12	Cap
	NOV	21	Aqu
	DEC	30	Pic
1953	FEB	8	Ari
	MAR	20	Tau
	MAY	1	Gem
	JUN	14	Can
	JUL	29	Leo
	SEP	14	Vir
	NOV	1	Lib
	DEC	20	Scp
1954	FEB	9	Sag
	APR	12	Cap
	JUL	3	Sag
	AUG	24	Cap
	OCT	21	Aqu
	DEC	4	Pic
1955	JAN	15	Ari
	FEB	26	Tau
	APR	10	Gem
	MAY	26	Can
	JUL	11	Leo
	AUG	27	Vir
	OCT	13	Lib
	NOV	29	Scp
1956	JAN	14	Sag
	FEB	28	Cap
	APR	14	Aqu
	JUN	3	Pic
	DEC	6	Ari
1957	JAN	28	Tau
	MAR	17	Gem
	MAY	4	Can
	JUN	21	Leo
	AUG	8	Vir
	SEP	24	Lib
	NOV	8	Scp
	DEC	23	Sag
1958	FEB	3	Cap
	MAR	17	Aqu
	APR	27	Pic
	JUN	7	Ari
	JUL	21	Tau

	SEP	21	Gem
	OCT	29	Tau
1959	FEB	10	Gem
	APR	10	Can
	JUN	1	Leo
	JUL	20	Vir
	SEP	5	Lib
	OCT	21	Scp
	DEC	3	Sag
1960	JAN	14	Cap
	FEB	23	Aqu
	APR	2	Pic
	MAY	11	Ari
	JUN	20	Tau
	AUG	2	Gem
	SEP	21	Can
1961	FEB	5	Gem
	FEB	7	Can
	MAY	6	Leo
	JUN	28	Vir
	AUG	17	Lib
	OCT	1	Scp
	NOV	13	Sag
	DEC	24	Cap
1962	FEB	1	Aqu
	MAR	12	Pic
	APR	19	Ari
	MAY	28	Tau
	JUL	9	Gem
	AUG	22	Can
	OCT	11	Leo
1963	JUN	3	Vir
	JUL	27	Lib
	SEP	12	Scp
	OCT	25	Sag
	DEC	5	Cap
1964	JAN	13	Aqu
	FEB	20	Pic
	MAR	29	Ari
	MAY	7	Tau
	JUN	17	Gem
	JUL	30	Can
	SEP	15	Leo
	NOV	6	Vir
1965	JUN	29	Lib
	AUG	20	Scp
	OCT	4	Sag
	NOV	14	Cap
	DEC	23	Aqu
1966	JAN	30	Pic
	MAR	9	Ari
	APR	17	Tau
	MAY	28	Gem
	JUL	11	Can
	AUG	25	Leo
	OCT	12	Vir
	DEC	4	Lib
1967	FEB	12	Scp
	MAR	31	Lib
	JUL	19	Scp
	SEP	10	Sag
	OCT	23	Cap
	DEC	1	Aqu
1968	JAN	9	Pic
	FEB	17	Ari
	MAR	27	Tau
	MAY	8	Gem
	JUN	21	Can
	AUG	5	Leo
	SEP	21	Vir
	NOV	9	Lib
	DEC	29	Scp
1969	FEB	25	Sag
	SEP	21	Cap
	NOV	4	Aqu
	DEC	15	Pic
1970	JAN	24	Ari
	MAR	7	Tau
	APR	18	Gem
	JUN	2	Can
	JUL	18	Leo
	SEP	3	Vir
	OCT	20	Lib
	DEC	6	Scp
1971	JAN	23	Sag
	MAR	12	Cap

Year	Month	Day	Sign
	MAY	3	Aqu
	NOV	6	Pic
	DEC	26	Ari
1972	FEB	10	Tau
	MAR	27	Gem
	MAY	12	Can
	JUN	28	Leo
	AUG	15	Vir
	SEP	30	Lib
	NOV	15	Scp
	DEC	30	Sag
1973	FEB	12	Cap
	MAR	26	Aqu
	MAY	8	Pic
	JUN	20	Ari
	AUG	12	Tau
	OCT	29	Ari
	DEC	24	Tau
1974	FEB	27	Gem
	APR	20	Can
	JUN	9	Leo
	JUL	27	Vir
	SEP	12	Lib
	OCT	28	Scp
	DEC	10	Sag
1975	JAN	21	Cap
	MAR	3	Aqu
	APR	11	Pic
	MAY	21	Ari
	JUL	1	Tau
	AUG	14	Gem
	OCT	17	Can
	NOV	25	Gem
1976	MAR	18	Can
	MAY	16	Leo
	JUL	6	Vir
	AUG	24	Lib
	OCT	8	Scp
	NOV	20	Sag
1977	JAN	1	Cap
	FEB	9	Aqu
	MAR	20	Pic
	APR	27	Ari
	JUN	6	Tau
	JUL	17	Gem
	SEP	1	Can
	OCT	26	Leo
1978	JAN	26	Can
	APR	10	Leo
	JUN	14	Vir
	AUG	4	Lib
	SEP	19	Scp
	NOV	2	Sag
	DEC	12	Cap
1979	JAN	20	Aqu
	FEB	27	Pic
	APR	7	Ari
	MAY	16	Tau
	JUN	26	Gem
	AUG	8	Can
	SEP	24	Leo
	NOV	19	Vir
1980	MAR	11	Leo
	MAY	4	Vir
	JUL	10	Lib
	AUG	29	Scp
	OCT	12	Sag
	NOV	22	Cap
	DEC	30	Aqu
1981	FEB	6	Pic
	MAR	17	Ari
	APR	25	Tau
	JUN	5	Gem
	JUL	18	Can
	SEP	2	Leo
	OCT	21	Vir
	DEC	16	Lib
1982	AUG	3	Scp
	SEP	20	Sag
	OCT	31	Cap
	DEC	10	Aqu
1983	JAN	17	Pic
	FEB	25	Ari
	APR	5	Tau
	MAY	16	Gem
	JUN	29	Can

	AUG	13	Leo
	SEP	30	Vir
	NOV	18	Lib
1984	JAN	11	Scp
	AUG	17	Sag
	OCT	5	Cap
	NOV	15	Aqu
	DEC	25	Pic
1985	FEB	2	Ari
	MAR	15	Tau
	APR	26	Gem
	JUN	9	Can
	JUL	25	Leo
	SEP	10	Vir
	OCT	27	Lib
	DEC	14	Scp
1986	FEB	2	Sag
	MAR	28	Cap
	OCT	9	Aqu
	NOV	26	Pic
1987	JAN	8	Ari
	FEB	20	Tau
	APR	5	Gem
	MAY	21	Can
	JUL	6	Leo
	AUG	22	Vir
	OCT	8	Lib
	NOV	24	Scp
1988	JAN	8	Sag
	FEB	22	Cap
	APR	6	Aqu
	MAY	22	Pic
	JUL	13	Ari
	OCT	23	Pic
	NOV	1	Ari
1989	JAN	19	Tau
	MAR	11	Gem
	APR	29	Can
	JUN	16	Leo
	AUG	3	Vir
	SEP	19	Lib
	NOV	4	Scp
	DEC	18	Sag
1990	JAN	29	Cap
	MAR	11	Aqu
	APR	20	Pic
	MAY	31	Ari
	JUL	12	Tau
	AUG	31	Gem
	DEC	14	Tau
1991	JAN	21	Gem
	APR	3	Can
	MAY	26	Leo
	JUL	15	Vir
	SEP	1	Lib
	OCT	16	Scp
	NOV	29	Sag
1992	JAN	9	Cap
	FEB	18	Aqu
	MAR	28	Pic
	MAY	5	Ari
	JUN	14	Tau
	JUL	26	Gem
	SEP	12	Can
1993	APR	27	Leo
	JUN	23	Vir
	AUG	12	Lib
	SEP	27	Scp
	NOV	9	Sag
	DEC	20	Cap
1994	JAN	28	Aqu
	MAR	7	Pic
	APR	14	Ari
	MAY	23	Tau
	JUL	3	Gem
	AUG	16	Can
	OCT	4	Leo
	DEC	12	Vir
1995	JAN	22	Leo
	MAY	25	Vir
	JUL	21	Lib
	SEP	7	Scp
	OCT	20	Sag
	NOV	30	Cap
1996	JAN	8	Aqu
	FEB	15	Pic

	MAR	24	Ari
	MAY	2	Tau
	JUN	12	Gem
	JUL	25	Can
	SEP	9	Leo
	OCT	30	Vir
1997	JAN	3	Lib
	MAR	8	Vir
	JUN	19	Lib
	AUG	14	Scp
	SEP	28	Sag
	NOV	9	Cap
	DEC	18	Aqu
1998	JAN	25	Pic
	MAR	4	Ari
	APR	13	Tau
	MAY	24	Gem
	JUL	6	Can
	AUG	20	Leo
	OCT	7	Vir
	NOV	27	Lib
1999	JAN	26	Scp
	MAY	5	Lib
	JUL	5	Scp
	SEP	2	Sag
	OCT	17	Cap
	NOV	26	Aqu
2000	JAN	4	Pic
	FEB	12	Ari
	MAR	23	Tau
	MAY	3	Gem
	JUN	16	Can
	AUG	1	Leo
	SEP	17	Vir
	NOV	4	Lib
	DEC	23	Scp
2001	FEB	14	Sag
	SEP	8	Cap
	OCT	27	Aqu
	DEC	8	Pic
2002	JAN	18	Ari

	MAR	1	Tau
	APR	13	Gem
	MAY	28	Can
	JUL	13	Leo
	AUG	29	Vir
	OCT	15	Lib
	DEC	1	Scp
2003	JAN	17	Sag
	MAR	4	Cap
	APR	21	Aqu
	JUN	17	Pic
	DEC	16	Ari
2004	FEB	3	Tau
	MAR	21	Gem
	MAY	7	Can
	JUN	23	Leo
	AUG	10	Vir
	SEP	26	Lib
	NOV	11	Sep
	DEC	25	Sag
2005	FEB	6	Cap
	MAR	20	Aqu
	MAY	1	Pic
	JUN	12	Ari
	JUL	28	Tau
2006	FEB	17	Gem
	APR	14	Can
	JUN	3	Leo
	JUL	22	Vir
	SEP	8	Lib
	OCT	23	Scp
	DEC	6	Sag
2007	JAN	16	Cap
	FEB	25	Aqu
	APR	6	Pic
	MAY	15	Ari
	JUNE	24	Tau
	AUG	7	Gem
	SEP	28	Can
	DEC	31	Gem*

*Repeat means planet is retrograde.

2008	MAR	4	Can
	MAY	9	Leo
	JUL	1	Vir
	AUG	19	Lib
	OCT	3	Scp
	NOV	16	Sag
	DEC	27	Cap

JUPITER SIGNS 1901–2008

1901	JAN	19	Cap
1902	FEB	6	Aqu
1903	FEB	20	Pic
1904	MAR	1	Ari
	AUG	8	Tau
	AUG	31	Ari
1905	MAR	7	Tau
	JUL	21	Gem
	DEC	4	Tau
1906	MAR	9	Gem
	JUL	30	Can
1907	AUG	18	Leo
1908	SEP	12	Vir
1909	OCT	11	Lib
1910	NOV	11	Scp
1911	DEC	10	Sag
1913	JAN	2	Cap
1914	JAN	21	Aqu
1915	FEB	4	Pic
1916	FEB	12	Ari
	JUN	26	Tau
	OCT	26	Ari
1917	FEB	12	Tau
	JUN	29	Gem
1918	JUL	13	Can
1919	AUG	2	Leo
1920	AUG	27	Vir
1921	SEP	25	Lib
1922	OCT	26	Scp
1923	NOV	24	Sag
1924	DEC	18	Cap
1926	JAN	6	Aqu
1927	JAN	18	Pic
	JUN	6	Ari
	SEP	11	Pic
1928	JAN	23	Ari
	JUN	4	Tau
1929	JUN	12	Gem
1930	JUN	26	Can
1931	JUL	17	Leo
1932	AUG	11	Vir
1933	SEP	10	Lib
1934	OCT	11	Scp
1935	NOV	9	Sag
1936	DEC	2	Cap
1937	DEC	20	Aqu
1938	MAY	14	Pic
	JUL	30	Aqu
	DEC	29	Pic
1939	MAY	11	Ari
	OCT	30	Pic
	DEC	20	Ari
1940	MAY	16	Tau
1941	MAY	26	Gem
1942	JUN	10	Can
1943	JUN	30	Leo
1944	JUL	26	Vir
1945	AUG	25	Lib
1946	SEP	25	Scp
1947	OCT	24	Sag
1948	NOV	15	Cap
1949	APR	12	Aqu
	JUN	27	Cap
	NOV	30	Aqu
1950	APR	15	Pic
	SEP	15	Aqu
	DEC	1	Pic
1951	APR	21	Ari

1952	APR	28	Tau
1953	MAY	9	Gem
1954	MAY	24	Can
1955	JUN	13	Leo
	NOV	17	Vir
1956	JAN	18	Leo
	JUL	7	Vir
	DEC	13	Lib
1957	FEB	19	Vir
	AUG	7	Lib
1958	JAN	13	Scp
	MAR	20	Lib
	SEP	7	Scp
1959	FEB	10	Sag
	APR	24	Scp
	OCT	5	Sag
1960	MAR	1	Cap
	JUN	10	Sag
	OCT	26	Cap
1961	MAR	15	Aqu
	AUG	12	Cap
	NOV	4	Aqu
1962	MAR	25	Pic
1963	APR	4	Ari
1964	APR	12	Tau
1965	APR	22	Gem
	SEP	21	Can
	NOV	17	Gem
1966	MAY	5	Can
	SEP	27	Leo
1967	JAN	16	Can
	MAY	23	Leo
	OCT	19	Vir
1968	FEB	27	Leo
	JUN	15	Vir
	NOV	15	Lib
1969	MAR	30	Vir
	JUL	15	Lib
	DEC	16	Scp
1970	APR	30	Lib
	AUG	15	Scp
1971	JAN	14	Sag
	JUN	5	Scp
	SEP	11	Sag
1972	FEB	6	Cap
	JUL	24	Sag
	SEP	25	Cap
1973	FEB	23	Aqu
1974	MAR	8	Pic
1975	MAR	18	Ari
1976	MAR	26	Tau
	AUG	23	Gem
	OCT	16	Tau
1977	APR	3	Gem
	AUG	20	Can
	DEC	30	Gem
1978	APR	12	Can
	SEP	5	Leo
1979	FEB	28	Can
	APR	20	Leo
	SEP	29	Vir
1980	OCT	27	Lib
1981	NOV	27	Scp
1982	DEC	26	Sag
1984	JAN	19	Cap
1985	FEB	6	Aqu
1986	FEB	20	Pic
1987	MAR	2	Ari
1988	MAR	8	Tau
	JUL	22	Gem
	NOV	30	Tau
1989	MAR	11	Gem
	JUL	30	Can
1990	AUG	18	Leo
1991	SEP	12	Vir
1992	OCT	10	Lib
1993	NOV	10	Scp
1994	DEC	9	Sag
1996	JAN	3	Cap
1997	JAN	21	Aqu
1998	FEB	4	Pic

1999	FEB	13	Ari
	JUN	28	Tau
	OCT	23	Ari
2000	FEB	14	Tau
	JUN	30	Gem
2001	JUL	14	Can
2002	AUG	1	Leo
2003	AUG	27	Vir
2004	SEP	24	Lib
2005	OCT	26	Scp
2006	NOV	24	Sag
2007	DEC	17	Cap
2008			Cap

SATURN SIGNS 1903–2008

1903	JAN	19	Aqu
1905	APR	13	Pic
	AUG	17	Aqu
1906	JAN	8	Pic
1908	MAR	19	Ari
1910	MAY	17	Tau
	DEC	14	Ari
1911	JAN	20	Tau
1912	JUL	7	Gem
	NOV	30	Tau
1913	MAR	26	Gem
1914	AUG	24	Can
	DEC	7	Gem
1915	MAY	11	Can
1916	OCT	17	Leo
	DEC	7	Can
1917	JUN	24	Leo
1919	AUG	12	Vir
1921	OCT	7	Lib
1923	DEC	20	Scp
1924	APR	6	Lib
	SEP	13	Scp
1926	DEC	2	Sag
1929	MAR	15	Cap
	MAY	5	Sag
	NOV	30	Cap
1932	FEB	24	Aqu
	AUG	13	Cap
	NOV	20	Aqu
1935	FEB	14	Pic
1937	APR	25	Ari
	OCT	18	Pic
1938	JAN	14	Ari
1939	JUL	6	Tau
	SEP	22	Ari
1940	MAR	20	Tau
1942	MAY	8	Gem
1944	JUN	20	Can
1946	AUG	2	Leo
1948	SEP	19	Vir
1949	APR	3	Leo
	MAY	29	Vir
1950	NOV	20	Lib
1951	MAR	7	Vir
	AUG	13	Lib
1953	OCT	22	Scp
1956	JAN	12	Sag
	MAY	14	Scp
	OCT	10	Sag
1959	JAN	5	Cap
1962	JAN	3	Aqu
1964	MAR	24	Pic
	SEP	16	Aqu
	DEC	16	Pic
1967	MAR	3	Ari
1969	APR	29	Tau
1971	JUN	18	Gem
1972	JAN	10	Tau
	FEB	21	Gem
1973	AUG	1	Can
1974	JAN	7	Gem
	APR	18	Can

1975	SEP	17	Leo
1976	JAN	14	Can
	JUN	5	Leo
1977	NOV	17	Vir
1978	JAN	5	Leo
	JUL	26	Vir
1980	SEP	21	Lib
1982	NOV	29	Scp
1983	MAY	6	Lib
	AUG	24	Scp
1985	NOV	17	Sag
1988	FEB	13	Cap
	JUN	10	Sag
	NOV	12	Cap
1991	FEB	6	Aqu
1993	MAY	21	Pic
	JUN	30	Aqu
1994	JAN	28	Pic
1996	APR	7	Ari
1998	JUN	9	Tau
	OCT	25	Ari
1999	MAR	1	Tau
2000	AUG	10	Gem
	OCT	16	Tau
2001	APR	21	Gem
2003	JUN	3	Can
2005	JUL	16	Leo
2007	SEP	2	Vir
2008			Vir

CHAPTER 7

The Leader of the Parade: Your Rising Sign

Your rising sign is the degree of the zodiac ascending over the eastern horizon at the time you were born. (That's why it's often called the ascendant.) It is important to know the rising sign, because it determines *where* things happen in the horoscope chart. It marks the first point in the horoscope, the beginning of the first house, one of twelve divisions of the horoscope, each of which represents a different area of life. After the rising sign, the other houses parade around the chart in sequence, with the following sign on the house cusp.

You can learn much about a person by the signs and interactions of the sun, moon, and planets in the horoscope, but you need to know the rising sign to determine where in that person's life an activity will take place. For example, you might know that a person has Mars in Aries, which will describe that person's dynamic, fiery energy. But if you also know that the person has a Capricorn rising sign, this Mars will fall in the fourth house of home and family, so you know where that energy will operate. Without a valid rising sign, the collection of planets have no homes. One would have no idea which area of life would be influenced by a particular planet.

Due to the earth's rotation, the rising sign changes every two hours, which means that even though other babies born later or earlier on the same day in the same hospital as you were will have most planets in the same signs as you, they may not have the same rising sign and their planets may fall in different houses in the chart. For instance, if Mars is in Gemini and your rising sign is Taurus, Mars will most likely be active in the second or financial house of your chart. Someone born later in the day, when the rising sign is Virgo, would have Mars positioned at the top of the chart, energizing the tenth house of career.

Most astrologers insist on knowing the exact time of a client's birth before analyzing a chart. The more accurate your birth time, the more accurately an astrologer can position the planets in your chart by determining the correct rising sign.

How Your Rising Sign Can Influence Your Sun Sign

Your rising sign has an important relationship with your sun sign. Some will complement the sun sign; others hide it under a totally different mask, as if playing an entirely different role, making it difficult to guess the person's sun sign from outer appearances. This may be the reason why you might not look or act like your sun sign's archetype. For example, a Leo with a conservative Capricorn ascendant would come across as much more serious than a Leo with a fiery Aries or Sagittarius ascendant.

Though the rising sign usually creates the first impression you make, there are exceptions. When the sun sign is reinforced by other planets in the same sign, this might overpower the impression of the rising sign. For instance, a Leo sun plus a Leo Venus and Leo Jupiter would counteract the more conservative image that would otherwise be conveyed by the person's Capricorn ascendant.

Those born early in the morning when the sun was on the horizon will be most likely to project the image of their sun sign. These people are often called a "double Aries" or a "double Virgo" because the same sun sign and ascendant reinforce each other.

Find Your Rising Sign

Look up your rising sign from the chart at the end of this chapter. Since rising signs change every two hours, it is important to know your birth time as close to the minute as possible. Even a few minutes' difference could change the rising sign and therefore the setup of your chart. If you are unsure about the exact time, but know within a few hours, check the following descriptions to see which is most like the personality you project.

Aries Rising: Alpha Energy

You are the most aggressive version of your sun sign, with boundless energy that can be used productively if it's channeled in the right direction. Watch a tendency to overreact emotionally and blow your top. You come across as openly competitive, a positive asset in business or sports. Be on guard against impatience, which could lead to head injuries. Your walk and bearing could have the telltale head-forward Aries posture. You may wear more bright colors, especially red, than others of your sign. You may also have a tendency to drive your car faster.

Can you see the alpha Aries tendency in Barbra Streisand (a sun-sign Taurus) and Bette Midler (a sun-sign Sagittarius)?

Taurus Rising: Down to Earth

You're slow-moving, with a beautiful (or distinctive) speaking or singing voice that can be especially soothing or melodious. You probably surround yourself with comfort, good food, luxurious environments, and other sensual pleasures. You prefer welcoming others into your home to gadding about. You may have a talent for business, especially in trading, appraising, and real estate. A Taurus ascendant gives a well-padded physique that gains weight easily, like Liza Minnelli. This ascendant can also endow females with a curvaceous beauty.

Gemini Rising: A Way with Words

You're naturally sociable, with lighter, more ethereal mannerisms than others of your sign, especially if you're female.

You love to communicate with people, and express your ideas and feelings easily, like British prime minister Tony Blair. You may have a talent for writing or public speaking. You thrive on variety, a constantly changing scene, and a lively social life. However, you may relate to others at a deeper level than might be suspected. And you will be far more sympathetic and caring than you project. You will probably travel widely, changing partners and jobs several times (or juggle two at once). Physically, your nerves are quite sensitive. Occasionally, you would benefit from a calm, tranquil atmosphere away from your usual social scene.

Cancer Rising: Nurturing Instincts

You are naturally acquisitive, possessive, private, a moneymaker, like Bill Gates or Michael Bloomberg. You easily pick up on others' needs and feelings—a great gift in business, the arts, and personal relationships. But you must guard against overreacting or taking things too personally, especially during full moon periods. Find creative outlets for your natural nurturing gifts, such as helping the less fortunate, particularly children. Your insights would be helpful in psychology. Your desire to feed and care for others would be useful in the restaurant, hotel, or child-care industries. You may be especially fond of wearing romantic old clothes, collecting antiques, and, of course, dining on exquisite food. Since your body may retain fluids, pay attention to your diet. To relax, escape to places near water.

Leo Rising: Diva Dazzle

You may come across as more poised than you really feel. However, you play it to the hilt, projecting a proud royal presence. A Leo ascendant gives you a natural flair for drama, like Marilyn Monroe, and you might be accused of stealing the spotlight. You'll also project a much more outgoing, optimistic, sunny personality than others of your sign. You take care to please your public by always projecting your best star quality, probably tossing a luxuriant mane of hair, sporting a striking hairstyle, or dressing to impress. Females often dazzle with spectacular jewelry. Since you may have a strong parental nature, you could well be the regal family matriarch or patriarch, like George W. Bush.

Virgo Rising: High Standards

Virgo rising masks your inner nature with a practical, analytical outer image. You seem neat, orderly, more particular than others of your sign. Others in your life may feel they must live up to your high standards. Though at times you may be openly critical, this masks a well-meaning desire to have only the best for loved ones. Your sharp eye for details could be used in the financial world, or your literary skills could draw you to teaching or publishing. The healing arts, health care, and service-oriented professions attract many with a Virgo ascendant. You're likely to take good care of yourself, with great attention to health, diet, and exercise, like Madonna. You might even show some hypochondriac tendencies, like Woody Allen. Physically, you may have a very sensitive digestive system.

Libra Rising: The Charmer

Libra rising gives you a charming, social public persona, like Bill Clinton. You tend to avoid confrontations in relationships, preferring to smooth the way or negotiate diplomatically rather than give in to an emotional reaction. Because you are interested in all aspects of a situation, you may be slow to reach decisions. Physically, you'll have good proportions and symmetry. You will move with natural grace and balance. You're likely to have pleasing, if not beautiful, facial features, with a winning smile, like Cary Grant. You'll show natural good taste and harmony in your clothes and home decor. Legal, diplomatic, or public relations professions could draw your interest.

Scorpio Rising: An Air of Mystery

You project an intriguing air of mystery with this ascendant, as the Scorpio secretiveness and sense of underlying power combines with your sun sign. As with Jackie O, there's more to you than meets the eye. You seem like someone who is always in control and who can move comfortably in the world of power. Your physical look comes across as intense. Many of you have remarkable eyes, with a direct, penetrating gaze. But you'll never reveal your private agenda, and you tend to keep your true feelings under wraps (watch a tendency toward paranoia). You may have an interesting romantic history with secret love affairs, like Grace Kelly. Many of you heighten your air of mystery by wearing black. You're happiest near water and should provide yourself with a seaside retreat.

Sagittarius Rising: The Explorer

You travel with this ascendant. You may also be a more outdoor, sportive type, with an athletic, casual, outgoing air. Your moods are camouflaged with cheerful optimism or a philosophical attitude. Though you don't hesitate to speak your mind, like Ted Turner, who was called the Mouth of the South, you can also laugh at your troubles or crack a joke more easily than others of your sign. A Sagittarius ascendant can also draw you to the field of higher education or to spiritual life. You'll seem to have less attachment to things and people, and may explore the globe. Your strong, fast legs are a physical bonus.

Capricorn Rising: Serious Business

This rising sign makes you come across as serious, goal-oriented, disciplined, and careful with cash. You are not one of the zodiac's big spenders, though you might splurge occasionally on items with good investment value. You're the traditional, conservative type in dress and environment, and you might come across as quite normal and businesslike, like Rupert Murdoch. You'll function well in a structured or corporate environment where you can climb to the top. (You are always aware of who's the boss.) In your personal life, you could be a loner or a single parent who is "father and mother" to your children.

Aquarius Rising: One of a Kind

You come across as less concerned about what others think and could even be a bit eccentric. You're more at ease with groups of people than others in your sign, and you may be attracted to public life, like Jay Leno. Your appearance may be unique, either unconventional or unimportant to you. Those of you whose sun is in a water sign (Cancer, Scorpio, Pisces) may exercise your nurturing qualities with a large group, an extended family, or a day-care or community center.

Pisces Rising: Romantic Roles

Your creative, nurturing talents are heightened and so is your ability to project emotional drama. And, like Antonio Banderas, your dreamy eyes and poetic air bring out the protective instinct in others. You could be attracted to the arts, especially theater, dance, film, and photography, or to psychology, spiritual practice, and charity work. You are happiest when you are using your creative ability to help others. Since you are vulnerable to mood swings, it is especially important for you to find interesting, creative work where you can express your talents and heighten your self-esteem. Accentuate the positive. Be wary of escapist tendencies, particularly involving alcohol or drugs to which you are supersensitive, like Whitney Houston.

RISING SIGNS—A.M. BIRTHS

	1 AM	2 AM	3 AM	4 AM	5 AM	6 AM	7 AM	8 AM	9 AM	10 AM	11 AM	12 NOON
Jan 1	Lib	Sc	Sc	Sc	Sag	Sag	Cap	Cap	Aq	Aq	Pis	Ar
Jan 9	Lib	Sc	Sc	Sag	Sag	Sag	Cap	Cap	Aq	Pis	Ar	Tau
Jan 17	Sc	Sc	Sc	Sag	Sag	Cap	Cap	Aq	Aq	Pis	Ar	Tau
Jan 25	Sc	Sc	Sag	Sag	Sag	Cap	Cap	Aq	Pis	Ar	Tau	Tau
Feb 2	Sc	Sc	Sag	Sag	Cap	Cap	Aq	Pis	Pis	Ar	Tau	Gem
Feb 10	Sc	Sag	Sag	Sag	Cap	Cap	Aq	Pis	Ar	Tau	Tau	Gem
Feb 18	Sc	Sag	Sag	Cap	Cap	Aq	Pis	Pis	Ar	Tau	Gem	Gem
Feb 26	Sag	Sag	Sag	Cap	Aq	Aq	Pis	Ar	Tau	Tau	Gem	Gem
Mar 6	Sag	Sag	Cap	Cap	Aq	Pis	Pis	Ar	Tau	Gem	Gem	Can
Mar 14	Sag	Cap	Cap	Aq	Aq	Pis	Ar	Tau	Tau	Gem	Gem	Can
Mar 22	Sag	Cap	Cap	Aq	Pis	Ar	Ar	Tau	Gem	Gem	Can	Can
Mar 30	Cap	Cap	Aq	Pis	Pis	Ar	Tau	Tau	Gem	Can	Can	Can
Apr 7	Cap	Cap	Aq	Pis	Ar	Ar	Tau	Gem	Gem	Can	Can	Leo
Apr 14	Cap	Aq	Aq	Pis	Ar	Tau	Tau	Gem	Gem	Can	Can	Leo
Apr 22	Cap	Aq	Pis	Ar	Ar	Tau	Gem	Gem	Gem	Can	Leo	Leo
Apr 30	Aq	Aq	Pis	Ar	Tau	Tau	Gem	Can	Can	Can	Leo	Leo
May 8	Aq	Pis	Ar	Ar	Tau	Gem	Gem	Can	Can	Leo	Leo	Leo
May 16	Aq	Pis	Ar	Tau	Gem	Gem	Can	Can	Can	Leo	Leo	Vir
May 24	Pis	Ar	Ar	Tau	Gem	Gem	Can	Can	Leo	Leo	Leo	Vir
June 1	Pis	Ar	Tau	Gem	Gem	Can	Can	Can	Leo	Leo	Vir	Vir
June 9	Ar	Ar	Tau	Gem	Gem	Can	Can	Leo	Leo	Leo	Vir	Vir
June 17	Ar	Tau	Gem	Gem	Can	Can	Can	Leo	Leo	Vir	Vir	Vir
June 25	Tau	Tau	Gem	Gem	Can	Can	Leo	Leo	Leo	Vir	Vir	Lib
July 3	Tau	Gem	Gem	Can	Can	Can	Leo	Leo	Vir	Vir	Vir	Lib
July 11	Tau	Gem	Gem	Can	Can	Leo	Leo	Leo	Vir	Vir	Lib	Lib
July 18	Gem	Gem	Can	Can	Can	Leo	Leo	Vir	Vir	Vir	Lib	Lib
July 26	Gem	Gem	Can	Can	Leo	Leo	Vir	Vir	Vir	Lib	Lib	Lib
Aug 3	Gem	Can	Can	Can	Leo	Leo	Vir	Vir	Vir	Lib	Lib	Sc
Aug 11	Gem	Can	Can	Leo	Leo	Leo	Vir	Vir	Lib	Lib	Lib	Sc
Aug 18	Can	Can	Can	Leo	Leo	Vir	Vir	Vir	Lib	Lib	Sc	Sc
Aug 27	Can	Can	Leo	Leo	Leo	Vir	Vir	Lib	Lib	Lib	Sc	Sc
Sept 4	Can	Can	Leo	Leo	Leo	Vir	Vir	Vir	Lib	Lib	Sc	Sc
Sept 12	Can	Leo	Leo	Leo	Vir	Vir	Lib	Lib	Lib	Sc	Sc	Sag
Sept 20	Leo	Leo	Leo	Vir	Vir	Vir	Lib	Lib	Sc	Sc	Sc	Sag
Sept 28	Leo	Leo	Leo	Vir	Vir	Lib	Lib	Lib	Sc	Sc	Sag	Sag
Oct 6	Leo	Leo	Vir	Vir	Vir	Lib	Lib	Sc	Sc	Sc	Sag	Sag
Oct 14	Leo	Vir	Vir	Vir	Lib	Lib	Lib	Sc	Sc	Sag	Sag	Cap
Oct 22	Leo	Vir	Vir	Lib	Lib	Lib	Sc	Sc	Sc	Sag	Sag	Cap
Oct 30	Vir	Vir	Vir	Lib	Lib	Sc	Sc	Sc	Sag	Sag	Cap	Cap
Nov 7	Vir	Vir	Lib	Lib	Lib	Sc	Sc	Sc	Sag	Sag	Cap	Cap
Nov 15	Vir	Vir	Lib	Lib	Sc	Sc	Sc	Sag	Sag	Cap	Cap	Aq
Nov 23	Vir	Lib	Lib	Lib	Sc	Sc	Sag	Sag	Sag	Cap	Cap	Aq
Dec 1	Vir	Lib	Lib	Sc	Sc	Sc	Sag	Sag	Cap	Cap	Aq	Aq
Dec 9	Lib	Lib	Lib	Sc	Sc	Sag	Sag	Sag	Cap	Cap	Aq	Pis
Dec 18	Lib	Lib	Sc	Sc	Sc	Sag	Sag	Cap	Cap	Aq	Aq	Pis
Dec 28	Lib	Lib	Sc	Sc	Sag	Sag	Sag	Cap	Aq	Aq	Pis	Ar

RISING SIGNS—P.M. BIRTHS

	1 PM	2 PM	3 PM	4 PM	5 PM	6 PM	7 PM	8 PM	9 PM	10 PM	11 PM	12 MID-NIGHT
Jan 1	Tau	Gem	Gem	Can	Can	Can	Leo	Leo	Vir	Vir	Vir	Lib
Jan 9	Tau	Gem	Gem	Can	Can	Leo	Leo	Leo	Vir	Vir	Vir	Lib
Jan 17	Gem	Gem	Can	Can	Can	Leo	Leo	Vir	Vir	Vir	Lib	Lib
Jan 25	Gem	Gem	Can	Can	Leo	Leo	Leo	Vir	Vir	Lib	Lib	Lib
Feb 2	Gem	Can	Can	Can	Leo	Leo	Vir	Vir	Vir	Lib	Lib	Sc
Feb 10	Gem	Can	Can	Leo	Leo	Leo	Vir	Vir	Lib	Lib	Lib	Sc
Feb 18	Can	Can	Can	Leo	Leo	Vir	Vir	Vir	Lib	Lib	Sc	Sc
Feb 26	Can	Can	Leo	Leo	Leo	Vir	Vir	Lib	Lib	Lib	Sc	Sc
Mar 6	Can	Leo	Leo	Leo	Vir	Vir	Vir	Lib	Lib	Sc	Sc	Sc
Mar 14	Can	Leo	Leo	Vir	Vir	Vir	Lib	Lib	Lib	Sc	Sc	Sag
Mar 22	Leo	Leo	Leo	Vir	Vir	Lib	Lib	Lib	Sc	Sc	Sc	Sag
Mar 30	Leo	Leo	Vir	Vir	Vir	Lib	Lib	Sc	Sc	Sc	Sag	Sag
Apr 7	Leo	Leo	Vir	Vir	Lib	Lib	Lib	Sc	Sc	Sc	Sag	Sag
Apr 14	Leo	Vir	Vir	Vir	Lib	Lib	Sc	Sc	Sc	Sag	Sag	Cap
Apr 22	Leo	Vir	Vir	Lib	Lib	Lib	Sc	Sc	Sc	Sag	Sag	Cap
Apr 30	Vir	Vir	Vir	Lib	Lib	Sc	Sc	Sc	Sag	Sag	Cap	Cap
May 8	Vir	Vir	Lib	Lib	Lib	Sc	Sc	Sag	Sag	Sag	Cap	Cap
May 16	Vir	Vir	Lib	Lib	Sc	Sc	Sc	Sag	Sag	Cap	Cap	Aq
May 24	Vir	Lib	Lib	Lib	Sc	Sc	Sag	Sag	Sag	Cap	Cap	Aq
June 1	Vir	Lib	Lib	Sc	Sc	Sc	Sag	Sag	Cap	Cap	Aq	Aq
June 9	Lib	Lib	Lib	Sc	Sc	Sag	Sag	Sag	Cap	Cap	Aq	Pis
June 17	Lib	Lib	Sc	Sc	Sc	Sag	Sag	Cap	Cap	Aq	Aq	Pis
June 25	Lib	Lib	Sc	Sc	Sag	Sag	Sag	Cap	Cap	Aq	Pis	Ar
July 3	Lib	Sc	Sc	Sc	Sag	Sag	Cap	Cap	Aq	Aq	Pis	Ar
July 11	Lib	Sc	Sc	Sag	Sag	Sag	Cap	Cap	Aq	Pis	Ar	Tau
July 18	Sc	Sc	Sc	Sag	Sag	Cap	Cap	Aq	Aq	Pis	Ar	Tau
July 26	Sc	Sc	Sag	Sag	Sag	Cap	Cap	Aq	Pis	Ar	Tau	Tau
Aug 3	Sc	Sc	Sag	Sag	Cap	Cap	Aq	Aq	Pis	Ar	Tau	Gem
Aug 11	Sc	Sag	Sag	Sag	Cap	Cap	Aq	Pis	Ar	Tau	Tau	Gem
Aug 18	Sc	Sag	Sag	Cap	Cap	Aq	Pis	Pis	Ar	Tau	Gem	Gem
Aug 27	Sag	Sag	Sag	Cap	Cap	Aq	Pis	Ar	Tau	Tau	Gem	Gem
Sept 4	Sag	Sag	Cap	Cap	Aq	Pis	Pis	Ar	Tau	Gem	Gem	Can
Sept 12	Sag	Sag	Cap	Aq	Aq	Pis	Ar	Tau	Tau	Gem	Gem	Can
Sept 20	Sag	Cap	Cap	Aq	Pis	Pis	Ar	Tau	Gem	Gem	Can	Can
Sept 28	Cap	Cap	Aq	Aq	Pis	Ar	Tau	Tau	Gem	Gem	Can	Can
Oct 6	Cap	Cap	Aq	Pis	Ar	Ar	Tau	Gem	Gem	Can	Can	Leo
Oct 14	Cap	Aq	Aq	Pis	Ar	Tau	Tau	Gem	Gem	Can	Can	Leo
Oct 22	Cap	Aq	Pis	Ar	Ar	Tau	Gem	Gem	Can	Can	Leo	Leo
Oct 30	Aq	Aq	Pis	Ar	Tau	Tau	Gem	Can	Can	Can	Leo	Leo
Nov 7	Aq	Aq	Pis	Ar	Tau	Tau	Gem	Can	Can	Can	Leo	Leo
Nov 15	Aq	Pis	Ar	Tau	Gem	Gem	Can	Can	Can	Leo	Leo	Vir
Nov 23	Pis	Ar	Ar	Tau	Gem	Gem	Can	Can	Leo	Leo	Leo	Vir
Dec 1	Pis	Ar	Tau	Gem	Gem	Can	Can	Can	Leo	Leo	Vir	Vir
Dec 9	Ar	Tau	Tau	Gem	Gem	Can	Can	Leo	Leo	Leo	Vir	Vir
Dec 18	Ar	Tau	Gem	Gem	Can	Can	Can	Leo	Leo	Vir	Vir	Vir
Dec 28	Tau	Tau	Gem	Gem	Can	Can	Leo	Leo	Vir	Vir	Vir	Lib

CHAPTER 8

Astrology's Magic Symbols: The Glyphs

One of the first things an astrology student learns is how to read the symbols on a horoscope chart. These symbols or *glyphs* represent a kind of code, a pictorial language understood by astrologers around the globe and used by all astrology software programs. You'll miss out if you don't learn the glyphs. Once you learn them, you can begin to find your way around the chart, beginning your journey to deeper understanding. You can also make use of free charts available on any number of Internet sites and perhaps purchase one of the many astrology software programs.

The glyphs are fascinating little pictures in themselves, with built-in clues to help you not only decipher which sign or planet each represents, but what the symbol means in a deeper, more esoteric sense. Actually the physical act of writing the symbol is a mystical experience in itself, a way to invoke the deeper meaning of the sign or planet through age-old visual elements that have been with us since time began.

Since there are only twelve signs and ten planets (not counting a few asteroids and other space objects some astrologers use), it's a lot easier than learning to read a foreign language. Here's a code cracker for the glyphs, beginning with the glyphs for the planets. To those who already know their glyphs, don't just skim over the chapter. These familiar graphics have hidden meanings you will discover!

The Glyphs for the Planets

The glyphs for the planets are easy to learn. They're simple combinations of the most basic visual elements: the circle, the semicircle or arc, and the cross. However, each component of a glyph has a special meaning in relation to the other parts of the symbol.

The circle, which has no beginning or end, is one of the oldest symbols of spirit or spiritual forces. Early diagrams of the heavens—spiritual territory—are shown in circular form. The never-ending line of the circle is the perfect symbol for eternity. The semicircle or arc is an incomplete circle, symbolizing the receptive, finite soul, which contains spiritual potential in the curving line.

The vertical line of the cross symbolizes movement from heaven to earth. The horizontal line describes temporal movement, here and now, in time and space. Combined in a cross, the vertical and horizontal planes symbolize manifestation in the material world.

The Sun Glyph ☉

The sun is always shown by this powerful solar symbol, a circle with a point in the center. The center point is you, your spiritual center, and the symbol represents your infinite personality incarnating (the point) into the finite cycles of birth and death.

The sun has been represented by a circle or disk since ancient Egyptian times when the solar disk represented the sun god, Ra. Some archaeologists believe the great stone circles found in England were centers of sun worship. This particular version of the symbol was brought into common use in the sixteenth century after German occultist and scholar Cornelius Agrippa (1486–1535) wrote a book called *Die Occulta Philosophia,* which became accepted as the authority in the field. Agrippa collected many medieval astrological and magical symbols in this book, which have been used by astrologers since then.

The Moon Glyph ☽

The moon glyph is the most recognizable symbol on a chart, a left-facing arc stylized into the crescent moon. As part of a circle, the arc symbolizes the potential fulfillment of the entire circle, the life force that is still incomplete. Therefore, it is the ideal representation of the reactive, receptive, emotional nature of the moon.

The Mercury Glyph ☿

Mercury contains all three elemental symbols: the crescent, the circle, and the cross in vertical order. This is the "Venus with a hat" glyph (compare with the symbol of Venus). With another stretch of the imagination, can't you see the winged cap of Mercury the messenger? Think of the upturned crescent as antennae that tune in and transmit messages from the sun, reminding you that Mercury is the way you communicate, the way your mind works. The upturned arc is receiving energy into the spirit or solar circle, which will later be translated into action on the material plane, symbolized by the cross. All the elements are equally sized because Mercury is neutral; it doesn't play favorites! This planet symbolizes objective, detached, unemotional thinking.

The Venus Glyph ♀

Here the relationship is between two components: the circle of spirit and the cross of matter. Spirit is elevated over matter, pulling it upward. Venus asks, "What is beautiful? What do you like best? What do you love to have done to you?" Consequently, Venus determines both your ideal of beauty and what feels good sensually. It governs your own allure and power to attract, as well as what attracts and pleases you.

The Mars Glyph ♂

In this glyph, the cross of matter is stylized into an arrowhead pointed up and outward, propelled by the circle of spirit. With a little imagination, you can visualize it as the shield and spear of Mars, the ancient god of war. You can deduce that Mars embodies your spiritual energy projected into the outer world. It's your assertiveness, your initiative, your aggressive drive, what you like to do to others, your temper. If you know someone's Mars, you know whether they'll blow up when angry or do a slow burn. Your task is to use your outgoing Mars energy wisely and well.

The Jupiter Glyph ♃

Jupiter is the basic cross of matter, with a large stylized crescent perched on the left side of the horizontal, temporal plane. You might think of the crescent as an open hand, because one meaning of Jupiter is "luck," what's handed to you. You don't have to work for what you get from Jupiter; it comes to you, if you're open to it.

The Jupiter glyph might also remind you of a jumbo jet plane, with a huge tail fin, about to take off. This is the planet of travel, mental and spiritual, of expanding your horizons via new ideas, new spiritual dimensions, and new places. Jupiter embodies the optimism and enthusiasm of the traveler about to embark on an exciting adventure.

The Saturn Glyph ♄

Flip Jupiter over, and you've got Saturn. This might not be immediately apparent because Saturn is usually stylized into an "h" form like the one shown here. The principle it expresses is the opposite of Jupiter's expansive tendencies. Saturn pulls you back to earth: the receptive arc is pushed down underneath the cross of matter. Before there are any rewards or expansion, the duties and obligations of the material world must be considered. Saturn says, "Stop, wait, finish your chores before you take off!"

Saturn's glyph also resembles the sickle of old "Father Time." Saturn was first known as Chronos, the Greek god of time, for time brings all matter to an end. When it was the most distant planet (before the discovery of Uranus), Saturn was believed to be the place where time stopped.

After the soul departed from earth, it journeyed back to the outer reaches of the universe and finally stopped at Saturn, or at "the end of time."

The Uranus Glyph ♅

The glyph for Uranus is often stylized to form a capital *H* after Sir William Herschel, who discovered the planet. But the more esoteric version curves the two pillars of the H into crescent antennae, or "ears," like satellite disks receiving signals from space. These are perched on the horizontal material line of the cross of matter and pushed from below by the circle of the spirit. To many sci-fi fans, Uranus looks like an orbiting satellite.

Uranus channels the highest energy of all, the white electrical light of the universal spiritual force that holds the cosmos together. This pure electrical energy is gathered from all over the universe. Because Uranus energy doesn't follow any ordinary celestial drumbeat, it can't be controlled or predicted (which is also true of those who are strongly influenced by this eccentric planet). In the symbol, this energy is manifested through the balance of polarities (the two opposite arms of the glyph) like the two polarized wires of a lightbulb.

The Neptune Glyph ♆

Neptune's glyph is usually stylized to look like a trident, the weapon of the Roman god Neptune. However, on a more esoteric level, it shows the large upturned crescent of the soul pierced through by the cross of matter. Neptune nails down, or materializes, soul energy, bringing impulses from the soul level into manifestation. That is why Neptune is associated with imagination or "imagining in," making an image of the soul. Neptune works through feelings, sensitivity, and the mystical capacity to bring the divine into the earthly realm.

The Pluto Glyph ♇

Pluto is written two ways. One is a composite of the letters *PL,* the first two letters of the word Pluto and coincidentally the initials of Percival Lowell, one of the planet's discoverers. The other, more esoteric symbol is a small circle above a large open crescent that surmounts the cross of matter. This depicts Pluto's power to regenerate. Imagine a new little spirit emerging from the sheltering cup of the soul. Pluto rules the forces of life and death. After this planet has passed a sensitive point in your chart, you are transformed, reborn in some way.

Sci-fi fans might visualize this glyph as a small satellite (the circle) being launched. It was shortly after Pluto's discovery that we learned how to harness the nuclear forces that made space exploration possible. Pluto rules the transformative power of atomic energy, which totally changed our lives and from which there is no turning back.

The Glyphs for the Signs

On an astrology chart, the glyph for the sign will appear after that of the planet. For example, when you see the moon glyph followed first by a number and then by another glyph representing the sign, this means that the moon was passing over a certain degree of that astrological sign at the time of the chart. On the dividing lines between the houses on your chart, you'll find the symbol for the sign that rules the house.

Because sun sign symbols do not contain the same basic geometric components of the planetary glyphs, we must look elsewhere for clues to their meanings. Many have been passed down from ancient Egyptian and Chaldean civilizations with few modifications. Others have been adapted over the centuries.

In deciphering many of the glyphs, you'll often find that the symbols reveal a dual nature of the sign, which is not always apparent in the usual sun sign descriptions. For instance, the Gemini glyph is similar to the Roman numeral for two, and reveals this sign's longing to discover a twin soul. The Cancer glyph may be interpreted as resembling either the nurturing breasts or the self-protective claws of a crab, both symbols associated with the contrasting qualities of this sign. Libra's glyph embodies the duality of the spirit balanced with material reality. The Sagittarius glyph shows that the aspirant must also carry along the earthly animal nature in his quest. The Capricorn sea goat is another symbol with dual emphasis. The goat climbs high, yet is always pulled back by the deep waters of the unconscious. Aquarius embodies the double waves of mental detachment, balanced by the desire for connection with others, in a friendly way. Finally, the two fishes of Pisces, which are forever tied together, show the duality of the soul and the spirit that must be reconciled.

The Aries Glyph ♈

Since the symbol for Aries is the Ram, this glyph is obviously associated with a ram's horns, which characterize one aspect of the Aries personality—an aggressive, me-first, leaping-headfirst attitude. But the symbol can be interpreted in other ways as well. Some astrologers liken it to a fountain of energy, which Aries people also embody. The first sign of the zodiac bursts on the scene eagerly, ready to go. Another analogy is to the eyebrows and nose of the human head, which Aries rules, and the thinking power that is initiated by the brain.

One theory of this symbol links it to the Egyptian god Amun, represented by a ram in ancient times. As Amun-Ra, this god was believed to embody the creator of the universe, the leader of all the other gods. This relates easily to the position of Aries as the leader (or first sign) of the zodiac, which begins at the spring equinox, a time of the year when nature is renewed.

The Taurus Glyph ♉

This is another easy glyph to draw and identify. It takes little imagination to decipher the bull's head with long curving horns. Like its symbol the Bull, the archetypal Taurus is slow to anger but ferocious when provoked, as well as stubborn, steady, and sensual. Another association is the larynx (and thyroid) of the throat area (ruled by Taurus) and the eustachian tubes running up to the ears, which coincides with the relationship of Taurus to the voice, song, and music. Many famous singers, musicians, and composers have prominent Taurus influences.

Many ancient religions involved a bull as the central figure in fertility rites or initiations, usually symbolizing the victory of man over his animal nature. Another possible origin is in the sacred bull of Egypt, who embodied the incarnate form of Osiris, god of death and resurrection. In early Christian imagery, the Taurus Bull represented St. Luke.

The Gemini Glyph ♊

The standard glyph immediately calls to mind the Roman numeral for two (II) and the Twins symbol, as it is called, for Gemini. In almost all drawings and images used for this sign, the relationship between two persons is emphasized. Usually one twin will be touching the other, which signifies communication, human contact, the desire to share.

The top line of the Gemini glyph indicates mental communication, while the bottom line indicates shared physical space.

The most famous Gemini legend is that of the twin sons, Castor and Pollux, one of whom had a mortal father while the other was the son of Zeus, king of the gods. When it came time for the mortal twin to die, his grief-stricken brother pleaded with Zeus, who agreed to let them spend half the year on earth in mortal form and half in immortal life, with the gods on Mount Olympus. This reflects a basic duality of humankind, which possesses an immortal soul yet is also subject to the limits of mortality.

The Cancer Glyph ♋

Two convenient images relate to the Cancer glyph. It is easiest to decode the curving claws of the Cancer symbol, the Crab. Like the crab's, Cancer's element is water. This sensitive sign also has a hard protective shell to protect its tender interior. The crab must be wily to escape predators, scampering sideways and hiding under rocks. The crab also responds to the cycles of the moon, as do all shellfish. The other image is that of two female breasts, which Cancer rules, showing that this is a sign that nurtures and protects others as well as itself.

In ancient Egypt, Cancer was also represented by the scarab beetle, a symbol of regeneration and eternal life.

The Leo Glyph ♌

Notice that the Leo glyph seems to be an extension of Cancer's glyph, with a significant difference. In the Cancer glyph, the lines curve inward protectively. The Leo glyph expresses energy outwardly. And there is no duality in the symbol, the Lion, or in Leo, the sign.

Lions have belonged to the sign of Leo since earliest times. It is not difficult to imagine the king of beasts with his sweeping mane and curling tail from this glyph. The upward sweep of the glyph easily describes the positive energy of Leo: the flourishing tail, the flamboyant qualities. Anther analogy, perhaps a stretch of the imagination, is that of a heart leaping up with joy and enthusiasm, also very typical of Leo, which also rules the heart. In early Christian imagery, the Leo Lion represented St. Mark.

The Virgo Glyph ♍

You can read much into this mysterious glyph. For instance, it could represent the initials of "Mary Virgin," or a young woman holding a staff of wheat, or stylized female genitalia, all common interpretations. The M shape might also remind you that Virgo is ruled by Mercury. The cross beneath the symbol reveals the grounded, practical nature of this earth sign.

The earliest zodiacs link Virgo with the Egyptian goddess Isis, who gave birth to the god Horus after her husband

Osiris had been killed, in the archetype of a miraculous conception. There are many ancient statues of Isis nursing her baby son, which are reminiscent of medieval Virgin and Child motifs. This sign has also been associated with the image of the Holy Grail, when the Virgo symbol was substituted with a chalice.

The Libra Glyph ♎

It is not difficult to read the standard image for Libra, the Scales, into this glyph. There is another meaning, however, that is equally relevant: the setting sun as it descends over the horizon. Libra's natural position on the zodiac wheel is the descendant, or sunset position (as the Aries natural position is the ascendant, or rising sign). Both images relate to Libra's personality. Libra is always weighing pros and cons for a balanced decision. In the sunset image, the sun (male) hovers over the horizontal earth (female) before setting. Libra is the space between these lines, harmonizing yin and yang, spiritual and material, male and female, ideal and real worlds. The glyph has also been linked to the kidneys, which are associated with Libra.

The Scorpio Glyph ♏

With its barbed tail, this glyph is easy to identify as the Scorpion for the sign of Scorpio. It also represents the male sexual parts, over which the sign rules. From the arrowhead, you can draw the conclusion that Mars was once its ruler. Some earlier Egyptian glyphs for Scorpio represent it as an erect serpent, so the Serpent is an alternate symbol.

Another symbol for Scorpio, which is not identifiable in this glyph, is the Eagle. Scorpios can go to extremes, either in soaring like the eagle or self-destructing like the scorpion. In early Christian imagery, which often used zodiacal symbols, the Scorpio Eagle was chosen to symbolize the intense apostle St. John the Evangelist.

The Sagittarius Glyph ♐

This is one of the easiest to spot and draw: an upward pointing arrow lifting up a cross. The arrow is pointing skyward, while the cross represents the four elements of the material world, which the arrow must convey. Elevating materiality into spirituality is an important Sagittarius quality, which explains why this sign is associated with higher learning, religion, philosophy, travel—the aspiring professions. Sagittarius can also send barbed arrows of frankness in the pursuit of truth, so the Archer symbol for Sagittarius is apt. (Sagittarius is also the sign of the supersalesman.)

Sagittarius is symbolically represented by the centaur, a mythological creature who is half man, half horse, aiming his arrow toward the skies. Though Sagittarius is motivated by spiritual aspiration, it also must balance the powerful appetites of the animal nature. The centaur Chiron, a figure in Greek mythology, became a wise teacher who, after many adventures and world travels, was killed by a poisoned arrow.

The Capricorn Glyph ♑

One of the most difficult symbols to draw, this glyph may take some practice. It is a representation of the sea goat: a mythical animal that is a goat with a curving fish's tail. The goat part of Capricorn wants to leave the waters of the emotions and climb to the elevated areas of life. But the fish tail is the unconscious, the deep chaotic psychic level that draws the goat back. Capricorn is often trying to escape the deep, feeling part of life by submerging himself in work, steadily ascending to the top. To some people, the glyph represents a seated figure with a bent knee, a reminder that Capricorn governs the knee area of the body.

An interesting aspect of this glyph is the contrast of the sharp pointed horns—which represent the penetrating, shrewd, conscious side of Capricorn—with the swishing tail—which represents its serpentine, unconscious, emotional force. One Capricorn legend, which dates from Roman times, tells of the earthy fertility god, Pan, who tried to save himself from uncontrollable sexual desires by jumping into the Nile. His upper body then turned into a goat, while the lower part became a fish. Later, Jupiter gave him a safe haven as a constellation in the skies.

The Aquarius Glyph ♒

This ancient water symbol can be traced back to an Egyptian hieroglyph representing streams of life force. Symbolized by the Water Bearer, Aquarius is distributor of the waters of life—the magic liquid of regeneration. The two waves can also be linked to the positive and negative charges of the electrical energy that Aquarius rules, a sort of universal wavelength. Aquarius is tuned in intuitively to higher forces via this electrical force. The duality of the glyph could also refer to the dual nature of Aquarius, a sign that runs hot and cold and that is friendly but also detached in the mental world of air signs.

In Greek legends, Aquarius is represented by Ganymede, who was carried to heaven by an eagle in order to become the cupbearer of Zeus and to supervise the annual flooding of the Nile. The sign later became associated with aviation and notions of flight.

The Pisces Glyph ♓

Here is an abstraction of the familiar image of Pisces, two Fishes swimming in opposite directions yet bound together by a cord. The Fishes represent the spirit—which yearns for the freedom of heaven—and the soul—which remains attached to the desires of the temporal world. During life on earth, the spirit and the soul are bound together. When they complement each other, instead of pulling in opposite directions, they facilitate the Pisces creativity. The ancient version of this glyph, taken from the Egyptians, had no connecting line, which was added in the fourteenth century.

In another interpretation, it is said that the left fish indicates the direction of involution or the beginning of a cycle, while the right fish signifies the direction of evolution, the way to completion of a cycle. It's an appropriate grand finale for Pisces, the last sign of the zodiac.

CHAPTER 9

High-Tech Astrology: The Best Software for Your Budget and Ability

After you've acquired some basic knowledge—the signs, houses, planets, and glyphs—you have the tools to take astrology to the next level by reading charts and relating the planets to the lives of friends, relatives, and daily events.

If you have a computer, the easiest way to do this is to use astrology software that can put a chart on the screen in seconds and even help you interpret it.

When it comes to astrology software, there are endless options. How do you make the right choice? First, define your goals. Do you want to do charts of friends and family, study celebrity charts, or check the aspects every day on your Palm Pilot? Do you want to invest in a more comprehensive program that adapts to your changing needs as you learn astrology?

The good news is that there's a program for every level of interest in all price points—starting with free. For the dabbler, there are the affordable Winstar Express and Time Passages. For the serious student, there are Astrolog (free), Solar Fire, Kepler, Winstar Plus—software that does every technique on planets and gives you beautiful chart printouts. You can do a chart of someone you've just met on your PDA with Astracadabra. If you're a Mac user, you'll be satisfied with the wonderful IO and Time Passages software.

However, since all the programs use the astrology symbols, or glyphs, for planets and signs, rather than written words, you should learn the glyphs before you purchase your software. Our chapter on the glyphs in this book will help you do just that. Here are some software options for you to explore.

Easy for Beginners

Time Passages

Designed for either a Macintosh or Windows computer, Time Passages is straightforward and easy to use. It allows you to generate charts and interpretation reports for yourself or friends and loved ones at the touch of a button. If you haven't yet learned the astrology symbols, this might be the program for you; just roll your mouse over any symbol of the planets, signs, or house cusps, and you'll be shown a description in plain English below the chart. Then click on the planet, sign, or house cusp and up pops a detailed interpretation. It couldn't be easier. A new basic edition, under fifty dollars at this writing, is bargain priced and ideal for beginners.

Time Passages
(866) 772-7876 (866-77-ASTRO)
Web site: www.astrograph.com

Growth Opportunities

Astrolabe

Astrolabe is one of the top astrology software resources. Check out the latest version of their powerful Solar Fire software for Windows. A breeze to use, it will grow with your increasing knowledge of astrology to the most sophisticated levels. This company also markets a variety of programs for all levels of expertise and a wide selection of computer-generated astrology readings. This is a good resource for innovative software as well as applications for older computers.

The Astrolabe Web site is a great place to start your astrology tour of the Internet. Visitors to the site are greeted with a chart of the time you log on. And you can get your chart calculated, also free, with an interpretation e-mailed to you.

Astrolabe
Box 1750-R
Brewster, MA 02631
Phone: (800) 843-6682
Web site: www.alabe.com

Matrix Software

You'll find a wide variety of software at student and advanced levels in all price ranges, demo disks, and lots of interesting readings. Check out Winstar Express, a powerful but reasonably priced program suitable for all skill levels. The Matrix Web site offers lots of fun activities for Web surfers, such as free readings from the *I Ching,* the runes, and the tarot. There are many free desktop backgrounds with astrology themes. Go here to connect with news groups and online discussions. Their online almanac helps you schedule the best day to sign on the dotted line, ask for a raise, or plant your tomatoes.

Matrix Software
126 South Michigan Avenue
Big Rapids, MI 49307
Phone: (800) 416-3924
Web site: www.astrologysoftware.com

Astro Communications Services (ACS)

Books, software for Mac and IBM compatibles, individual charts, and telephone readings are offered by this California company. Their freebies include astrology greeting cards and new moon reports. Find technical astrology materials here, such as *The American Ephemeris* and PC atlases. ACS will calculate and send charts to you, a valuable service if you do not have a computer.

ACS Publications
P.O. Box 1646
El Cajon, CA 92022-1646
Phone: (800) 514-5070
Fax: (619) 631-0180
Web site: www.astrocom.com

Air Software

Here you'll find powerful, creative astrology software, and current stock market analysis. Financial astrology programs for stock market traders are a specialty. There are some interesting freebies at this site; check out the maps of eclipse paths for any year and a free astrology clock program.

Air Software
115 Caya Avenue
West Hartford, CT 06110
Phone: (800) 659-1247
Web site: www.alphee.com

Kepler: State of the Art

Here's a program that has everything. Gorgeous graphic images, audio-visual effects, and myriad sophisticated chart options are built into this fascinating software. It's even got an astrological encyclopedia, plus diagrams and images to help you understand advanced concepts. This program is expensive, but if you're serious about learning astrology, it's an investment that will grow with you! Check out its features at www.astrologysoftwareshop.com.

Time Cycles Research: For Mac Users

Here's where Mac users can find astrology software that's as sophisticated as it gets. If you have a Mac, you'll love their beautiful graphic IO Series programs.

Time Cycles Research
P.O. Box 797
Waterford, CT 06385
Web site: www.timecycles.com
(800) 827-2240

Shareware and Freeware: The Price Is Right!

Halloran Software: A Super Shareware Program

Check out Halloran Software's Web site (www.halloran.com), which offers several levels of Windows astrology software. Beginners should consider their Astrology for Windows shareware program, which is available in unregistered demo form as a free download and in registered form for a very reasonable price.

Halloran Software
P.O. Box 75713
Los Angeles, CA 90075
(800) 732-4628

Astrolog

If you're computer-savvy, you can't go wrong with Walter Pullen's amazingly complete Astrolog program, which is offered absolutely free at the site. The Web address is www.astrolog.org/astrolog.htm.

Astrolog is an ultrasophisticated program with all the features of much more expensive programs. It comes in versions for all formats—DOS, Windows, Mac, UNIX—and has some cool features, such as a revolving globe and a constellation map. If you are looking for astrology software with bells and whistles that doesn't cost big bucks, this program has it all!

Programs for the Pocket PDA and Palm Pilot

Would you like to have astrology at your fingertips everywhere you go? No need to drag along your laptop. You can check the chart of the moment or of someone you've just met on your pocket PDA or Palm Pilot. As with most other programs, you'll need to know the astrological symbols in order to read the charts.

For the pocket PC that has the Microsoft Pocket PC 2002 or the Microsoft Windows Mobile 2003 operating system, there is the versatile Astracadabra, which can interchange charts with the popular Solar Fire software. It can be ordered at www.leelehman.com or www.astrologysoftwareshop.com.

For the Palm OS5 and compatible handheld devices, there is Astropocket from www.yves.robert.org/features.html. This is a shareware program, which allows you to use all the features free. However, you cannot store more than one chart at a time until you pay a mere twenty-eight-dollar registration fee for the complete version.

CHAPTER 10

Travel the World of Astrology

There's a world of astrology waiting to welcome you, and thanks to the Internet, it's now possible to connect instantly with astrology fans and events around the globe. There are so many ways out there to expand your knowledge and share with others. Consider studying with a famous astrologer or attending a local astrology club or regional workshop. You could even combine your vacation with an astrological workshop in an exotic locale such as Bali or Mexico.

You need only type the word *astrology* into any Internet search engine and watch hundreds of listings of astrology-related sites pop up. There are local meetings and international conferences where you can connect with other astrologers, and books and tapes to help you study at home.

To help you sort out the variety of options available, here are our top picks of the Internet and the astrological community at large.

Nationwide Astrology Organizations and Conferences

Meet the World's Best Astrologers at UAC!

From May 14 to 21, 2008, the best astrologers from around the world will gather in Denver, Colorado, site of the United

Astrology Conference. UAC is jointly sponsored by three nonprofit educational organizations: AFAN (Association for Astrological Networking), ISAR (International Society for Astrological Research), and NCGR (National Council for Geocosmic Research). This conference attracts astrology fans from North and South America, Europe, Russia, India, Japan, South Africa, Australia, and New Zealand.

Here's your chance to meet and socialize with the world's top astrologers, who'll be participating in a global forum on modern astrology. There will be an all-star lineup of lectures on a variety of financial, metaphysical, psychological, and scientific topics for astrology professionals, students, and beginners. Whatever your level of expertise, there's a track for you at UAC.

Preview the conference at the convention site Web site, www.uacastrology.com.

National Council for Geocosmic Research (NCGR)

Whether you'd like to know more about such specialties as financial astrology or techniques for timing events, or if you'd prefer the psychological or mythological approach, you'll meet the top astrologers at conferences sponsored by the National Council for Geocosmic Research. NCGR is dedicated to providing quality education, bringing astrologers and astrology fans together at conferences, and promoting fellowship. Their course structure provides a systematized study of the many facets of astrology. The organization sponsors educational workshops, taped lectures, conferences, and a directory of professional astrologers. For an annual membership fee, you get their excellent publications and newsletters, plus the opportunity to network with other astrology buffs at local chapter events. (At this writing there are chapters in twenty-six states and four countries.)

To join NCGR for the latest information on upcoming events and chapters in your city, consult their Web site: www.geocosmic.org.

American Federation of Astrologers (AFA)

Established in 1938, this is one of the oldest astrological organizations in the United States. AFA offers conferences, conventions, and a thorough correspondence course. If you are looking for a reading, their interesting Web site will refer you to an accredited AFA astrologer.

AFA
6535 S. Rural Road
Tempe, AZ 85283
Phone: (888) 301-7630 or (480) 838-1751
Fax: (480) 838-8293
Web site: www.astrologers.com

Association for Astrological Networking (AFAN)

Did you know that astrologers are still being harassed for practicing astrology? AFAN provides support and legal information and works toward improving the public image of astrology. AFAN's network of local astrologers links with the international astrological community. Here are the people who will go to bat for astrology when it is attacked in the media. Everyone who cares about astrology should join!

AFAN
8306 Wilshire Boulevard
PMB 537
Beverly Hills, CA 90211
Phone: (800) 578-2326
E-mail: info@afan.org
Web site: www.afan.org

International Society for Astrology Research (ISAR)

An international organization of professional astrologers dedicated to encouraging the highest standards of quality in the field of astrology with an emphasis on research. Among ISAR's benefits are a quarterly journal, a weekly e-mail newsletter, frequent conferences, and a free membership directory.

ISAR
P.O. Box 38613
Los Angeles, CA 90038
Fax: (805) 933-0301
Web site: www.isarastrology.com

Astrology Magazines

In addition to articles by top astrologers, most of these have listings of astrology conferences, events, and local happenings.

Horoscope Guide
Kappa Publishing Group
6198 Butler Pike
Suite 200
Blue Bell, PA 19422-2600
Web site: www.kappapublishing.com/astrology

Dell Horoscope
Their Web site (www.dellhoroscope.com) features a listing of local astrological meetings.

Customer Service
6 Prowitt Street
Norwalk, CT 06855
(800) 220-7443

The Mountain Astrologer

A favorite magazine of astrology fans! *The Mountain Astrologer* also has an interesting Web site featuring the latest news from an astrological point of view, plus feature articles from the magazine.

The Mountain Astrologer
P.O. Box 970
Cedar Ridge, CA 95924
Phone: (800) 247-4828
Web site: www.mountainastrologer.com

Astrology College

Kepler College of Astrological Arts and Sciences

A degree-granting college, which is also a center of astrology, has long been the dream of the astrological community and is a giant step forward in providing credibility to the profession. Therefore, the opening of Kepler College in 2000 was a historical event for astrology. It is the only college in the western hemisphere authorized to issue B.A. and M.A. degrees in Astrological Studies. Here is where to study with the best scholars, teachers, and communicators in the field. A long-distance study program is available for those interested.

For more information, contact:

Kepler College of Astrological Arts and Sciences
4630 200th Street SW
Suite A-1
Lynnwood, WA 98036
Phone: (425) 673-4292
Fax: (425) 673-4983
Web site: www.kepler.edu

Our Favorite Web Sites

Of the thousands of astrological Web sites that come and go on the Internet, these have stood the test of time and are likely to still be operating when this book is published.

Astrodienst (www.astro.com)

Don't miss this fabulous international site that has long been one of the best astrology resources on the Internet. It's also a great place to view and download your own astrology chart. The world atlas on this site will give you the accurate longitude and latitude of your birthplace for setting up your horoscope. Then you can print out your free chart in a range of easy-to-read formats. Other attractions: a list of famous people born on your birth date, a feature that helps you choose the best vacation spot, plus articles by world-famous astrologers.

AstroDatabank (www.astrodatabank.com)

When the news is breaking, you can bet this site will be the first to get accurate birthdays of the headliners. The late astrologer Lois Rodden was a stickler for factual information and her meticulous research is being continued, much to the benefit of the astrological community. The Web site specializes in charts of current newsmakers, political figures, and international celebrities. You can also participate in discussions and analysis of the charts and see what some of the world's best astrologers have to say about them. Their AstroDatabank program, which you can purchase at the site, provides thousands of verified birthdays sorted into categories. It's an excellent research tool.

StarIQ (www.stariq.com)

Find out how top astrologers view the latest headlines at the must-see StarIQ site. Many of the best minds in astrology comment on the latest news, stock market ups and downs, political contenders. You can sign up to receive e-mail forecasts at the most important times keyed to your individual chart. (This is one of the best of the many online forecasts.)

Astro-Noetics (www.astro-noetics.com)

For those who are ready to explore astrology's interface with politics, popular culture, and current events, here is a sophisticated site with in-depth articles and personality profiles. Lots of depth and content here for the astrology-savvy surfer.

Astrology Books (www.astroamerica.com)

The Astrology Center of America sells a wide selection of books on all aspects of astrology, from the basics to the most advanced, at this online bookstore. Also available are many hard-to-find and recycled books.

Astrology Scholars' Sites

See what one of astrology's great teachers, Robert Hand, has to offer on his site: www.robhand.com. A leading expert on the history of astrology, he's on the cutting edge of the latest research.

The Project Hindsight group of astrologers is devoted to restoring the astrology of the Hellenistic period, the primary source for all later Western astrology. There are fascinating articles for astrology fans on this site, www.project-hindsight.com.

Financial Astrology Sites

Financial astrology is a hot specialty, with many tipsters, players, and theorists. There are online columns, newsletters, specialized financial astrology software, and mutual funds run by astrology seers. One of the more respected financial astrologers is Ray Merriman, whose stock market comments on www.mmacycles.com are a must read for those following the bulls and bears. Other top financial astrologers offer tips and forecasts at the www.afund.com and www.alphee.com sites.

CHAPTER 11

Is It Time for a Personal Reading?

Looking for answers to a burning personal question? A reading with a professional astrologer might help. A reading can be an empowering experience if you want to reach your full potential. You could use it for sizing up a lover or business situation to find out what the future has in store. If you're in a quandary about a problem, some astrological perspective could be an eye-opener. It might help you make over your life by choosing a more satisfying career or moving to a more favorable location. You could use it to find the optimum time for an important event such as a wedding or get the competitive edge in a meeting.

Another good reason for a reading is to refine your knowledge of astrology by consulting with someone who has years of experience analyzing charts. You might choose someone with a special technique that intrigues you. Armed with the knowledge of your chart that you have acquired so far, you can then learn to interpret subtle nuances or gain insight on your talents and abilities.

How do you choose when there are so many different kinds of readings available, especially since the Internet has brought astrology into the mainstream? Besides individual one-on-one readings with a professional astrologer, there are personal readings by mail, telephone, Internet, and tape. Well-advertised computer-generated reports and celebrity-sponsored readings are sure to attract your attention on commercial Web sites and in magazines. Then there are astrologers who specialize in certain areas such as finance or medical astrology. And unfortunately, there are many questionable practitioners who range from streetwise gypsy fortune-tellers to unscrupulous scam artists.

The following basic guidelines can help you sort out your options to find the reading that's right for you.

One-on-One Consultations with a Professional Astrologer

Nothing compares to a one-on-one consultation with a professional astrologer who has analyzed thousands of charts and can pinpoint the potential in yours. During your reading, you can get your specific questions answered. For instance, how to get along better with your mate or coworker. There are many astrologers who now combine their skills with training in psychology and are well-suited to help you examine your alternatives.

To give you an accurate reading, an astrologer needs certain information from you: the date, time, and place where you were born. (A horoscope can be cast about anyone or anything that has a specific time and place.) Most astrologers will then enter this information into a computer, which will calculate a chart in seconds. From the resulting chart, the astrologer will do an interpretation.

If you don't know your exact birth time, you can usually locate it at the Bureau of Vital Statistics at the city hall or county seat of the state where you were born. If you still have no success in getting your time of birth, some astrologers can estimate an approximate birth time by using past events in your life to determine the chart. This technique is called *rectification*.

How to Find an Astrologer

Choose your astrologer with the same care as you would any trusted adviser such as a doctor, lawyer, or banker. Unfortunately, anyone can claim to be an astrologer—to date, there is no licensing of astrologers or universally established professional criteria. However, there are nationwide organizations of serious, committed astrologers that can help you in your search.

Good places to start your investigation are organizations such as the American Federation of Astrologers (AFA) or the National Council for Geocosmic Research (NCGR), which offer a program of study and certification. If you live near a major city, there is sure to be an active NCGR chapter or astrology club in your area; many are listed in astrology magazines available at your local newsstand. In response to many requests for referrals, both the AFA and the NCGR have directories of professional astrologers listed on their Web sites; these directories include a glossary of terms and an explanation of specialties within the astrological field. Contact the NCGR and AFA headquarters for information (see chapter 10 in this book).

Warning Signals

As a potentially lucrative freelance business, astrology has always attracted self-styled experts who may not have the knowledge or the counseling experience to give a helpful reading. These astrologers can range from the well-meaning amateur to the charlatan or street-corner gypsy who has for many years given astrology a bad name. Be very wary of astrologers who claim to have occult powers or who make pretentious claims of celebrated clients or miraculous achievements. You can often tell from the initial phone conversation if the astrologer is legitimate. He or she should ask for your birthday time and place, then conduct the conversation in a professional manner. Any astrologer who gives a reading based only on your sun sign is highly suspect.

When you arrive at the reading, the astrologer should be prepared. The consultation should be conducted in a private, quiet place. The astrologer should be interested in your problems of the moment. A good reading involves feedback on your part. So if the reading is not relating to your concerns, you should let the astrologer know. You should feel free to ask questions and get clarifications of technical terms. The more you actively participate, rather than expecting the astrologer to carry the reading or come forth with oracular predictions, the more meaningful your experience will be. An astrologer should help you validate your current experience and be frank about possible negative happenings, but also suggest a positive course of action.

In their approach to a reading, some astrologers may be more literal, others more intuitive. Those who have had counseling training may take a more psychological approach. Though some astrologers may seem to have an almost psychic ability, extrasensory perception or any other parapsychological talent is not essential. A very accurate picture can be drawn from the data in your horoscope chart.

An astrologer may do several charts for each client, including one for the time of birth and a *progressed chart,* showing the evolution from birth to the present time. According to your individual needs, there are many other possibilities, such as a chart for a different location if you are contemplating a change of place. Relationships between any two people, things, or events can be interpreted with a chart that compares one partner's horoscope with the other's. A composite chart, which uses the midpoint between planets in two individual charts to describe the relationship, is another commonly used device.

An astrologer will be particularly interested in transits, those times when cycling planets activate the planets or sensitive points in your birth chart. These indicate important events in your life.

Many astrologers offer tape-recorded readings, another option to consider, especially if the astrologer you choose lives at a distance. In this case, you'll be mailed a taped reading based on your birth chart. This type of reading is more personal than a computer printout and can give you valuable insights, though it is not equivalent to a live dialogue with the astrologer when you can discuss your specific interests and issues of the moment.

The Telephone Reading

Telephone readings come in two varieties: a dial-in taped reading, usually recorded in advance by an astrologer, or a live consultation with an "astrologer" on the other end of the line. The taped readings are general daily or weekly forecasts, applied to all members of your sign and charged by the minute. The quality depends on the astrologer. One caution: Be aware that these readings can run up quite a telephone bill, especially if you get into the habit of calling every day. Be sure that you are aware of the per-minute cost of each call beforehand.

Live telephone readings also vary with the expertise of the astrologer. Ideally, the astrologer at the other end of the line enters your birth date into a computer, which then quickly calculates your chart. This chart will be referred to during the consultation. The advantage of a live telephone reading is that your individual chart is used and you can ask about a specific problem. However, before you invest in any reading, be sure that your astrologer is qualified and that you fully understand in advance how much you will be charged. There should be no unpleasant financial surprises later.

Computer-Generated Reports

Companies that offer computer programs (such as ACS, Matrix, Astrolabe) also offer a variety of computer-generated horoscope readings. These can be quite comprehensive, offering a beautiful printout of the chart plus many pages of detailed information about each planet and aspect of the chart. You can then study it at your convenience. Of course, the interpretations will be general, since there is no personal input from you, and may not cover your immediate concerns. Since computer-generated horoscopes are much lower in cost than live consultations, you might consider one as either a supplement or a preparation for an eventual live reading. You'll then be more familiar with your chart and able to plan specific questions in advance. They also make terrific gifts for astrology fans. There are several companies, listed in chapter 9, that offer computerized readings prepared by reputable astrologers.

Whichever option you decide to pursue, may your reading be an empowering one!

CHAPTER 12

Your Baby-scope: Children Born in 2008

Parents of several children may see a marked difference between children born in 2008 and their older siblings, as the cosmic atmosphere is changing, which should imprint the personalities of this year's children.

Astrologers look to the slow-moving outer planets—Uranus, Neptune, and Pluto—to describe a generation. This year, Uranus and Neptune are still passing through Pisces and Aquarius, both visionary and spiritual signs. However, there is also much more earth-sign emphasis than in previous years due to the earthly pull of Pluto in Capricorn, plus the closer planets, Jupiter and Saturn, also in earth signs, which will counterbalance this spirituality with extreme practicality and pragmatism. This generation will be focused on getting the job done, on fixing up the planet, and on making things work.

Astrology can be an especially helpful tool that can be used to design an environment that will enhance and encourage each child's positive qualities. Some parents start before conception, planning the birth of their child as far as possible to harmonize with the signs of other family members. However, each baby has its own schedule, so if yours arrives a week early or late, or elects a different sign than you'd planned, recognize that the new sign may be more in line with the mission your child is here to accomplish. In other words, if you were hoping for a Libra child and he arrives during Virgo, that Virgo energy may be just what is needed to stimulate or complement your family. Remember that there are many astrological elements besides the sun sign that indicate strong family ties. Usually each child will share a particular planetary placement, an emphasis on a particular sign or house, or a certain chart configuration with his parents and other family members. Often there is a significant planetary angle that will define the parent-child relationship, such as family sun signs that form a T-square or a triangle.

One important thing you can do is to be sure the exact moment of birth is recorded. This will be essential in calculating an accurate astrological chart. The following descriptions can be applied to the sun or moon sign (if known) of a child—the sun sign will describe basic personality and the moon sign indicates the child's emotional needs.

The Aries Child

Baby Aries is quite a handful! This energetic child will walk—and run—as soon as possible and perform daring feats of exploration. Caregivers should be vigilant. Little Aries seems to know no fear (and is especially vulnerable to head injuries). Many Aries children, in their rush to get on with life, seem hyperactive and are easily frustrated when they can't get their own way. Violent temper tantrums and dramatic physical displays are par for the course with these children, necessitating a time-out chair.

The very young Aries should be monitored carefully, since he is prone to take risks and may injure himself. An Aries loves to take things apart and may break toys easily, but with encouragement, the child will develop formidable coordination. Aries's bossy tendencies should be molded into leadership qualities, rather than bullying. Otherwise, the me-first Aries will have many clashes with other strong-willed youngsters. Encourage these children to take out aggressions and frustrations in active, competitive sports, where they usually excel. When a young Aries learns to focus his energies long enough to master a subject and learns consideration for others, the indomitable Aries spirit will rise to the head of the class.

Aries born in 2008 will be a more subdued version of

this sign, but still loaded with energy. The Capricorn effect should make little Aries easier to discipline and more focused on achievement. A natural leader!

The Taurus Child

This is a cuddly, affectionate child who eagerly explores the world of the senses, especially the senses of taste and touch. The Taurus child can be a big eater and will put on weight easily if not encouraged to exercise. Since this child likes comfort and gravitates to beauty, try coaxing little Taurus to exercise to music or take him outdoors for hikes or long walks. Though Taurus may be a slow learner, this sign has an excellent retentive memory and generally masters a subject thoroughly. Taurus is interested in results and will see each project patiently through to completion, continuing long after others have given up. This year's earth-sign planet will give him a wonderful sense of support and accomplishment.

Choose Taurus toys carefully to help develop innate talents. Construction toys, such as blocks or erector sets, appeal to their love of building. Paints or crayons develop their sense of color. Many Taurus have musical talents and love to sing, which is apparent at a young age.

This year's Taurus will want a pet or two and a few plants of his own. Give little Taurus a minigarden and watch the natural green thumb develop. This child has a strong sense of acquisition and an early grasp of material value. After filling a piggy bank, Taurus graduates to a savings account, before other children have started to learn the value of money.

This year's Taurus gets a bonanza of good luck and support from Jupiter, Pluto, and Saturn—all in compatible earth signs. These should give little Taurus an especially easygoing disposition and provide many opportunities to live up to his sign's potential.

The Gemini Child

Little Gemini will talk as soon as possible, filing the air with questions and chatter. This is a friendly child who enjoys social contact, seems to require company, and adapts quickly to different surroundings. Geminis have quick minds that easily grasp the use of words, books, and telephones and will probably learn to talk and read at an earlier age than most. Though they are fast learners, Gemini may have a short attention span, darting from subject to subject. Projects and games that help focus the mind could be used to help them concentrate. Musical instruments, typewriters, and computers help older Gemini children combine mental with manual dexterity. Geminis should be encouraged to finish what they start before they go on to another project. Otherwise, they can become jack-of-all-trade types who have trouble completing anything they do. Their dispositions are usually cheerful and witty, making these children popular with their peers and delightful company at home.

This year's Gemini baby should go to the head of the class. Uranus in Pisces could inspire Gemini to make an unusual career choice, perhaps in a financial field. When he grows up, this year's Gemini may change jobs several times before he finds a position that satisfies his need for stimulation and variety.

The Cancer Child

This emotional, sensitive child is especially influenced by patterns set early in life. Young Cancers cling to their first memories as well as their childhood possessions. They thrive in calm emotional waters, with a loving, protective mother, and usually remain close to her (even if their relationship with her was difficult) throughout their lives. Divorce, death—anything that disturbs the safe family unit—

are devastating to Cancers, who may need extra support and reassurance during a family crisis.

They sometimes need a firm hand to push the positive, creative side of their personality and discourage them from getting swept away by emotional moods or resorting to emotional manipulation to get their way. Praised and encouraged to find creative expression, Cancer will be able to express his positive side consistently on a firm, secure foundation.

This year's Cancer baby should be a social, cooperative child, oriented toward others, thanks to Jupiter and Pluto blessing relationships.

The Leo Child

Leo children love the limelight and will plot to get the lion's share of attention. These children assert themselves with flair and drama and can behave like tiny tyrants to get their way. But in general, they have sunny, positive dispositions and are rarely subject to blue moods. At school, they're the ones who are voted most popular, head cheerleader, or homecoming queen. Leo is sure to be noticed for personality, if not for stunning looks or academic work; the homely Leo will be a class clown and the unhappy Leo may be the class bully.

Above all, a Leo child cannot tolerate being ignored for long. Drama or performing-arts classes, sports, and school politics are healthy ways for Leo to be a star. But Leos must learn to take lesser roles occasionally, or they will have some painful put-downs in store. Usually, the popularity of Leos is well earned; they are hard workers who try to measure up to their own high standards—and usually succeed.

This year's Leo should be a less flamboyant, more down-to-earth version of his sign, as the earthy planets exert their influence. This should add more financial and practical talents to the expressive Leo personality.

The Virgo Child

The young Virgo can be a quiet, rather serious child, with a quick, intelligent mind. Early on, little Virgo shows far more attention to detail and concern with small things than other children do. Little Virgo has a built-in sense of order and a fascination with how things work. It is important for these children to have a place of their own, which they can order as they wish and where they can read or busy themselves with crafts and hobbies.

This child's personality can be very sensitive. Little Virgo may get hyper and overreact to seemingly small irritations, which can take the form of stomach upsets or delicate digestive systems. But this child will flourish where there is mental stimulation and a sense of order. Virgos thrive in school, especially in writing or language skills, and seem truly happy when buried in books. Chances are, young Virgo will learn to read ahead of classmates. Hobbies that involve detail work or that develop fine craftsmanship are especially suited to young Virgos.

Baby Virgo of 2008 is likely to be an especially high achiever with Saturn also in Virgo, adding focus and discipline, while Jupiter transiting the house of self-expression endows extra creativity.

The Libra Child

The Libra child learns early about the power of charm and appearance. This is often a very physically appealing child with an enchanting dimpled smile, who is naturally sociable and enjoys the company of both children and adults. It is a rare Libra child who is a discipline problem, but when their behavior is unacceptable, they respond better to calm discussion than displays of emotion, especially if the discussion revolves around fairness. Because young Libras without a strong direction tend to drift with the mood of the group, these children should be encouraged to develop their unique talents and powers of discrimination so they can later stand on their own.

In school, this child is usually popular and will often have to choose between social invitations and studies. In the teen years, social pressures mount as the young Libra begins to look for a partner. This is the sign of best friends, so Libra's choice of companions can have a strong effect on his future direction. Beautiful Libra girls may be tempted to go steady or have an unwise early marriage. Chances are, both sexes will fall in and out of love several times in their search for the ideal partner.

Little Libra of 2008 is an especially social, talkative child who gets along well with siblings because Jupiter in Capricorn enhances family life. This child is endowed with much imagination and creativity, as well as communication skills.

The Scorpio Child

The Scorpio child may seem quiet and shy, but will surprise others with intense feelings and formidable willpower. Scorpio children are single-minded when they want something and intensely passionate about whatever they do. One of a caregiver's tasks is to teach this child to balance activities and emotions, yet at the same time to make the most of his or her great concentration and intense commitment.

Since young Scorpios do not show their depth of feelings easily, parents will have to learn to read almost imperceptible signs that troubles are brewing beneath the surface. Both Scorpio boys and girls enjoy games of power and control on or off the playground. Scorpio girls may take an early interest in the opposite sex, masquerading as tomboys, while Scorpio boys may be intensely competitive and loners. When their powerful energies are directed into work, sports, or challenging studies, Scorpio is a superachiever, focused on a goal. With trusted friends, young Scorpio is devoted and caring—the proverbial friend through thick and thin, loyal for life.

Scorpio 2008 has a strong financial emphasis, which could make these children big money earners in adulthood. Uranus in Pisces in their house of creativity should put them on the cutting edge of whichever field they choose.

The Sagittarius Child

This restless, athletic child will be out of the playpen and off on adventures as soon as possible. Little Sagittarius is remarkably well-coordinated, attempting daredevil feats on any wheeled vehicle from scooters to skateboards. These natural athletes need little encouragement to channel their energies into sports. Their cheerful, friendly dispositions earn them popularity in school, and once they have found a subject where their talent and imagination can soar, they will do well academically. They love animals, especially horses, and will be sure to have a pet or two, if not a home zoo. When they are old enough to take care of themselves, they'll clamor to be off on adventures of their own, away from home, if possible.

This child loves to travel, will not get homesick at summer camp, and may sign up to be a foreign-exchange student or spend summers abroad. Outdoor adventure appeals to little Sagittarius, especially if it involves an active sport, such as skiing, cycling, or mountain climbing. Give them enough space and encouragement, and their fiery spirit will propel them to achieve high goals.

Baby Sagittarius of 2008 has a natural generosity of spirit and an optimistic, expansive nature. He will also demand a great deal of freedom. He may need reality checks from time to time, since he may be a risk taker, especially in the financial area. He should learn early in life how to handle money.

The Capricorn Child

These purposeful, goal-oriented children will work to capacity if they feel this will bring results. They're not ones who enjoy work for its own sake—there must be an end in sight. Authority figures can do much to motivate these children, but once set on an upward path, young Capricorns will mobilize energy and talent and work harder, and with more perseverance, than any other sign. Capricorn has built-in self-discipline that can achieve remarkable results, even if lacking the flashy personality, quick brain power, or penetrating insight of others. Once involved, young Capricorn will stick to a task until it is mastered. These children also know how to use others to their advantage and may well become team captains or class presidents.

A wise parent will set realistic goals for the Capricorn child, paving the way for the early thrill of achievement. Youngsters should be encouraged to express their caring, feeling side to others, as well as their natural aptitude for leadership. Capricorn children may be especially fond of grandparents and older relatives and will enjoy spending time with them and learning from them. It is not uncommon for young Capricorns to have an older mentor or teacher who guides them. With their great respect for authority, Capricorn children will take this influence very much to heart.

The Capricorn born in 2008 will have an upbeat, cheerful personality, thanks to the presence of lucky Jupiter in Capricorn. This child should have a generous, expansive nature and be more outgoing than the usual member of this sign.

The Aquarius Child

The Aquarius child has an innovative, well-focused mind that often streaks so far ahead of those of peers that this child seems like an oddball. Routine studies never hold the restless youngster for long; he will look for another, more experimental place to try out his ideas and develop his inventions. Life is a laboratory to the inquiring Aquarius mind. School politics, sports, science, and the arts offer scope for such talents. But if there is no room for expression within approved social limits, Aquarius is sure to rebel. Questioning institutions and religions comes naturally, so these children may find an outlet elsewhere, becoming rebels with a cause. It is better not to force this child to conform, but rather to channel forward-thinking young minds into constructive group activities.

This year's Aquarius will have far-out glamour as well as charisma, thanks to his ruler, Uranus, in a friendly bond with Neptune. This could be a rock star, a statesman, or a scientist.

The Pisces Child

Give young Pisces praise, applause, and a gentle, but firm, push in the right direction. Lovable Pisces children may be abundantly talented, but may be hesitant to express themselves, because they are quite sensitive and easily hurt. It is a parent's challenge to help them gain self-esteem and self-confidence. However, this same sensitivity makes them trusted friends who'll have many confidants as they develop socially. It also endows many Pisces with spectacular creative talent.

Pisces adores drama and theatrics of all sorts; therefore, encourage them to channel their creativity into art forms rather than indulging in emotional dramas. Understand that they may need more solitude than other children, as they develop their creative ideas. But though daydreaming can be creative, it is important that these natural dreamers not dwell too long in the world of fantasy. Teach them practical coping skills for the real world. Since Pisces are physically sensitive, parents should help them build strong bodies with proper diet and regular exercise. Young Pisces may gravitate to more individual sports, such as swimming, sailing, and skiing, rather than to team sports. Or they may prefer more artistic physical activities like dance or ice skating.

Born givers, these children are often drawn to the underdog (they fall quickly for sob stories) and attract those who might take advantage of their empathic nature. Teach them to choose friends wisely and to set boundaries in relationships, to protect their emotional vulnerability—invaluable lessons in later life.

With the planet Uranus now in Pisces, the 2008 baby

belongs to a generation of Pisces movers and shakers. This child may have a rebellious streak that rattles the status quo. But this generation also has a visionary nature, which will be much concerned with the welfare of the world at large.

CHAPTER 13

Your Leap Year Guide to Love

The year 2008 is a leap year, when ladies traditionally make the first romantic moves. However, it's no longer unusual for women to pursue the object of their desire aggressively, no matter what the year. So if you want to charm a Capricorn, hook a Pisces, or corral a Taurus, here are sun-sign seduction tips guaranteed to keep your lover begging for more.

How to Love Every Sign

Aries: Daredevil Lover

This highly physical sign is walking dynamite with a brief attention span. Don't be too easy to get, ladies. A little challenge, a lively debate, and a merry chase only heat up your admirers. They want to see what you're made of. Once you've lured them into your lair, be a challenge, a bit of a daredevil, and pull out your X-rated tricks. Don't give your all—let them know there's more where that came from. Make it exciting, show you're up for adventure. Wear bright red somewhere interesting. Since Aries rules the head and face, be sure to focus on these areas in your lovemaking. Use your lips, tongue, breath, and even your eyelashes to the max. Practice scalp massages and deep-kissing techniques. Aries won't wait, so when you make your move, be sure you're ready to follow through. No head games or teasing!

To keep you happy, you've got to voice your own needs, because this lover will be focused on his. Teach him how to please, or this could be a one-sided adventure.

Taurus: Sweet Treats

Taurus wins as the most sensual sign, with the most sexual stamina. This man is earthy and lusty in bed; he can go on all night. This is not a sign to tease. Like the Bull, he'll see red, not bed. So make him comfortable, then bombard all his senses. Good food gets Taurus in the mood. So do the right music and fragrance, revealing clothes, and luxurious bed linens. Give him a massage with delicious-smelling and -tasting oils; focus on the neck area.

Don't forget to turn off the phone! Taurus hates interruptions. Since they can be very vocal lovers, choose a setting where you won't be disturbed. And don't ever rush; enjoy a long, slow, delicious encounter.

Gemini: Playtime

Playful Gemini loves games, so make your seduction fun. Be their lost twin soul, their confidant. Good communication is essential, so share deep secrets, live out fantasies. This sign adores variety. Nothing bores Gemini more than making love the same way all the time, or bringing on the heavy emotions. So trot out all the roles you've been longing to play. Here's the perfect partner. But remember to keep it light and fun. Gemini's turn-on zone is the hands, and this sign gives the best massages. Gadgets that can be activated with a touch amuse Gemini. This sign is great at doing two things at once, like making love while watching an erotic film. Turn the cell phone off unless you want company. On the other hand, Gemini is your sign for superhot phone sex.

Gemini loves a change of scene. So experiment on the floor, in the shower, or on the kitchen table. Borrow a friend's apartment or rent a room in a hotel for variety.

Cancer: In the Mood

The key to Cancer is to get this moon child in the mood. Consult the moon—a full moon is best. Wining, dining, old-fashioned courtship, and breakfast in bed are turn-ons. Whatever makes your Cancer feel secure will promote shedding inhibitions in the sack. (Don't try any of your Aries daredevil techniques here!) Cancer prefers familiar, comfortable, homey surroundings. Cancer's turn-on zone is the breasts. Cancer women often have naturally inflated chests. Cancer men may fantasize about a well-endowed playmate. If your breasts are enhanced, show them off. Cancer will want to know all your deepest secrets, so invent a few good ones. But lots of luck delving into their innermost thoughts!

A sure thing: Take your Cancer near water. The sight and sound of the sea can be their aphrodisiac. A moonlit beach, a deserted swimming pool, a Jacuzzi, and a bubble bath are good seduction spots. Listen to the rain patter on the roof in a mountain cabin.

Leo: The Royal Treatment

Leo must be the best and hear it from you often. In return, they'll perform for you, telling you just what you want to hear (true or not). They like a lover with style and endurance, to be swept off their feet and into bed. Leos like to go first-class all the way, so build them up with lots of attention, wining and dining, special gifts.

Never mention other lovers or make them feel like second best. A sure signal for Leo to look elsewhere is a competitive spouse. Leos take great pride in their body, so you should pour on the admiration. A few well-placed mirrors could inspire them. So would a striptease of beautiful lingerie, expensive fragrance on the sheets, and, if female, an occasional luxury hotel room, with champagne and caviar delivered by room service. Leo's erogenous zone is the lower back, so a massage with expensive oils would make your lion purr with pleasure.

Virgo: Pedestal Perfect

Virgo's standards are so sky-high that you may feel intimidated at first. The key to pleasing fussy Virgo lovers is to look for the hot fantasy beneath their cool surface. Secret tip: They're really looking for someone to make over. So let Virgo play teacher and you play willing student; the doctor-patient routine works as well.

Let Virgo help you improve your life, quit smoking, learn French, or diet. Read an erotic book together, then practice the techniques. Or study the esoteric, erotic exercises from Asia.

The Virgo erogenous zone is the tummy area, which should be your base of operations. Virgo likes things pristine and clean. Fall into crisp, immaculate white sheets. Wear a sheer white nightie. Smell shower-fresh with no heavy perfume. Be sure your surroundings pass the hospital test. A shower together afterward (with great-smelling soap) could get the ball rolling again.

Libra: The Beauty Lover

Libra must be turned on aesthetically. Make sure you look as beautiful as possible and wear something stylishly seductive but never vulgar. Have a mental affair first, as you flirt and flatter this sign. Then proceed to the physical. Approach Libra like a dance partner, ready to waltz or tango.

Libra must be in the mood for love; otherwise, forget it. Any kind of ugliness is a turnoff. Provide the right atmosphere, elegant and harmonious. No loud noise, clashing colors, or uncomfortable beds. Libra is not an especially spontaneous lover, so it is best to spend time warming them up. Libra's back is his erogenous zone, your cue to provide back rubs with scented potions. Once in bed, you can be a bit aggressive sexually. Libra loves strong, decisive moves. Set the scene, know what you want, and let Libra be happy to provide it.

Scorpio: The Legendary Lover

Scorpio is legendary in bed, often called the sex sign of the zodiac. But seducing them is often a power game. Scorpio likes to be in control, even the quiet, unassuming ones. Scorpio loves a mystery, so don't tell all. Keep them guessing about you, offering tantalizing hints along the way. The hint of danger often turns Scorpio on, so you'll find members of this sign experimenting with the exotic and highly erotic forms of sex. Sadomasochism and bondage, anything that tests the limits of power could be a turn-on for Scorpio.

Invest in some sexy black leather and some powerful music (depending on your tastes). Clothes that lace, buckle, or zip tempt Scorpio to untie you. Present yourself as a mysterious package just waiting to be unwrapped.

Once in bed, there are no holds barred with Scorpio. They'll find your most pleasurable pressure points and touch you as you've never been touched before. They are quickly aroused (the genital area belongs to this sign) and willing to try anything. But they can be possessive. Don't expect your Scorpio to share you with anyone. It's all or nothing for them.

Sagittarius: The Sexual Athletes

Sagittarius men are the Don Juans of the zodiac, love-'em-and-leave-'em types who are difficult to pin down. Your seduction strategy is to join them in their many pursuits, then hook them with love on the road. Sagittarius enjoys sex in venues that suggest movement: planes, SUVs, or boats. But a favorite turn-on place is outdoors, in nature. A deserted hiking path, a field of tall grass, a remote woodland glade all give the Centaur sexy ideas. Athletic Sagittarius might go for some personal training in an empty gym. Join your Sagittarius for amorous aerobics, meditate together, or explore the tantric forms of sex. Lovemaking after hiking and skiing would be healthy fun.

Sagittarius enjoys lovers from exotic ethnic backgrounds or lovers met in spiritual pursuits or on college campuses. Sagittarius are great cheerleaders and motivators, and will enjoy feeling that they have inspired you to be all that you can be.

There may be a canine or feline companion sharing your Sagittarius lover's bed with you, so check your allergies. And bring Fido or Felix a toy to keep him occupied.

Capricorn: Animal Instincts

The great news about Capricorn lovers is that they improve with age. They are probably the sexiest seniors. So stick around, if you have a young one. They're lusty in bed (it's not the sign of the Goat for nothing), and can be quite raunchy and turned on by X-rated words and deeds. If this is not your thing, let them know. The Capricorn erogenous zone is the knees. Some discreet fondling in public places could be your opener. Capricorn tends to think of sex as part of a game plan for the future. They are well-organized, and might regard lovemaking as relaxation after a long day's work. This sign often combines business with pleasure. So look for a Capricorn where there's a convention, trade show, or work-related conference.

Getting Capricorn's mind off his agenda and onto yours could take some doing. Separate him from his buddies by whispering sexy secrets in his ear. Then convince him you're an asset to his image and a boon to his health. Though he may seem uptight at first, you'll soon discover he's a love animal who makes a wonderful and permanent pet.

Aquarius: Far-Out Lover

This sign really does not want an all-consuming passion or an all-or-nothing relationship. Aquarius need space. But once they feel free to experiment with a spontaneous and exciting partner, Aquarius can give you a far-out sexual adventure.

Passion begins in the mind, so a good mental buildup is key. Aquarius is an inventive sign who believes love is a playground without rules. Plan surprise, unpredictable encounters in unusual places. Find ways to make love transcendental, an extraordinary and unique experience. Be ready to try anything Aquarius suggests, if only once. Calves and ankles are the special Aquarius erogenous zones, so perfect your legwork.

Be careful not to be too possessive. Your Aquarius needs lots of space, tolerance for friends (including old lovers), and their many outside interests.

Pisces: Fantasy Time

Pisces is the sign of fantasy and imagination. This sign has great theatrical talent. Pisces looks for lovers who will take care of them. Pisces will return the favor! Here is someone who can psych out your deepest desires without mentioning them. Pisces falls for sob stories and is always ready to empathize. It wouldn't hurt to have a small problem for Pisces to help you overcome. It might help if you cry on his shoulder, for this sign needs to be needed. Use your imagination when setting the scene for love. A dramatic setting brings out Pisces theatrical talents. Or creatively use the element of water. Rain on the roof, waterfalls, showers, beach houses, waterbeds, and Jacuzzis could turn up the heat. Experiment with pulsating jets of water. Skinny-dip at midnight in deserted pools.

The Pisces erogenous zone is the feet. This is your cue to give a sensuous foot massage using scented lotions. Let him paint your toes. Beautiful toenails in sexy sandals are a special turn-on.

Your Hot Planets: Mars and Venus Tango Together

Here's a tip for finding your hottest love match. If your lover's Mars sign makes favorable aspects to your Venus, is in the same element (earth, air, fire, water), or is in the same sign, your lover will do what you want done! Mars influences how we act when we make love, while Venus shows what we like done to us. Sometimes fighting and making up is the sexiest fun of all. If you're the type who needs a spark to keep lust alive (you know who you are!), then look for Mars and Venus in different signs of the same quality (fixed or cardinal or mutable). For instance, a fixed sign (Taurus, Leo, Scorpio, Aquarius) paired with another fixed sign can have a sexy standoff, a hot tug of war before you finally surrender. Two cardinal signs (Aries, Cancer, Libra, Capricorn) set off passionate fireworks when they clash. Mutable signs (Gemini, Virgo, Sagittarius, Pisces) play a fascinating game of cat and mouse, never quite catching each other.

The Best Time for Love

The best time for love is when Venus is in your sign, making you the most desirable sign in the zodiac. This only lasts about three weeks (unless Venus is retrograde), so don't waste time! And find out the time this year when Venus is in your sign by consulting the Venus chart at the end of chapter 6.

Who's the Sexiest Sign of the Zodiac?

It depends on what sign you are. Astrology has traditionally given this honor to Scorpio, the sign associated with the sex organs. However, we are all a combination of different signs (and turn-ons). Gemini's communicating ability and manual dexterity could deliver the magic touch. Cancer's tenderness and understanding could bring out your passion more than regal Leo.

Who'll Be Faithful?

The earth signs of Capricorn, Taurus, and Virgo are usually the most faithful. They tend to be more home-oriented and family-oriented, and they are usually choosy about their mates. It's impractical, inconvenient, and probably expensive to play around, so they think.

Who's Most Likely to Cheat?

The mutable signs of Gemini, Pisces, and Sagittarius win the playboy or playgirl sweepstakes. These signs tend to be changeable, fickle, and easily bored. But they're so much fun!

CHAPTER 14

Signs of Success: Wealth-Building Advice from the Stars

Are you a serial spender or a savvy saver? Here's where to find out your sign's bottom line when it comes to managing money. Though no sign wins the financial sweepstakes—all have their share of billionaires and paupers—the signs of success are those who make the most of their particular financial talents. This year's financial winners are the earth signs (Taurus, Virgo, and especially Capricorn), who should profit from the lucky rays of Jupiter in Capricorn. Yet all of us could benefit from some of Capricorn's self-discipline when it comes to spending wisely and budgeting carefully.

Aries

You've got a taste for fast money, quick turnover, and edgy investments, with no patience for gradual long-term gains. You're an impulse buyer with the nerve for risky tactics that could backfire. On the other hand, you're a pioneer who can see into the future, who dares to take a gamble on a new idea or product that could change the world . . . like Sam Walton of the Wal-mart stores who changed the way we shop. You need a backup plan in case one of your big ideas burns out. To protect your money, get a backup plan you can follow without thinking about it. Have an automatic percentage of your income put into a savings or retirement plan. Then give yourself some extra funds to play with. Your weak point is your impatience; you're not one to wait out a slow market or watch savings slowly accumulate.

Taurus

You're a saver who loves to see your cash accumulate, as well as your possessions. You have no qualms about steadily increasing your fortune. You're a savvy trader and a shrewd investor, in there for long-term gains. You have low toleration for risk, hate to lose anything. But you do enjoy luxuries, may need to reward yourself frequently. You might pass up an opportunity because it seems too risky. Take a chance once in a while. You're especially lucky in real estate.

Gemini

With Gemini, the cash can flow in and then out just as quickly. You naturally multitask and are sure to have several projects going at once, as well as several credit cards, which can easily get out of hand. Saving is not one of your strong points . . . too boring. You fall in and out of love with different ideas, have probably tried a round of savings techniques. Diversification is your best strategy. Have several different kinds of investments—at least one should be a long-term plan. Set savings goals and then regularly deposit small amounts into your accounts.

Cancer

You can be a natural moneymaker with your peerless intuition. You can spot a winner that everyone else misses. Consider Cancer success stories like those of cosmetics queen Estée Lauder and Roxanne Quimby, of Burt's Bees, who turned her friend's stash of beeswax into a thriving cosmetics business. Who knew? So trust your intuition. You are a saver who always has a backup plan just in case. Remember to treat and nurture yourself as well as others. Investments in the food industry, restaurants, hotels, shipping, and water-related industries are Cancer territory.

Leo

You love the first-class lifestyle, but may not always have the resources to support it. Finding a way to fund your extravagant tastes is the Leo challenge. Some courses in money management or an expert financial coach could set you on the right track. However, you're also a terrific salesperson, fabulous in high-profile jobs that pay a lot. You're the community tastemaker. Satisfy your appetite for "the best" by working for a quality company that sells luxury goods, splendid real estate, dream vacations, first-class travel—that way you'll have access to the lifestyle without having to pay for it.

Virgo

Your sign is a stickler for details and that includes your money management. You like to follow your spending and saving closely and enjoy planning and budgeting and price comparison. Your sign usually has no problem sticking to a savings or investment plan. You have a critical eye for quality and like to bargain—shop to get the best value. In fact, Virgo billionaire Warren Buffet is known for value investing. You buy cheap and sell at a profit. Investing in health care and organic products and food could be profitable for you.

Libra

Oh, do you ever love to shop! And you often have an irresistible urge to acquire an exquisite object, like a designer dress you can't really afford, or splurge on the perfect antique armoire once you've found it. You don't like to settle for second-rate or bargain buys. Learning to prioritize your spending is especially difficult for your sign, so try to find a good money manager to do it for you. Following a strictly balanced budget is your key to financial success. With Libra's keen eye for quality and good taste, you are a savvy picker at auctions and antiques fairs, so you might be able to turn around your purchase for a profit.

Scorpio

Scorpios prefer to stay in control of their finances at all times. You're sure to have a financial-tracking program on your computer. You're not an impulse buyer, unless you see something that immediately turns you on. Rely on your instincts! Scorpio is the sign of credit cards, taxes, and loans, so you are able to use these tools cleverly. Investing for Scorpio is rarely casual. You'll do extensive research and track your investments—reading the financial pages, annual reports, and profit-and-loss statements.

Sagittarius

Sagittarius is a natural gambler, with a high tolerance for risk. It's important for you to learn when to hold 'em, and when to fold 'em, as the song goes, by setting limits on your risk taking and covering your assets. You enjoy the thrill of playing the stock market, where you could win big and lose big. Money itself is rarely the object for Sagittarius—it's the game that counts. Since your sign rarely saves for a rainy day, your best strategy might be an automatic-savings plan that deducts a certain amount without your knowing it. Regular bill-paying plans are another strategy to keep you on track. You could benefit from an inspirational money manager who gets you fired up about an investment plan.

Capricorn

You're one of the strongest money managers in the zodiac, which should serve you well this year when Jupiter, the planet of luck and expansion, is blessing Capricorn. You're a born bargain hunter and clever negotiator, a saver rather than a spender. You are the sign of self-discipline, which works well when it comes to sticking with a budget and living frugally while waiting for resources to accumulate. You are likely to plan carefully for your elder years, profiting from long-term investments. You have a keen sense of value and will pick up a bargain, then turn it around at a nice profit.

Aquarius

The Aquarius trait of unpredictability extends to your financial life, where you surprise us all with your ability to turn something totally unique into a money spinner. Consider your wealthy sign mates Oprah Winfrey and Paris Hilton, who are able to intuit what the public will buy at a given moment. Some of your ideas might sound far-out, but turn out to be right on the money. Investing in high-tech companies that are on the cutting edge of their field is good for Aquarius. You'll probably intuit which ones will stay the course. You'll feel good about investing in companies that improve the environment, such as new types of fuel, or ones that are related to your favorite cause.

Pisces

The typical Pisces is probably the sign least interested in money management. However, there are many billionaires born under your sign, such as Michael Dell, David Geffen, and Steve Jobs. Generally they have made money from innovative ideas and left the details to others. That might work for you. Find a Scorpio, Capricorn, or Virgo to help you set a profitable course and systematically save (which is not in your nature). Sign up for automatic bill paying, so you won't have to think about it. If you keep in mind how much less stressful life will be and how much more you can do when you're not worried about paying bills, you might be motivated enough to stick to a sensible budget. Investmentwise, consider anything to do with water—offshore drilling, water conservation and purifying, shipping, and seafood. Petroleum is also ruled by your sign, as are institutions related to hospitals.

CHAPTER 15

Keep Father Time in His Place: Antiaging Tips

In 2008, both Jupiter and Pluto enter the sign of Capricorn, the Saturn-ruled sign associated with Father Time and the elder years. This is especially meaningful for the baby boomer generation, the millions of Americans born between 1946 and 1964. For the post–World War II generation, who are looking forward to a long and vital life span, age sixty is the beginning of middle age, not old age. This active generation will be reinventing our concept of how to spend the senior years, as they play a much more vocal and demanding role in society.

It will not be unusual to live to be over one hundred, say the experts, but baby boomers will be concerned with how well they live, not just how long. Innovative medical technologies in areas such as joint replacement and management of cardiovascular disease assure this generation of more pep and productivity, while drugs like Viagra boost their sex lives. Americans will be well able to skip retirement and continue in the workforce or choose to start a second, more rewarding career.

Astrology has many ideas for keeping baby boomers healthy and happy. Each sign is associated with a part of the body that could become vulnerable in later years. Within the personality of a sign are other clues for having a productive old age.

Aries

The Aries baby boomer is one who plans on staying forever young. You'll stay up-to-date and may identify with the younger generation rather than your peers. If something is wrong physically, you'll fix it quickly with the latest medical technology. It's important, Aries, that you learn to pace yourself and be realistic about what you can do. (You are the sign that goes snowboarding at age sixty.) Be sure to take physical precautions to safeguard yourself when doing sports. Guard your head area with the right gear and rein in your impulsiveness when in crowded or traffic situations. More patience could be the greatest gift of your elder years.

Taurus

As the zodiac's gourmet, Taurus needs to watch your diet and craving for sweets as you grow older, since you're more likely to overindulge and gain weight. Exercise is not your favorite activity, so trick yourself by combining a workout with a walk in a beautiful nature preserve or bike path. Since you are a great shopper, you could combine bargain hunting with a power walk in your local mall. Gardening and playing with a lively pet are pleasant ways to get moving or get a fun workout playing with young grandchildren. Combining movement with your everyday activities is the key for sedentary Taurus.

Gemini

Yours is one of the active signs that rarely has a serious weight problem. Your lungs may be vulnerable, however, so do everything you can to stop smoking, get regular flu shots, and improve the air quality in your home. Gemini thrives on social contact and mental stimulation and should remain active in the community. Expand your social network as much as possible to include young people with innovative ideas. Take courses at your local college and challenge yourself by learning new skills. It is important for Gemini to protect your nerve pathways, so be sure your chairs are ergonomic and watch for carpal tunnel syndrome if you use a computer.

Cancer

Cancer is family-oriented in the elder years and thrives on close contact with loving relatives. It is even better if your home is near water, where you can exercise with long walks on the beach and swimming. If not, join a local water-aerobics class at your local pool. Cancer can be moody, so combat any tendency to get depressed by doing creative projects and spending time with loved ones. A positive attitude is one of your best antiaging techniques.

Leo

Leo's vulnerable area is the heart, which you should check frequently as you grow older, even if you appear to be the picture of health, like Leos Arnold Schwarzenegger and Bill Clinton, who have had cardiac surgery. Adopting a heart-healthy diet will help stave off problems. Sun-ruled Leos should take preventive measures to avoid skin cancer by using a high SPF sunscreen, especially if you live in a Southern climate. Leos thrive on the attention they get from performing, so why not share skills by lecturing or teaching a local class. Share that hard-won wisdom!

Virgo

As one of the most health-conscious signs, Virgo usually sticks to a sensible diet and gets regular checkups. Staying mentally active can ward off age-related depression, so investigate your local community college, take education-oriented trips, and expand your social circle with new friends. Virgo thrives when being of service to the community and should seek opportunities to do volunteer work. Teaching or coaching young people can be especially rewarding to your sign.

Libra

Libra's key to youth is to keep the social, family, mental, and physical areas of your life in balance. Strengthen your body with balancing exercises like tai chi and yoga or artistic and social exercises like dancing. Exercises done in a sociable group are more to Libra's liking. Your back and kidneys are vulnerable areas to keep in good condition. In later years, Libra has the time to become more involved in intellectual pursuits and arts and crafts. Libra enjoys entertaining and throwing parties for friends and family. Cultivating relationships with like-minded friends by joining a club or group with a common cause is a good idea.

Scorpio

You're the sexy senior! The sign of Scorpio is associated with the sex organs and known for having an active sex life in the senior years. Your partner may well need Viagra! Scorpio is often likened to a phoenix rising from the ashes for your ability to survive illness and regain health. However, you should pay special attention to the elimination and sexual functions of the body with regular examinations and colonoscopies. Water sports and vacations near the sea are excellent therapy for stressed-out Scorpios. Getting involved in something you care passionately about keeps Scorpio young at heart.

Sagittarius

You're no stay-at-home senior! You'll enjoy the independence you have, which gives you the chance to pursue your many interests, including travel to places you've always wanted to explore and having fun times with pals. Active Sagittarius is one of the most athletic signs and may continue to play your favorite sports in senior years, right alongside your grandchildren. Now's your time to motivate the younger generation, so find ways to pass on your hard-won wisdom via teaching or writing, perhaps continuing your career on a part-time basis. Many Sagittarius will get involved in promoting an idealistic or political cause.

Capricorn

The Capricorn senior likes to stay actively involved in community life. Yours is a disciplined, organized sign that may not retire from business or may continue your career on a part-time basis. Some may pursue an entirely different career, with great success. You could well represent the seniors in your community on boards and committees. It is important for Capricorn to continue doing productive work, even if it is on a volunteer basis. Physically Capricorn is one of the longer-lived signs. It is associated with bones and knees, so protect these areas and watch a tendency toward arthritis and osteoporosis.

Aquarius

Aquarius is on the cutting edge and usually on top of the latest trends, even later in life. You won't let advanced years hold you back! You're likely to play computer games with grandchildren and even have your own Web site. You remain young if you stay involved in a cause and pursue your multiple interests. You'll share your wisdom by teaching a class, lecturing, or writing. Physically, protect yourself against airborne allergies, and exercise to prevent circulation problems. Group activities appeal to Aquarius, especially if you are promoting a cause.

Pisces

Elder Pisces is happiest when pursuing creative activities, such as filmmaking, painting, writing, or a hobby or craft in which you can express your imagination. Places near water are particularly healthful for Pisces. Water sports, especially swimming, can maintain your health. Avoid addictive substances and stick to a balanced diet of organic foods, including plenty of fish. Lymphatic drainage massage is good therapy for Pisces, which is associated with the lymphatic system. Pay special attention to the condition of your feet, and wear the appropriate shoes for each activity.

CHAPTER 16

The Mystic Properties of Your Birthstone

Who hasn't at one time or another received a special piece of jewelry with a birthstone? We enjoy the idea that wearing a special gem resonates with our personality and might even bring us luck. However, there is quite a bit of confusion over which stone is best for each sign, because we are often given birthstones according to the month of our birthday rather than our zodiac sign. You may be wondering if the amethyst is more suitable for a February-born Pisces than the aquamarine, or you might prefer the gems associated with your moon sign, which resonate with your emotional nature, or your Venus sign, which appeal to your sense of fashion and good taste.

There are many ways to approach the subject of birthstones. Lovers of precious gems could choose one that reflects the element of your sun sign. Earth signs (Taurus, Virgo, Capricorn) resonate to the bright green emerald. Fire signs (Aries, Leo, Sagittarius) belong to the flaming ruby. Water signs (Cancer, Scorpio, Pisces) might prefer the deep blue sapphire. And air signs (Gemini, Libra, Aquarius) may gravitate to the clear, brilliant diamond.

If you don't care for your birthstone, you could choose a talisman by color. Choose a stone that is associated with your sun, moon, or Venus sign. An Aries with moon in Cancer might prefer a pale lunar jewel like the pearl or moonstone. A Pisces with Venus in Aries might love to wear bright red stones like ruby or spinel.

In ancient India, Egypt, and Babylonia, rare and beautiful gemstones were thought to have magical properties. People are said to have consulted astrologers for advice on wearing the appropriate gem for each occasion. Ancient Egyptians carried scarabs and tiny figures of their gods for protection and luck. These were carved in semi-precious stones like lapis lazuli, carnelian, and turquoise. In India, one of the most powerful talismans was an amulet designed with precious stones representing the known planets at the time. Another astrological connection was the wearing of gems associated with a planet on that planet's special day. Mars-ruled rubies would be worn on the Mars day, Tuesday, for instance. It is still possible to find special astrological talismans created by astrologer-jewelers, who will make up a special pendant or necklace displaying your horoscope's special stones in a beautiful design.

In the Judeo-Christian tradition, the astrological association with gemstones dates from the sacred twelve-gem breastplate of Aaron, recorded in Exodus. Each gem symbolized one of the twelve tribes of Israel. Later these gems became connected with the twelve signs of the zodiac. However, it was not until the eighteenth century that people began to wear their special birthstones. For more information on the history and mystery of gemstones, including their astrological use, read *The Curious Lore of Precious Stones* by George Frederick Kunz.

Here are some suggestions for choosing stones associated with a given zodiac sign. Bear in mind that there are no hard-and-fast rules; you might find yourself attracted to a certain gem without fully understanding why. That might well be the gem you are supposed to wear, regardless of your sign.

Aries

Though most sources give the birthstone for April as the diamond, Aries may feel more affinity for Mars-ruled stones with red hues, such as ruby, spinels, fire opals, garnets, coral, and carnelian.

Taurus

Emeralds are most associated with Taurus. However, Taurus might gravitate toward some of the earthy agates and green stones such as tourmaline, jade, serpentine (which is believed to draw good fortune), and green quartz.

Gemini

Pearls and agates are associated with Gemini, but you might prefer fascinating gems like alexandrite or tanzanite, which change color according to the angle of light. Or watermelon tourmaline, which has dual colorations. Interesting rutilated quartzes with fine hairlike inclusions are associated with communication and might be perfect for your sign.

Cancer

July has often been linked with the ruby; however, that fiery stone might be better suited to Leos born in late July. Cancer seems to resonate more with the elegant blue sapphire, moonstone, chalcedony, and the deep blue flashes of laboradorite and rainbow moonstone.

Leo

The yellow-green peridot and all golden stones belong to sun-ruled Leos. You may also love the ruby, yellow diamonds, amber, and citrine. Go for the golden tones!

Virgo

Sapphires, which come in many colors, carnelian, onyx, and pink jasper are associated with Virgo. You may also respond to the earthy agates and the green tones of emerald and jade.

Libra

Opal, which was once considered exclusive to Libra, comes in many variations. In fact, the opal was deemed unlucky for any other sign. This beautiful stone comes in many color variations, from the deeper Australian opals to the pale Russian opals. You might try the blue-and-pink Peruvian opal or the mysterious, earthy boulder opal. Libra is also associated with the color pink, as in rose quartz, pink sapphires, pink diamonds, and kunzite. Apple green chrysoprase is another beautiful choice.

Scorpio

This mysterious sign was given the topaz, which comes in blue or golden variations. You might also respond to the deep tones of smoky quartz, tiger's eye, black onyx, rainbow obsidian, black diamonds, or black South Sea pearls.

Sagittarius

Visionary Sagittarius responds to turquoise, the mystical stone of Native Americans and Tibetans. No medicine man's outfit was complete without a turquoise. It was treasured by the Persians, who believed that turquoise could protect from evil and bring good fortune. Also consider lapis lazuli, blue topaz, and ruby.

Capricorn

The burgundy red garnet is the usual stone for Capricorn, but garnets are now available in many other colors, such as the green tsavorite garnet. Also consider the beautifully marked green malachite. Onyx in all its color variations is compatible with Capricorn.

Aquarius

Aquarius is associated with the purple amethyst, a type of quartz that was once thought to prevent drunkenness. This sign might respond to some of the newer stones on the market, such as laboradorite, a gray stone that flashes electric blue, or to some of the other purple stones, such as sugilite, tanzanite, or purple jade. The colorful quartzes, which are able to conduct electricity, could be your gem. Diamonds of all kinds also resonate with Aquarius, according to the glamorous Aquarius Gabor sisters and Carol Channing, who sang "Diamonds Are a Girl's Best Friend."

Pisces

The blue-green aquamarine and the earthy bloodstone are usually associated with Pisces. During the sixteenth century, bloodstone was believed to cure hemorrhages caused by the plague. Jasper is also a Pisces stone, now available in many beautiful colors such as "picture jasper" and "poppy jasper," which look like miniature paintings. Pisces also responds to jewels from the sea: pearls and coral and ocean blue sapphires. Elizabeth Taylor, a great Pisces jewel collector, owns the famous Peregrina pearl as well as many deep blue sapphires.

CHAPTER 17

Give the Perfect Gift to Every Sign

So often we're in a quandary about what to give a loved one, someone who has everything, that hard-to-please friend, or a fascinating new person in your life, or about the right present for a wedding, birthday, or hostess gift. Why not let astrology help you make the perfect choice by appealing to each sun sign's personality. When you're giving a gift, you're also making a memory, so it should be a special occasion. The gift that's most appreciated is one that touches the heart, reminds you both of a shared experience, or shows that the giver has really cared enough to consider the recipient's personality.

In general, the water signs (Cancer, Pisces, Scorpio) enjoy romantic, sentimental, and imaginative gifts given in a very personal way. Write your loved one a poem or a song to express your feelings. Assemble an album of photos or mementos of all the good times you've shared. Appeal to their sense of fantasy. Scorpio Richard Burton had the right idea when he gave Pisces Elizabeth Taylor a diamond bracelet hidden in lavender roses (her favorite color).

Fire signs (Aries, Leo, Sagittarius) appreciate a gift presented with lots of flair. Pull out the drama, like the actor who dazzled his Aries sweetheart by presenting her with trash cans overflowing with daisies.

Air signs (Gemini, Libra, Aquarius) love to be surprised with unusual gifts. The Duke of Windsor gave his elegant Gemini duchess, Wallis Windsor, fabulous jewels engraved with love notes and secret messages in their own special code.

Earth signs (Taurus, Virgo, Capricorn) value solid, tangible gifts or ones that appeal to all the senses. Delicious gourmet treats, scented body lotions, the newest CDs, the gift of a massage, or stocks and bonds are sure winners! Capricorn Elvis Presley once received a gold-plated piano from his wife.

Here are some specific ideas for each sign:

Aries

These are the trendsetters of the zodiac, who appreciate the latest thing! For Aries, it's the excitement that counts, so present your gift in a way that will knock their socks off. Aries is associated with the head, so a jaunty hat, hair ornaments, chandelier earrings, sunglasses, and hair-taming devices are good possibilities. Aries love games of any kind that offer a real challenge, like war video games, military themes, or rousing music with a beat. Anything red is a good bet: red flowers, red gems, and red accessories. How about giving Aries a way to let off steam with a gym membership or aerobic-dancing classes? Monogram a robe with a nickname in red.

Taurus

These are touchy-feely people who love things that appeal to all their senses. Find something that sounds, tastes, smells, feels, or looks good. And don't stint on quality or comfort. Taurus know the value of everything and will be aware of the price tag. Taurus foodies will appreciate chef-worthy kitchen gadgets, the latest cookbook, and gourmet treats. Taurus is a great collector. Find out what their passion is and present them with a rare item or a beautiful storage container such as an antique jewelry box. Green-thumb Taurus would love some special plants or flowers, garden tools, beautiful plant containers. Appeal to their sense of touch with fine fabrics—high-thread-count sheets, cashmere, satin, and mohair. One of the animal-loving signs, Taurus might appreciate a retractable leash or soft bed for the dog or cat. Get them a fine wallet or checkbook cover. They'll use it often.

Gemini

Mercury-ruled Gemini appreciates gifts that appeal to their mind. The latest book or novel, a talked-about film, a CD from a hot new singer, or a high-tech gadget might appeal. A beautiful diary or a tape recorder would record their adventures. Since Geminis often do two things at once, a telephone gadget that leaves their hands free would be appreciated. In fact, a new telephone device or superphone would appeal to these great communicators. Gloves, rings, and bracelets accent their expressive hands. Clothes from an interesting new designer appeal to their sense of style. You might try giving Gemini a variety of little gifts in a beautiful box or a Christmas stocking. A tranquil massage at a local spa would calm Gemini's sensitive nerves. Find an interesting way to wrap your gift. Nothing boring, please!

Cancer

Cancer is associated with home and family, so anything to do with food, entertaining at home, and family life is a good bet. Beautiful dishes or serving platters, silver items, fine crystal and linen, gourmet cookware, cooking classes or the latest DVD from a cooking teacher might be appreciated. Cancer designers Vera Wang and Giorgio Armani have perfected the Cancer style and have many home products available, as well as their elegant designer clothing. Naturally, anything to do with the sea is a possibility: pearls, coral, or shell jewelry. Boat and water-sports equipment might work. Consider cruise wear for traveling Cancers. Sentimental Cancer loves antiques and silver frames for family photos. Cancer people are often good photographers, so consider frames, albums, and projectors to showcase their work. Present your gift in a personal way with a special note.

Leo

Think big with Leo and appeal to this sign's sense of drama. Go for the gold (Leo's color) with gold jewelry, designer clothing, or big attention-getting accessories. Follow their signature style, which could be superelegant, like Jacqueline Onassis, or superstar, like Madonna or Jennifer Lopez. This sign is always ready for the red carpet and stays beautifully groomed, so stay within these guidelines when choosing your gift. Feline motifs and animal prints are usually a hit. The latest grooming aids, high-ticket cosmetics, and mirrors reflect their best image. Beautiful hairbrushes tame their manes. Think champagne, high-thread-count linens, and luxurious loungewear or lingerie. Make Leo feel special with a custom portrait or photo shoot with your local star photographer. Be sure to go for spectacular wrapping, with beautiful paper and ribbons. Present your gift with a flourish!

Virgo

Virgo usually has a special subject of interest and would appreciate relevant books, films, lectures, or classes. Choose health-oriented things: gifts to do with fitness and self-improvement. Virgo enjoys brainteasers, crossword puzzles, computer programs, organizers, and digital planners. Fluffy robes, bath products, and special soaps appeal to Virgo's sense of cleanliness. Virgo loves examples of good, practical design: efficient telephones, beautiful briefcases, computer cases, desk accessories. Choose natural fibers and quiet colors when choosing clothes for Virgo. Virgo has high standards, so go for quality when choosing a gift.

Libra

Whatever you give this romantic sign, go for beauty and romance. Libra loves accessories, decorative objects, whatever makes him or his surroundings more aesthetically pleasing. Beautiful flowers in pastel colors are always welcome. Libras are great hosts and hostesses, who might appreciate a gift related to fine dining: serving pieces, linens, glassware, flower vases. Evening or party clothes please since Libra has a gadabout social life. Interesting books, objets d'art, memberships to museums, and tickets to cultural events are good ideas. Fashion or home-decorating magazine subscriptions usually please Libra women. Steer away from anything loud, garish, or extreme. Think pink, one of their special colors, when giving Libra jewelry, clothing, or accessories. It's a very romantic sign, so be sure to remember birthdays, holidays, and anniversaries with a token of affection.

Scorpio

Scorpios love mystery, so bear that in mind when you buy these folks a present. You could take this literally and buy them a good thriller DVD, novel, or video game. Scorpios are power players, so a book about one of their sign might please. Bill Gates, Jack Welch, Condoleezza Rice, and Hillary Clinton are hot Scorpio subjects. Scorpios love black leather, suede, fur, anything to do with the sea, power tools, tiny spy tape recorders, and items with secret compartments or intricate locks. When buying a handbag for Scorpio, go for simple shapes with lots of interior pockets. Sensuous Scorpios appreciate hot lingerie, sexy linens, body lotions, and perfumed candles. Black is the favored color for Scorpio clothing—go for sexy textures like cashmere and satin in simple shapes by designers like Calvin Klein. This sign is fascinated with the occult, so give them an astrology or tarot-card reading, beautiful crystals, or an astrology program for the computer.

Sagittarius

For these outdoor people, consider adventure trips, designer sportswear, gear for their favorite sports. A funny gift or something for their pets pleases Sagittarius. For clothing and accessories, the fashionista of this sign tends to like bright colors and dramatic innovative styles. Otherwise, casual sportswear is a good idea. These travelers usually have a favorite getaway place; give them a travel guide, DVD, novel, or history book that would make their trip more interesting. Luggage is also a good bet. Sleek carry-ons, travel wallets, ticket holders, business-card cases, and wheeled computer bags might please these wanderers. Anything that makes travel more comfortable and pleasant is good for Sagittarius, including a good book to read en route. This sign is the great gambler of the zodiac, so gifts related to their favorite gambling venue would be appreciated.

Capricorn

For this quality-conscious sign, go for a status label from the best store in town. Get Capricorns something good for their image and career. They could be fond of things Spanish, like flamenco or tango music, or of country-and-western music and motifs. In the bookstore, go for biographies of the rich and famous, or advice books to help Capricorn get to the top. Capricorns take their gifts seriously, so steer away from anything too frivolous. Garnet, onyx, or malachite jewelry, Carolina Herrera fragrance and clothing, and beautiful briefcases and wallets are good ideas. Glamorous status tote bags carry business gear in style. Capricorns like golf, tennis, and sports that involve climbing, cycling, or hiking, so presents could be geared to their outdoor interests. Elegant evening accessories would be fine for this sign, which often entertains for business.

Aquarius

Give Aquarius a surprise gift. This sign is never impressed with things that are too predictable. So use your imagination to present the gift in an unusual way or at an unexpected time. With Aquarius, originality counts. When in doubt, give them something to think about, a new electronic gadget, perhaps a small robot, or an advanced computer game. Or something New Age, like an amethyst-crystal cluster. Aquarius like innovative materials with a space-age look. They are the ones with the wraparound glasses, the titanium computer cases. This air sign loves to fly—an airplane ticket always pleases. Books should be on innovative subjects, politics, or adventures of the mind. Aquarius goes for unusual color combinations—especially electric blue or hot pink—and abstract patterns. They like the newest, coolest looks on the cutting edge of fashion and are not afraid to experiment. Think of Paris Hilton's constantly changing looks. Look for an Aquarius gift in an out-of-the-way boutique or local hipster hangout. They'd be touched if you find out Aquarius's special worthy cause and make a donation. Spirit them off to hear their favorite guru.

Pisces

Pisces respond to gifts that have a touch of fantasy, magic, and romance. Look for mystical gifts with a touch of the occult. Romantic music (a customized CD of favorite love songs) and love stories appeal to Pisces sentimentalists. Pisces is associated with perfume and fragrant oils, so help this sign indulge with their favorite scent in many forms. Anything to do with the ocean, fish, and water sports appeals to Pisces. How about a whirlpool, a water-therapy spa treatment, or a sea salt rub. Appeal to this sign with treats for the feet: foot massages, pedicures, ballet tickets, and dance lessons. Cashmere socks and metallic evening sandals are other Pisces pleasers. A romantic dinner overlooking the water is Pisces paradise. A case of fine wine or another favorite liquid is always appreciated. Write a love poem and enclose it with your gift.

CHAPTER 18

The Meaning of Numbers

What exactly is a number 9 day, and how did it get to be that number? If you've been reading the dailies, you've no doubt seen such numerological references. Usually you'll find these numbers on the days when the moon is transiting from one sign to another.

If you're familiar with numerology, you probably know your life-path number, which is derived from your birth date. That number represents who you were at birth and the traits that you'll carry throughout your life. There are numerous books and Web sites that will provide you with details on what the numbers mean regarding your life path.

The numbers used in the dailies are found by adding the numbers related to the astrological sign (1 for Aries, 2 for Taurus, etc.), the year, the months, and the day. For example, June 14, 2008 for a Libra would be 7 for Libra, plus 1 (adding together the numbers in 2008), plus 6 for June, plus 7 (1+6) for the day. That would be 7+1+6+5 (sign+year+month+day)=19=1 (1+9=10 [1+0=1]).

So on that number 1 day, you might be advised that you're getting a fresh start, a new beginning. You can take the lead on something new. Stress originality and creativity. Explore and discover. You're inventive and make connections that others overlook.

Briefly, here are the meanings of the numbers, which are included in more detail in the dailies themselves.

1: taking the lead, getting a fresh start, a new beginning
2: cooperation, partnership, a new relationship, sensitivity
3: harmony, beauty, pleasures of life, warm, receptive

4: getting organized, hard work, being methodical, rebuilding, fulfilling your obligations
5: freedom of thought and action, change, variety, thinking outside the box
6: a service day, being diplomatic, generous, tolerant, sympathetic
7: mystery, secrets, investigations, research, detecting deception, exploration of the unknown, of the spiritual realms
8: your power day, financial success, unexpected money, a windfall
9: finishing a project, looking beyond the immediate, setting your goals, reflection, expansion

—Rob MacGregor

Rob MacGregor is the author of seventeen novels and ten nonfiction books, including *Psychic Power*, *Star Power for Teens*, and *Romancing the Raven*. For more information, go to www.robmacgregor.net.

CHAPTER 19

All About Aries: Your Personality, Family, Career, Relationships, and Lifestyle

Have you tapped in to your Aries power? Knowing and using your positive Aries sun-sign traits (and downplaying the negative ones) could be your key to achieving more happiness and success in all areas of your life. That's because every part of your life has a strong Aries influence, including what and whom you like, your family relationships, your strengths on the job, even the decor of your home. The more you understand the Aries in you, the better you can use your personal solar power to help you make good decisions. You can use it every day from something as basic as choosing what to wear to more important issues, such as getting along with your boss or spicing up your love life.

So get ready for your close-up! In the following chapters, you'll be empowered with tools to control your destiny and make your dreams come true by moving in harmony with your natural inclinations.

Before we begin, here's how we determine what an Aries personality is. Astrologers describe an Aries using a type of recipe. First, there's your Aries element: fire. Fire signs are passionate go-getters, full of energy and ambition. Aries functions like a cardinal sign, a doer who must be active. Then there's your sign's polarity, which adds a positive, masculine, yang dimension. Let's not forget your planetary ruler: Mars, the planet of action, drive, forward movement. Add your sign's location in the zodiac: first, placed in the house of personality and will. Finally, stir in your symbol, the aggressive Ram.

This recipe influences everything we say about Aries. For example, you could easily deduce that a fire sign ruled by Mars would be out there making things happen, rather than sitting around the house. The red shades of Mars should flatter your vibrant looks. And you might be impatient, a bit pushy, in your desire to be first. But your individual astrological personality contains a blend of many other planets, colored by the signs they occupy, plus factors such as the sign coming over the horizon at the exact moment of your birth. However, the more Aries planets in your horoscope, the more likely you'll follow your sun sign's prototype. On the other hand, if many planets are grouped together in a different sign, they will color your horoscope accordingly, sometimes making a dynamic sign like yours come on as much more mellow. So if the Aries traits mentioned here don't describe you, there might be other factors flavoring your cosmic stew. (Look up your other planets in the tables in this book to find out what they might be!)

The Aries Man: The Take-Charge Leader

The archetypal Aries man dares to dream those impossible dreams, fight against the toughest odds, take on the roughest bullies. You see life as an adventure. You thrive on challenges that would wear out most other signs. Because conflict situations bring out the best in you, you sometimes seek them. When there's a bad guy to catch, a problem to solve, a tyrant to be cut down to size, a dragon to slay, you jump on that white horse and charge forward!

The Aries man is an optimist, a risk taker, a hard-driving pioneer who expects a great deal from others but always gives equal or better himself. In business and in life, he aims high. "High expectations are the key to everything," believed one of the most successful Aries businessmen of all time—Sam Walton, the founder of Wal-Mart.

You are not known for sensitivity, patience, tact, or consideration of other people's wants and needs. Instead, you expect others to play to your script. You have little patience with the realities of life or with the demands of others that would slow you down. This attitude forces many Aries males to learn lessons of patience the hard way.

The most successful Aries recognizes the need for people who will help you see projects through to completion, who will keep you organized as you speed along, and who will smooth ruffled feelings after you've spoken your mind. Diplomacy, which sometimes wins more points than combat, is not your strong point. You are more likely to tell it like it is, then take the consequences head-on. Headstrong is one adjective that suits you, as the sign of Aries is associated with the head. And many Aries bear head scars of battle to prove it!

Professionally, few Aries are ever content behind a desk doing routine work. What is stable and secure to others is just plain boring—or worse, unbearably stifling—to you. You'll find a way to make a job interesting, striking out in new directions and following your nose for hot news in order to capitalize on the most promising friends. (Use that powerful antenna, Aries—it's one of your greatest assets!)

You love adventure and challenge so much that when there is no action, you'll create it yourself. Used positively, your powerhouse energy and vibrant personality will recharge those who are flagging and motivate everyone to be the best they can be.

In a Relationship

Often, you'll leap into a relationship without bothering to test the temperature first, and so you will sometimes get burned. Aries sometimes worships the airbrushed ideal of woman—the princess or the goddess on a pedestal—then becomes let down by a real-life woman with pimples and ongoing problems. Many Aries finally find your ideal lady after you've been burned a few times; you may settle down at fifty-plus to a mellow matrimonial life.

One of your favorite roles is that of the rescuer. You'll become a daring crusader who charges out to the battlefield to fight for the cause or the fair lady. And the smart fair lady should never make your conquest too easy! It is the long-term maintenance of a relationship that becomes a challenge. Aries men often find the role of playboy much easier than that of the devoted husband.

Though you're not the easiest to land, once committed, you're a proud and passionate lover. However, you can also be a demanding one who may find it difficult to accept an equal partnership. You insist on being head of the household and the number-one priority in your partner's life.

Your ideal lady is not easy to find. But if you do find someone who can manage to live up to your standards and never dampen your enthusiasm, you can be an exciting partner who never loses your enthusiasm, spirit of adventure, or joie de vivre. The most likely lady to qualify is one who's half playmate and half Girl Scout. She's someone who never rains on your parade, who can follow through on your impulsive decisions and mobilize for spur-of-the-moment plans, and who can have a positive, adventurous point of view. Look for a Sagittarius, Gemini, Aquarius, or Leo; these enthusiastic, upbeat, energetic signs love adventure, as you do. Sometimes, however, you'll wind up with a sign that loves to organize and take care of you, like Virgo, who will give you the challenge of measuring up to her high standards.

When it comes to family life, you become surprisingly conservative and take your position as head of the house seriously, so it is also important that your partner share your point of view on domestic matters. With similar interests, outlook, and goals, you'll be much less likely to flare up over who's the boss.

The Aries Woman: The Action Heroine

To see the Aries woman in action, rent a video of the vintage film *All About Eve*. Bette Davis, the legendary Hollywood star, embodied the courageous, fiery, confrontational spirit of Aries. Bette's memorable line, "Fasten your seat belts, it's going to be a bumpy night," describes the Aries-influenced experience, which often seems like a thrilling roller-coaster ride.

A natural leader, with drive to spare, you need a challenge or a competitor to light your fire and direct your energy. Otherwise, you can ignite with enthusiasm over a dazzling opportunity one day and be supercharged about another the next. As the immortal Bette once explained: "If it's too easy, where's the challenge?"

Once you've found your worthy cause of the moment, you are instantly able to mobilize and move forward. Under ideal conditions, while your enthusiasm runs high, you'll take the helm with military flair, working quickly and efficiently, convinced that nobody does it better. You could be right—your energy, speed, and drive are tough to beat! Follow-through is not as easy, perhaps because you get so quickly steamed up over frustrations and delays. It's more appealing to change direction and start anew than to slog along patiently in a stalled situation. Sometimes burning your bridges is the right tactic. But there are other times when lack of perseverance leaves you with much energy expended and little actually accomplished. If you find yourself repeating the same situation with slightly different variations, you'll know you've fallen into an old Aries trap.

Your sign was liberated long before the women's movement. You'll be the first to fight for respect in male-dominated territory, as assertive Aries women are famous for doing. Many Aries have pioneered in breaking sex barriers, from Gloria Steinem to Supreme Court Justice Sandra Day O'Connor. Though easily the equal of any man, you sometimes succeed in the world at the cost of close emotional relationships. (It is nearly impossible for you to play a submissive feminine role.)

If you're not the conquering heroine, you're the unsinkable optimist who sings in the rain when the odds are against you, or the pioneer woman who'll shoot 'em up with the best of the cowboys, like the roles Doris Day, Jane Powell, and Debbie Reynolds played so well in the 1950s. You're likely to see men as competitors, which is part of your enormous sex appeal. When you boldly throw down the gauntlet, challenging a man to keep up with you, it's catnip to the macho kind of guy.

Today's Aries woman finds plenty of worthy challenges, whether she heads her own company or fights sexual harassment and discrimination in the workplace. Though most Aries are ardent feminists at heart, you really prefer the company of men, perhaps because you don't care for the emotional tactics women often use. Since your way is to confront problems head-on, your energy can be deflated or worn away by those who use subtle maneuvers, emotional manipulations, or constant pressures.

In a Relationship

You must choose your partners carefully. Like the male Aries, you tend to be an impulsive idealist in love. Long, lingering courtships, where you gradually get to know each other, are not for you! But you can be thrilled by a slightly dangerous man who sweeps you off your feet—the proverbial knight on a white horse (or a red motorcycle). Though you only respect a man who's as strong-willed and courageous as you are, you'll often fall for someone who merely treats you rough or plays cool to your charms, mistaking his detached attitude for a sign of strength. Fortunately, you are able to recover from a broken heart more swiftly than most other signs. Starting over is easier for you than hanging on to a losing relationship, and your upbeat personality usually attracts new admirers quickly.

One of your greatest virtues in a relationship is your lack of emotional possessiveness. Though you can be fiery and passionate, you rarely try to live your life through your partner. You'll hold your own, never clinging or depending on him to provide for you. Usually, you're a career woman who is well able to fend for herself. You'll have a schedule filled with outside activities. Or you'll share equal responsibilities with your husband, perhaps as partners in business or professional work. Common interests are usually the bond that holds your relationship together.

If you're willing to put in the time, effort, and energy,

you can keep the flames of love burning. If you're expected to toe the line, however, you're likely to turn up the tension by pushing all the red buttons you can find. You need a husband who supports your talents and activities, and doesn't expect you to sit by the fire at night when you have a meeting to attend. When you do meet someone who enjoys your strong points and lets you run your own show, you make an energetic, youthful partner well into later life.

Aries in the Family

The Aries Parent

For an Aries, who usually has a compelling personal agenda, children change the focus of your life. They add a whole new dimension and stretch your capacity for growth and tolerance in directions you've never anticipated. Children require you to react to their needs, and so teach you valuable lessons of patience and tolerance. Children can transform a gadabout Aries into a devoted parent who passionately espouses family values. Always young at heart, you relive the spontaneity and joy of your own childhood as you keep pace with the kids, playing roughhouse games or matching wits. You'll thoroughly enjoy this injection of youth into your life.

The dependent infant and toddler stages of your children, which could restrict your freedom and test your patience, could be your greatest challenge as a parent. You'll much prefer the grade-school years when you can share your hard-won wisdom and regale kids with your battle stories. In spite of your impatience with youngsters' clinging and whining, you'll love being a hero and you'll play the role with aplomb. You are often quite skilled in handling teenagers as well, since you sympathize with rebellious adolescent feelings and can motivate teenagers toward positive goals.

The child who is quick, strong-willed, competitive, and athletic will be your pride and joy. However, you have more to learn from the challenging, slower, more sensitive children. By allowing these children to develop at their own speed, you may expand your own capacity for equanimity and tolerance.

Most Aries parents stay active outside the home, which encourages the child to develop independence and self-sufficiency. You'll set house rules (sometimes with military discipline), delegating chores to each child and expecting them to fulfill their duties—or else! Aries is a boss who commands respect and a parent whose high energy motivates children to do their personal best.

The Aries Stepparent

Creating a harmonious new family situation is a challenge to Aries, after you've set up your new home in record time. You'll confront problems head-on, leaving no time for resentment to build or for emotional manipulation to take place. Instead, you'll redirect everyone's attention to the exciting activities your new family can share. And your Aries optimism and enthusiasm can quickly dispel any initial awkwardness. However, since you are so open yourself, you may not be aware of a child's inner vulnerability or personal agenda, and you may become impatient if a warm, enthusiastic response is not soon expressed. Allow time for the relationship to develop and be especially tolerant. Then you'll find that the difficult stepchild will eventually respond to your indomitable spirit, infectious energy, and warm enthusiasm.

The Aries Grandparent

The Aries grandparent is the peppy, unsinkable oldster with at least as much energy as the younger generations. Since you usually stay in good health and remain physically fit, you won't let age slow you down one bit. You'll work as long as possible, rather than retire. Or you might start a second career, pursuing an interest you had no time for before. Your strong preference is to remain independent, living by yourself if necessary. Since you've learned many lessons in patience over the years, you'll find being with young children much easier this time around, with strong clashes of will less evident. And though you'll have strong opinions about how the children should be raised, you'll probably see the wisdom in letting others learn the hard way. (There are Aries grandparents, however, who still take over the family reins.) You'll be most effective as the enthusiastic grandparent who cheers the kids on to higher achievements. After all, the kids are chips off the old block!

CHAPTER 20

The Aries Lifestyle: How to Make Your Aries Sign Shine

Astrology's personal insights follow through to the way you dress and live. Here's how to polish your Aries image with tips tailored specifically for your sign, improve your atmosphere by using your best colors and surrounding yourself with Aries-loving sounds. Find out how to create a living environment that reflects your personality and where you'll feel totally at home. And how to make the most of your sign's special fashion flair. Even your vacations might be more fun and relaxing if you tailor them to your sun sign's natural inclinations.

The Aries Fashion Image

Aries truly has fun with fashion. You love to make a strong statement, turn heads, and be the first to pick up on a fashion trend, the one everyone else copies. Get a head start (Aries rules the head) with the sharpest hairstyle or a head-turning hat. Aries can get away with unusual headgear, and sometimes is known for a signature hat style, like Ali MacGraw's knit caps.

Aries should always keep hair shining and healthy, then make a statement with a clever cut or dramatic coloring effects, as Sarah Jessica Parker does. (At least once you should be a redhead or put some red highlights in your hair, like Marcia Cross of *Desperate Housewives* or Cynthia Nixon of *Sex and the City*). Be sure your hairstyle and makeup plays up your strong eyebrows and well-shaped forehead. It might be a good idea to have your eyebrows shaped professionally, especially if they grow together in a unibrow, which often happens with female rams.

Structured clothes often suit the Aries better than flowing styles. The tailored military look with prominent shoulders (think Joan Crawford) belongs to you, male or female. Dramatic jewelry (leave the little chain collection or demure string of pearls to someone else) is another Aries attention getter. Go for one stunning piece and keep the rest of your outfit simple.

Aries Fashion Colors

A full blast of red is the Aries trademark. Slick on the red lipstick, like Aries Paloma Picasso, who made it her trademark. Try red shoes or a red pocket scarf with conservative outfits. All shades of red, from fire engine red through burgundy, are yours to play with. So always wear a bit of red somewhere (even if it doesn't show). Don't be red shy in your wardrobe. Own at least one knockout stunner in scarlet, like a military coat, a clingy sheath dress, or a dramatic cape. (No one will mistake you for Little Red Riding Hood!)

Your Aries Fashion Role Models

Aries celebrities Sarah Jessica Parker of *Sex and the City*, singer Mariah Carey, Kate Hudson, Ashley Judd, and Reese Witherspoon have become fashion icons. Like their Aries forebears, Joan Crawford, Doris Day, and Ali MacGraw, they seem to sense the mood of the moment and make it their own.

Aries fashion designers are sure to have your sign's special flair. Liz Claiborne is a top-notch Aries fashion designer who does the sportswear look you love. Marc Jacobs is a favorite with A-list Aries celebrities and regular folks as well. Paloma Picasso's fragrance, jewelry, red lipstick, and accessories have your kind of drama.

Aries at Home

Your home is the ideal place to express your Aries personality. If your rooms don't suit you, you probably don't feel as comfortable as you should in your environment, which could adversely affect your health and well-being. Put some Aries spice in your rooms. Make them colorful, lively places that reflect your dynamic personality.

Your cardinal Aries fire sign is a cue to bring warmth and excitement into your environment. A big stone fireplace, potbellied stove, or outdoor hearth would comfort you. Or use candles to evoke your fire element. Show off your spirit of adventure with clever displays of your hobbies, crafts, trophies, and awards. Why not devote a wall to photos of your exploits and conquests? Aries heroes and heroines should show off their military memorabilia, sports trophies, antique weapons, and model planes or cars.

You need brightness—not dark caves for you! The atmosphere should be upbeat and exciting rather than bland and neutral. Vibrant upholstery, futuristic furniture, exotic pieces from your travels express your Aries nature. Experiment with shades of red and trendy high-tech Italian furniture. Add splashes of red velvet upholstery, red satin sheets, and Chinese red enameled furniture.

The Aries man should be catered to in his environment, with a masculine domain to call your own. You may be a collector of machinery, power tools, kitchen tools, or cars—one is sure to be a shade of red. (At some point in your life, indulge in a bright red sports car!) Your lair might be a well-stocked garage, a basement workroom, or a command control center with a high-tech computer environment.

Your Aries Background Music

You like it loud and dramatic, with a definite beat, whether it's rock, soul, conga drums, or the marching tunes of John Philip Sousa. You take your music with you personalized on your iPod. Your Aries song stylists are the divas of the music business who specialize in passionate vocalizing: Elton John, Celine Dion, Mariah Carey, Reba McIntire, Aretha Franklin, and Diana Ross. Salsa and flamenco guitar music also get you moving. You may have to soundproof your music room or put up with complaints from neighbors. Get a good pair of earphones so you can enjoy the full blast of sound without disturbing others. In classical music, you'll go for the drama of grand opera or sweeping symphonies with spectacular sound effects.

Aries Travel Guide

Sometimes you just have to get away from it all, though what unwinds an Aries would exhaust many other signs. You're likely to take off on the spur of the moment—a good case for getting a travel agent to smooth the roadblocks.

Your best kind of vacation provides not only a change in scenery but also an exciting challenge. You don't mind a bit of discomfort, so you might prefer sleeping under the stars to a posh hotel. Since you're not one for lounging around the beach or pool, if you do go to a beach resort, be sure it offers plenty of high-action options like parasailing, waterskiing, or scuba diving, and samba dancing at night.

You take a childlike joy in natural wonders, breathtaking waterfalls, hiking trails along steep cliffs, running the rapids of a churning river. The view is even more beautiful if you've had to trek through the jungle or climb a mountain to see it. Best of all is when you're the first in your crowd to have been there. Try exploring the rugged coast of Ireland, hiking the moors of England, biking through Denmark, scuba-diving off Puerto Rico, trekking in the Canadian Rockies—all of these are Aries-favored places.

For the spur-of-the-moment getaway, pack a special travel bag with necessities, and don't forget a few soft-brimmed hats for sun protection and swagger, a disposable camera, sunglasses, sun block, and a bathing suit. By traveling with lightweight carry-on luggage, you can skip the baggage claim. Reserve in advance a rental car or have a car service waiting to whisk you away.

Outwit travel delays productively, with a great book or stationery and postcards to catch up on your correspondence. Or power walk the terminal. (Or practice your flirting arts on attractive fellow passengers!) If you're traveling on business, find out what business services are available, so you can get some work done or surf the Internet. Some research in advance could keep travel headaches to a minimum.

CHAPTER 21

Aries Health and Well-Being

Astrology can clue you in to the tendencies that contribute to good or ill health (especially when it comes to controlling your appetite). So follow these tips on how best to lose those extra pounds and make this your healthiest year ever.

Avoid the Quick Fix

Thanks to your hyperactive Mars-ruled lifestyle, you're sometimes too busy to bother with healthy meals in a calm atmosphere. You're more likely to grab carbohydrate-laden, calorie-packed fast foods for instant energy on the run. You need a regimen that gives you sustained energy, rather than a quick fix or a caffeine-fueled jump start. Aim for frequent small meals and carry healthy snacks with you to recharge your batteries. Protein and fruit smoothies in the morning might provide you with a quick, healthy head start to the day.

Wear Protective Headgear

Aries is associated with the head, your most vulnerable area, which you should be especially careful to protect by wearing the appropriate headgear during risky activities and sports. Headaches warn you to slow down and take it easy for a while. If you've been stocking up on headache remedies, it might be time to consult a nutritionist for expert dietary advice.

Sports Are Your Best Exercise Outlet

Superbusy, impatient Aries tends to overschedule and stress out when others don't, won't, or can't keep up the pace. Sports to the rescue! Swatting a ball, cheering on your favorite team, training for a marathon, or just running around the block can be the best remedies for whatever ails an Aries. Sports allow you to let off steam in an atmosphere of excitement and competition where you can feel the joy of winning. Your daring moves and Mars-powered energy should earn you a stellar spot on any team. If you're older, volunteer to coach local youngsters.

Martial arts of any kind appeal to your love of action. The slower, more flowing forms such as tai chi can be done throughout life. You don't have to be Jackie Chan or Russell Crowe to show your Aries flair for action heroics. Try racket sports (any sport that involves hitting or working with a swordlike object), fencing, tap dancing, or aerobics if martial arts don't give you a kick. However, do remember to take time to check your equipment, do the proper warm-ups, and wait until you're properly conditioned before you jump to expert-level challenges.

Once you've found a sport you love, try not to push yourself too hard. Listen to your body when it tells you it's time to quit (never easy for Aries). Finally, know the difference between well-exercised, fatigued muscles and the pain that signals trouble.

CHAPTER 22

Your Aries Career Guide: What It Takes to Succeed in 2008

Find the Right Career for You

Aries has a special combination of talents and abilities that can make you a natural winner. Develop and nurture these sun-sign strengths, and you'll be likely to find a career you truly enjoy, one where you'll be most successful. The great Aries philosopher and teacher Joseph Campbell gave you the best advice: Follow your bliss!

Your Ideal Work Environment

Adventurous Aries can put up with hardship and difficult working conditions if there is enough challenge! You should be inspired by Jane Goodall, the great Aries explorer, who was content to live alone in the African wilderness in order to do pioneering work with chimpanzees. The feeling of being stuck in a job is what you must avoid at all costs. Look for a position with action and challenge where you can use your natural ability to make lightning-fast decisions and mobilize instantly. Stock and bond trading, emergency medicine, the military, police work, rescue work, surgery, sales, promotion, show business, journalism, retail, or sports and fitness fields would provide the fast pace and excitement Aries thrives on.

Like other fire signs, you often gravitate to careers that require heat, either literally or figuratively. Intense competition that would scorch others actually turns you on, and you'll blaze right through office politics because you thrive under pressure. Chefs with a busy restaurant kitchen, firefighters, iron workers (work that requires a blowtorch), and heating contractors are other hot jobs for Aries.

As one of the zodiac's pioneers, you flourish when developing or promoting new, improved products and services. Though you can be a big money earner, thanks to your tireless work ethic, financial rewards alone are not enough to satisfy your fiery spirit. You must believe in what you're doing and be able to move ahead at your own pace.

The Aries Leader

Sam Walton is the perfect example of the Aries leader with innovative spirit and the courage to follow his dream. Walton revolutionized the way we shop by setting up huge megastores. Today, there are thousands of Wal-Mart stores across the country. This self-made Aries billionaire should inspire you to take a new idea and run with it.

As a supervisor, Aries is the take-charge office dynamo who is at ease running the show. Because you naturally take the driver's seat, you can be an exciting person to work for. You'll motivate others to perform at their peak (in fact, you have no patience with slowpokes). Because you get everyone moving and energized, you are best at starting projects. However, you can become extremely frustrated when a project or a person requires patience, tactful handling, and perseverance.

With your Aries megadose of energy, learning to delegate is one of your biggest challenges. Avoid taking an "I can do it better" attitude that may leave you overextended, doing everyone else's work. However, you're on target when it comes to spotting a trend, and you'll try to be the first out with the newest product. You're always open to innovative methods, and no one is better at getting the job done in record time!

The Aries Team Player

You really work best alone, in charge of your own territory. You're a natural leader, not a follower, though you will fulfill your company's expectations if the job is challenging enough. In fact, problems that might discourage others will actually stimulate you. You thrive on competition rather than routine, and you should look for the chance to use your assertive qualities in a positive way. Find an action spot where you can move around from place to place rather than stay rooted to one desk all day long. But do control your wanderlust long enough to reap your due rewards.

The Aries Way to Get Ahead

As an Aries, you bring some important assets to the table, such as your ability to think on your feet, to act quickly, and to get results. It's up to you to decide how to best utilize your talents and abilities to bring you the very highest return on the investment of your time and energy. Look for a job with plenty of challenge, stimulating competition, and decision-making freedom. Play up these attributes:

- Energy
- Enthusiasm
- Optimism
- Ability to spot trends
- Decisiveness
- Initiative

CHAPTER 23

Aries on the Red Carpet

Are you a fan of tabloids and gossip columns? Your fascination with the rich and famous could have a fringe benefit. It's also a terrific way to learn more about astrology. A celebrity's attraction for the public tells much about the planetary influences of a given time and the special star quality of his or her sun sign. You may even have a celebrity astro twin who shares both your birthday and the same year.

You're sure to have many of the same traits as your famous sun-sign siblings. Do you share the confrontational Aries temper of Russell Crowe, Marlon Brando, or Star Jones? How did they face scandal and reinvent themselves? Do you swagger with the cutting-edge Aries sense of style like Sarah Jessica Parker or Marcia Cross? Maybe you're an adventurous pioneer or an activist like Gloria Steinem or Jane Goodall. There are many heroes born under Aries whose lives can inspire you to follow your bliss, as the great Aries philosopher and teacher Joseph Campbell advised.

The lives of the famous can be fascinating textbooks with full-color illustrations of the different planetary combinations. If someone intrigues you, explore his personality further by looking up his other planets using the tables in this book. Then apply the effects of Venus, Mars, Saturn, and Jupiter to his sun-sign traits. It's a fun way to get up close and personal with your famous friend, maybe learn some secrets not revealed to the public.

Then why not move on from the red carpet to world leaders and current newsmakers? You can find accurate data online at Internet sites such as www.Stariq.com or www.astrodatabank.com, which have the charts of world events and headline makers. Then compare notes with other fans, including many professional astrologers, who frequent the forums on these sites.

Aries Celebrities

Timothy Dalton (3/21/44)
Matthew Broderick (3/21/62)
Rosie O'Donnell (3/21/62)
Gary Oldman (3/21/68)
Kevin Federline (3/21/78)
Andrew Lloyd Webber (3/22/48)
Lena Olin (3/22/55)
Pat Robertson (3/22/30)
William Shatner (3/22/31)
Stephanie Mills (3/22/57)
Matthew Modine (3/22/59)
Keira Knightley (3/22/74)
Reese Witherspoon (3/22/76)
Joan Crawford (3/23/1904)
Amanda Plummer (3/23/57)
Kelly LeBrock (3/24/60)
Star Jones (3/24/62)
Lara Flynn Boyle (3/24/70)
Simone Signoret (3/25/21)
Gloria Steinem (3/25/34)
Aretha Franklin (3/25/42)
Elton John (3/25/47)
Brenda Strong (3/25/58)
Marcia Cross (3/25/62)
Sarah Jessica Parker (3/25/65)
Sandra Day O'Connor (3/26/30)
Leonard Nimoy (3/26/31)
James Caan (3/26/39)
Diana Ross (3/26/44)
Steven Tyler (3/26/48)
Leeza Gibbons (3/26/57)
Talisa Soto (3/27/67)
Mariah Carey (3/27/70)

Dianne Wiest (3/28/48)
Reba McIntire (3/28/55)
Julia Stiles (3/28/81)
Sam Walton (3/29/18)
Lucy Lawless (3/29/68)
Elle Macpherson (3/29/64)
Vincent van Gogh (3/30/1853)
Warren Beatty (3/30/37)
Eric Clapton (3/30/45)
Celine Dion (3/30/68)
Mark Consuelos (3/30/70)
Liz Claiborne (3/31/29)
Shirley Jones (3/31/34)
Richard Chamberlain (3/31/35)
Herb Alpert (3/31/35)
Christopher Walken (3/31/43)
Al Gore (3/31/48)
Rhea Perlman (3/31/48)
Paul Reiser (3/31/65)
Debbie Reynolds (4/1/32)
Ali MacGraw (4/1/39)
Marvin Gaye (4/2/39)
Linda Hunt (4/2/45)
Emmylou Harris (4/2/47)
Dana Carvey (4/2/55)
Marlon Brando (4/3/24)
Doris Day (4/3/24)
Jane Goodall (4/3/34)
Marsha Mason (4/3/42)
Alec Baldwin (4/3/58)
David Hyde Pierce (4/3/59)
Eddie Murphy (4/3/61)
Jennie Garth (4/3/72)
Maya Angelou (4/4/28)
Anthony Perkins (4/4/32)
Kitty Kelley (4/4/42)
Christine Lahti (4/4/50)
Robert Downey, Jr. (4/4/65)
Heath Ledger (4/4/79)
Bette Davis (4/5/1908)
Gregory Peck (4/5/16)

Colin Powell (4/5/37)
Harry Houdini (4/6/1874)
Merle Haggard (4/6/37)
Marilu Henner (4/6/52)
Francis Ford Coppola (4/7/39)
David Frost (4/7/39)
Jackie Chan (4/7/54)
Russell Crowe (4/7/64)
Julian Lennon (4/8/63)
Robin Wright Penn (4/8/66)
Hugh Hefner (4/9/26)
Dennis Quaid (4/9/54)
Marc Jacobs (4/9/63)
Cynthia Nixon (4/9/66)
Omar Sharif (4/10/32)
Steven Seagal (4/10/51)
Joel Grey (4/11/32)
Ann Miller (4/12/23)
David Letterman (4/12/47)
Scott Turow (4/12/49)
Andy Garcia (4/12/56)
Shannen Doherty (4/12/71)
Clare Danes (4/12/79)
Howard Keel (4/13/19)
Lyle Waggoner (4/13/35)
Ron Perlman (4/13/50)
Sarah Michelle Gellar (4/14/77)
Julie Christie (4/14/41)
Kareem Abdul-Jabbar (4/15/47)
Emma Thompson (4/15/59)
Ellen Barkin (4/16/54)
Pete Shelley (4/17/55)
Liz Phair (4/17/67)
Victoria "Posh Spice" Beckham (4/17/74)
Conan O'Brien (4/18/63)
James Woods (4/18/47)
Jane Leeves (4/18/63)
Dudley Moore (4/19/35)
Tim Curry (4/19/46)
Ashley Judd (4/19/66)
Kate Hudson (4/19/79)

CHAPTER 24

Star Wars or Passionate Supernovas? How Aries Partners with Every Other Sign

After learning all about your own sun sign, it's time to consider how you interact with others. Knowing how your sun sign works with other signs can give you valuable insight into the future of all your relationships. Once you understand how another sun sign is likely to view yours, you'll be in a much better position to judge whether this combination will crash and burn or have lasting happiness potential.

The celebrity couples are used as examples to help you visualize each sun-sign combination. Note that some legendary couples have stood the test of time, others blazed brightly and then burned out, and a few existed only in the fantasy world of film or television (but still captured our imagination). Is there a magic formula for compatibility? Traditional astrological wisdom holds that signs of the same element, in your case other fire signs (Leo and Sagittarius), are naturally compatible. So are signs of complementary elements, such as fire signs with air signs. In these relationships communication supposedly flows easily and you'll feel most comfortable with each other. However, there are no hard-and-fast rules with sun-sign combinations. Many lasting marriages happen between incompatible sun signs, while some ideally matched couples fizzle after a few years.

When sparks fly and an irresistible magnetic pull draws you together, when disagreements and challenges fuel intrigue, mystery, passion, and sexy sparring matches, don't rule the relationship out. That person may provide the diversity, excitement, and challenge you need for an unforgettable romance, a stimulating friendship, or a successful business partnership!

Aries/Aries

THE ATTRACTION:

At last, here's someone who can keep up with you! This is the Scarlett O'Hara/Rhett Butler combination of two risk takers ready to take on the world. If you have the same mission in life, but you have staked out separate territory, you can function as passionate partners.

THE ISSUES:

The burning question between two fire signs is: "Who's the boss?" You may be so preoccupied with your own agenda that you may not have time for each other after the initial blaze of passion. And when you need backup support, better look for it elsewhere. You can't fight fire with fire, so this romance could burn out.

SIGN MATES:

Aries Sarah Jessica Parker and Matthew Broderick

Aries/Taurus

THE ATTRACTION:

You'll get slow-moving Taurus up and at 'em by waving a red flag before the bull. Taurus will be excited and ready to charge just where you direct. Your payoff is when Taurus keeps you on course, follows through, and provides solid backup support, as well as a warm, loving sensual companion who is devoted and loyal. With the Taurus focus to steady you, you'll get things done!

THE ISSUES:

Adapting to each other's pace calls for compromise, especially when Aries learns that Taurus cannot be pushed or rushed and when Taurus learns that Aries likes instant gratification, not slow decision making. You could lock horns over short-term versus long-term goals. Taurus might prefer comfortable surroundings, while Aries happily sacrifices comfort for adventure. Separate vacations might be the only solution.

SIGN MATES:

Aries Victoria (Posh Spice) Beckham and Taurus David Beckham

Aries/Gemini

THE ATTRACTION:

There's plenty of excitement and fast-paced action with this duo. You're energetic enough to keep up with Gemini's constant changes. You're both spontaneous, optimistic, energetic, and life-affirming. Sure, there are differences of opinion, but this only keeps the atmosphere charged and mentally stimulating.

THE ISSUES:

Juggling life with changeable Gemini could have Aries seeing double. Aries is direct and to the point, while Gemini can't be pinned down. And they change their mind at the drop of an Aries hat! This hyperactive combination could get on both your nerves, unless you give each other plenty of space. Aries, you must realize you probably won't be number one with Gemini. Be willing to share, and don't fly off the handle when Gemini flirts—it's their favorite pastime.

SIGN MATES:

Aries Warren Beatty and Gemini Annette Bening

Aries/Cancer

THE ATTRACTION:

Cancer will give you all the hero worship and nurturing you deeply desire, plus a shrewd business sense and a solid base to operate from. (Cancer knows what people want before they do!) Your flair for romance, enthusiasm, positive energy, and courage will coax out the cautious crab. If your relationship can provide the home and financial security Cancer desires, this relationship could last.

THE ISSUES:

Aries detests complaining or whining, so Cancer will have to suffer in silence. Sulking and possessive behavior will also turn you off. Cancer may balk when you get pushy, and might find your behavior too insensitive and self-centered for their delicate feelings or stomach to bear. And when Cancer starts with the emotional dreams or heavy mood swings, you're out the door!

SIGN MATES:

Aries Betty Ford and Cancer President Gerald Ford

Aries/Leo

THE ATTRACTION:

The heat's on with you two romantics. You both share high hopes, high energy, and high ideals. You both can express your finest qualities. If you can learn to feed each other's egos and costar, rather than compete for center stage, this could be a long-run relationship.

THE ISSUES:

The problems appear when romance turns to reality. Both of you are delegators—neither likes to do the nitty-gritty follow-through. If either gets overly bossy, this romance could explode. Leo may long to be fussed over, while Aries will also want to feel like number one once in a while. These two self-centered signs have to learn to give and occasionally give in to each other.

SIGN MATES:

Aries Robin Wright Penn and Leo Sean Penn
Aries Jennifer Garner and Leo Ben Affleck
Aries Jesse James and Leo Sandra Bullock

Aries/Virgo

THE ATTRACTION:

Your magnetism and positive energy warm up Virgo, who is thrilled by your energy and ardent pursuit of excellence. You both share high ideals in love and tend to put lovers on a pedestal. Virgo sees their beloved as perfect. Your honesty and directness will earn Virgo's trust.

THE ISSUES:

Aries can be recklessly impatient, which Virgo will find a serious weakness. Virgo dedication to selfless service gets no credit from self-centered Aries, who wants recognition. Virgo may get tired, sick, and feel martyred. Unsympathetic Aries will see Virgo as a downer.

SIGN MATES:

Aries Reese Witherspoon and Virgo Ryan Phillipe

Aries/Libra

THE ATTRACTION:

This attraction of opposites is about sharing versus going it alone, the judge versus the crusader, cool judgment versus hot activity. Libra admires the decision maker in Aries and adores having a true romantic lead. In this combination, you'll supply the push and energy; Libra, the charm and diplomacy. Libra learns to take a stand; Aries learns to see and appreciate the opposite point of view.

THE ISSUES:

Libra indecisiveness can make Aries see red or take over. Aries views vacillation as a serious weakness—he who hesitates is lost or last! Libra believes in looking at both sides of the question. To Aries there's only one side. The Aries lack of consideration and pushy manner is a Libra no-no. Aries enjoys a rousing confrontation, while Libra prefers quiet debate. Get your problems out on the table calmly in an elegant setting.

SIGN MATES:

Aries Mark Consuelos and Libra Kelly Ripa
Aries Deryck Whibley and Libra Avril Lavigne

Aries/Scorpio

THE ATTRACTION:

One of the zodiac's most challenging pairs, your mutual Mars-ruled chemistry could thrive on a battle of the sexes. And you both love a dare! While neither of you gives in, you'll never bore each other (though you might eventually wear out). Your direct, uncomplicated forcefulness especially intrigues Scorpio, who's caught off-guard for once.

THE ISSUES:

You could both play so hard to get that you never really connect! Aries never quite trusts secretive Scorpio, while the Scorpio subtle intrigues and backstage power plays can fizzle under direct Aries fire. You are both jealous and controlling, but this dynamic duo can work if you transcend the trivial by focusing on high ideals and mutual respect.

SIGN MATES:

Aries Rhea Perlman and Scorpio Danny DeVito

Aries/Sagittarius

THE ATTRACTION:

You're good buddies who love the great outdoors, risk-taking adventures, travel, and a high-action lifestyle. You'll happily support each other's goals. This combination works especially well if you share spiritual ideals. You're both independent and understand each other's need for space. Neither of you can abide a possessive, clingy partner and you won't find one here.

THE ISSUES:

You both tend to be self-involved and may not invest enough time in maintaining the relationship. Common goals may not be enough to keep you together, especially if you lack solid financial backup. Unless you become more available to each other, you may find yourself heading off in different directions, in search of more ego support.

SIGN MATES:

Aries Alec Baldwin and Sagittarius Kim Basinger
Aries Talisa Soto and Sagittarius Benjamin Bratt
Aries Kevin Federline and Sagittarius Britney Spears

Aries/Capricorn

THE ATTRACTION:

You're both high achievers and hard workers who admire each other's stamina. Capricorn provides the solid organizational skills, while you'll provide enthusiasm and pioneering ideas. The mature Capricorn outlook could offer the stable backup that Aries needs to get there first. In return, the Aries innovativeness could pull Capricorn out of the ordinary.

THE ISSUES:

Capricorn values the traditional; Aries, the trendy. Aries can seem like a self-centered baby; Capricorn, an old fuddy-duddy. Capricorn rules and structure can seem confining to Aries, whose headstrong methods seem foolhardy to Capricorn.

SIGN MATES:

Aries Heath Ledger and Capricorn Michelle Williams
Aries Celine Dion and Capricorn René Angelil

Aries/Aquarius

THE ATTRACTION:

You're both visionaries who are turned on by the avant-garde. Anything goes with you two. Aquarius will find Aries a willing and experimental partner who also loves surprises. Both freedom-loving, you'll give each other plenty of space.

THE ISSUES:

Aries may resent being constantly surrounded by an Aquarius squadron of friends and associates, unless you are both united by common ideals and goals. You'll never be the focus of this sign's attention, but then, no one else will either! A bossy Aries and a know-it-all Aquarius could clash mightily. The cool Aquarius detachment could send Aries looking for attention elsewhere.

SIGN MATES:

Aries Ryan O'Neal and Aquarius Farrah Fawcett
Aries Vince Vaughn and Aquarius Jennifer Aniston

Aries/Pisces

THE ATTRACTION:

Pisces love to be swept off their feet and you're happy to comply! Here is someone who appreciates your Aries dynamism and is not threatened by your Aries aggressiveness. Aries will be number one with Pisces, who'll have wonderful, romantic ideas to contribute. Aries tempts Pisces to swim in new waters, to follow that dream!

THE ISSUES:

Supersensitive Pisces feelings are the problem here. Pushy, bossy, or inconsiderate partners turn Pisces into martyrs or monsters who could rain on your Aries parade or simply tune you out. Balancing positive and negative energies is the key to success. Aries needs to apply brakes, to slow down and consider the consequences before you blurt out that rash remark, while Pisces sometimes needs a strong charge to be jolted into action.

SIGN MATES:

Aries Sarah Michelle Gellar and Pisces Freddy Prinze Jr.

CHAPTER 25

The Big Picture for Aries in 2008

Welcome to 2008, Aries! It's your year for cooperation, partnerships, patience, arbitration, and relationships. Given your independence and need for action, there could be some inherent challenges in what's called for this year. But no challenge is big enough to daunt your pioneering spirit.

You have major, positive changes coming up this year in your career. Whether you're just starting out on a career path, in the middle of it, or nearing retirement, Jupiter and Pluto in your tenth house of careers both expand and radically change what you're doing. New opportunities that are more in line with your spiritual and personal beliefs come your way. Individuals who may act as guides or mentors enter your life, or you may fulfill that role for someone else. You'll do well in business partnerships this year, as long as you don't get into power plays with other people.

Other areas to watch for this year concern Saturn, the planet that represents rules, restrictions, and karma. For the past 2.5 years, Saturn has been in your fifth house of romance. You may have experienced delays or restrictions related to romance, or your joy may have been squashed for some reason. Even if other areas of your life have flourished, you may have been disappointed in the love department.

That ended late last year, when Saturn moved into Virgo for a run of 2.5 years. So this year, you may experience restrictions related to your daily work routine. You could be saddled with more responsibility. Just do the work, Aries. The payoff comes two years up the line. Since the sixth house also represents your daily health, it's important to keep yourself in good shape this year. Pay close attention to your nutrition and exercise routines.

Uranus, the planet that symbolizes sudden, unexpected change, is still in your twelfth house this year. It's been there for quite a while, so you should be well acquainted with its energies. You may experience events or relationships that touch upon deeply buried issues and allow you to confront these issues and resolve them once and for all. Since the twelfth house symbolizes what we can't see, you could have some associations with people in hospitals, nursing homes, or other institutions. Your dreams could be particularly vivid this year and can bring you intuitive information, insight into your own unconscious, and answers to questions.

Best Time for Romance

Mark the dates between April 6 and 29, when Venus is in your sign. Your romantic quota soars. You're also more artistic then, and others see you in a whole new light. You feel more confident and your sex appeal soars. Great backup dates for romance fall between July 12 and August 4, when Venus is transiting your fifth house of love and forming a beautiful angle to your sun.

Best Time for Career Decisions

Make career decisions between the first of the year and May 8 or between September 8 and the end of the year, when Jupiter is moving direct through your tenth house. During the four-month period between early May and early September, Jupiter is moving retrograde—it's essentially dormant.

The are some especially lucky days this year for career decision. They fall between May 11–13, and September 3–5, when the sun and Jupiter see eye to eye and there's a nice flow of energy between them.

Mercury Retrogrades

Every year, there are three periods when Mercury—the planet of communication and travel—turns retrograde. During these periods, it's wisest not to negotiate or sign contracts, to travel, to submit manuscripts, or to make major decisions. Granted, we can't live our lives entirely by Mercury retrogrades! However, if you have to travel during the periods listed below, expect changes in your itinerary. If you have to sign a contract, expect to revisit it.

It's also a good idea to back up computer files before Mercury turns retrograde. Quite often, computers and other communication devices act up. Be sure your virus software is up-to-date. Pay special attention to the house in which a Mercury retrograde falls. It will tell you the area of your life most likely to be impacted. The periods to watch for in 2008 are:

January 28–February 18: retrograde in Aquarius, your eleventh house of friends.

May 26–June 19: retrograde in Gemini, your third house of communication and travel.

September 24–October 15: retrograde in Libra, your seventh house of partnerships.

Eclipses

Every year, there are four eclipses, two solar and two lunar. Solar eclipses trigger external events that allow us to see what eluded us before. When an eclipse hits one of your natal planets, it's especially important. Take note of the sign and house placement. Lunar eclipses bring up emotional issues related to the sign and house in which they fall.

Here are the dates to watch for:

February 6: Solar eclipse at 17 degrees Aquarius, your eleventh house of friends, wishes, and dreams. Those of you who were born between April 6–8 are likely to feel the greatest impact, in a positive way. But check your natal chart to find out if you have any planets at 17 degrees.

February 20: Lunar eclipse at 10 degrees Virgo, in your sixth house of daily work and health.

August 1: Solar eclipse, 9 degrees Leo, in your fifth house of romance. If you were born between March 29–31, this eclipse will impact you strongly, in a positive way.

August 16: Lunar eclipse at 24 degrees Aquarius, your eleventh house of friends, wishes, and dreams.

Luckiest Days in 2008

Every year, Jupiter forms a beneficial angle with the sun, usually a conjunction, when both planets are in the same sign. In 2008, the angle is a lovely trine and it occurs during two time periods: May 11–13 and September 3–5. If you're going to buy a Lotto ticket, do it during these periods!

Now let's take a look at what 2008 has in store for you day by day.

CHAPTER 26

Eighteen Months of Day-by-Day Predictions—July 2007 to December 2008

Moon sign times are calculated for Eastern Standard Time and Eastern Daylight Time. Please adjust for your local time zone.

JULY 2007

Sunday, July 1 (Moon in Capricorn) If you're a politician, huddle with your advisers, your managers, and even some of your constituents and brainstorm. You're laying a strategy for more than just today; your vision is for tomorrow and the next day and even ten years from now.

Monday, July 2 (Moon in Capricorn to Aquarius 1:25 a.m.) This moon provides insights into your relationships with friends and acquaintances. Are these solid connections? Are they based on illusions? With Neptune also in Aquarius in your eleventh house, even you can be deceived, Aries.

Tuesday, July 3 (Moon in Aquarius) You're preparing for the Independence Day holiday. If you have family or friends coming into town, be sure you've done the basics before this evening. A Gemini or a Libra helps you out. One of them may play into your dreams.

Wednesday, July 4 (Moon in Aquarius to Pisces 4:53 a.m.) Happy Independence Day! You spend the day with family or friends. Someone you haven't seen for a long time shows up again. This person may stir up buried feelings, and you have to decide whether to resolve the feelings or ignore them.

Thursday, July 5 (Moon in Pisces) When the moon joins Uranus in your solar twelfth house, your emotional responses to certain things are unusual. Your spiritual beliefs snap into focus, and by tomorrow, you will figure out a way to factor these beliefs into who you are and what you do.

Friday, July 6 (Moon in Pisces to Aries 10:57 a.m.) With the moon in your sign, life suddenly seems remarkably less complicated. This feeling will be intensified even more after Mercury turns direct on July 9. Your self-confidence attracts the attention of a special someone.

Saturday, July 7 (Moon in Aries) You get out with family or friends to enjoy summer activities—the riskier, the better, as far as you're concerned. Forget a sedate hike; you're more the extreme-sports type: rock climbing, white-water rafting. You and your significant other take in dinner and a show this evening.

Sunday, July 8 (Moon in Aries to Taurus 1:54 p.m.) How far can you stretch your finances, Aries? Pretty far, as it turns out, but you may have to purchase a big-ticket item on credit. Better yet, wait until the day after tomorrow to buy the item. Mercury will be moving direct by then.

Monday, July 9 (Moon in Taurus) Mercury turns direct. This movement greatly alleviates any miscommunication issues you've been experiencing. Expected checks and contracts should arrive in the next few days. Things at home start straightening out as well.

Tuesday, July 10 (Moon in Taurus to Gemini 4:10 p.m.) By this afternoon, you feel the shift in lunar energies. The Gemini moon stimulates your intellect, attracts more interaction with neighbors, relatives, and siblings, and certainly favors writing and other forms of communication. You may need all those skills to convince someone to change his mind.

Wednesday, July 11 (Moon in Gemini) You do a lot today—running errands, visiting friends, tying up some loose ends related to neighborhood projects. Your love life has improved and will continue to do so.

Thursday, July 12 (Moon in Gemini to Cancer 6:40 p.m.) The moon joins Mercury in your solar fourth house, bringing your attention squarely to family and home. Your mother or another nurturing female in your life plays an important role. In less than a month, Jupiter in Sagittarius will turn direct again; that will be the time to take your overseas trip.

Friday, July 13 (Moon in Cancer) You're investigating a mystery that has puzzled you for years. It may be related to your family's genealogy. Persist. Don't get discouraged. You're closer than you believe to the truth.

Saturday, July 14 (Moon in Cancer to Leo 10:44 p.m.) Venus moves into Virgo and remains there until September 8. Until July 27, this transit favors romance and love with a coworker or someone you meet through work. After that, you may have to revisit issues you thought were settled.

Sunday, July 15 (Moon in Leo) The energy of the Leo moon is compatible with Aries. All that fire triggers your passion for pleasure. Don't get involved beyond what you're willing to commit to. Some issue with your children may need attention.

Monday, July 16 (Moon in Leo) If you're involved with a new romance, keep things light and fun. That probably won't be a big problem for you since you aren't in the mood for commitment. But be sure your new partner understands your ground rules.

Tuesday, July 17 (Moon in Leo to Virgo 5:40 a.m.) The moon joins Venus in your sixth house. This combination could be the ideal recipe for a romance at work or with someone you meet through work. It's time to see the dentist or catch up on health appointments you've been putting off.

Wednesday, July 18 (Moon in Virgo) You're watching what you eat; whether you're counting calories or carbs, it behooves you to start exercising regularly. Pick an activity that you know you'll be able to do daily. Make it part of your regular daily routine.

Thursday, July 19 (Moon in Virgo to Libra 3:54 p.m.) Your marriage or partnership is highlighted. Even though communication shouldn't go awry, be sure to state your position clearly and honestly. Establish your base together; don't procrastinate.

Friday, July 20 (Moon in Libra) It's Friday, and as the song goes, living is easy. Romance is in the air, your aesthetic sensitivity is acute, and you're in a very social mood. Even though this moon is opposed to your sun, the air and fire energies blend well.

Saturday, July 21 (Moon in Libra) Art museums, music, literature—all of these areas play roles in your life. You and your significant other spend quality time together this evening and the excellent rapport between you continues throughout the rest of the weekend.

Sunday, July 22 (Moon in Libra to Scorpio 4:19 a.m.) You're more secretive than you usually are. Your secrets revolve around assets you share with others—or vice versa—and how you really feel about this sharing. If you're in the midst of a divorce, now is the time to negotiate for what is fairly yours.

Monday, July 23 (Moon in Scorpio) Be sure that your insurance payments are up-to-date. It's a good day to apply for a mortgage, a car loan, or any other kind of loan. In fact, you should do this before Venus turns retrograde on July 27.

Tuesday, July 24 (Moon in Scorpio to Sagittarius 4:31 p.m.) This moon triggers your lust for travel. Any number of overseas destinations would suit you, Aries. Get out your world map and your monthly planner and decide where you want to go. Set your plans in motion after August 6, when Jupiter in Sagittarius turns direct.

Wednesday, July 25 (Moon in Sagittarius) You're able to see the larger picture of an issue or a relationship. Regardless of whether you like what you see, information empowers you. You're now able to make an informed decision.

Thursday, July 26 (Moon in Sagittarius) As the moon closes in on the career sector of your chart, you're gearing up for a major presentation. Have your plan ready. Tomorrow is the big day! Tonight, information may come to you through dreams, so have your journal handy.

Friday, July 27 (Moon in Sagittarius to Capricorn 2:23 a.m.) Venus turned retrograde in Virgo, so the romance that started last month could be in for a bumpy ride. Just take it all in stride, Aries. The retrograde also could produce physically uncomfortable conditions at work or compel you to take up your exercise routine again.

Saturday, July 28 (Moon in Capricorn) With the moon in the career sector of your chart, you're in an excellent position to implement a plan or strategy. Keep to the course you've set and don't allow others to deter you. You're in the driver's seat professionally.

Sunday, July 29 (Moon in Capricorn to Aquarius 9:14 a.m.) You enjoy this moon. The air element is compatible with the Aries fire. It allows you to detach emotionally where friendships and group associations are concerned. Take an honest look at your wishes and dreams.

Monday, July 30 (Moon in Aquarius) You meet with your writing group, and you are pleased with the feedback you receive on your manuscript or screenplay. It's time to implement what you've learned.

Tuesday, July 31 (Moon in Aquarius to Pisces 1:41 p.m.) The moon moves into your twelfth house. This transit may feel uncomfortable. It urges you to look within for answers. It's an excellent moon, however, for dream recall, past-life regressions, and any sort of psychic experimentation.

AUGUST 2007

Wednesday, August 1 (Moon in Pisces) If you're more of a loner than usual, don't obsess about it. It's healthy to step out of the chaotic center of your life. You need the downtime. Start planning for what you will do tomorrow and the next day when the moon moves into your sign.

Thursday, August 2 (Moon in Pisces to Aries 4:43 p.m.) You feel the shift this afternoon when the moon moves into your sign. This transit is always a high peak of the month. Your self-confidence sweeps you along and helps attract new opportunities.

Friday, August 3 (Moon in Aries) With Venus still retrograde in Virgo and your sixth house, you may have to deal with a disgruntled coworker. Exhibit patience. If the job isn't done the way you want it, step in and do it yourself.

Saturday, August 4 (Moon in Aries to Taurus 7:16 p.m.) Mercury moves into Leo and your fifth house. Your thoughts turn to your children, enjoyment, love affairs, and creative endeavors. For the next two weeks, work on your own creative projects. You'll make tremendous strides.

Sunday, August 5 (Moon in Taurus) If the check has cleared, start shopping for the big-ticket item you've been eyeing for several months. Compare prices. Mars is in your solar second house of finances, so money is burning a hole through your pocket!

Monday, August 6 (Moon in Taurus to Gemini 10:02 p.m.) Jupiter turns direct in Sagittarius and your ninth house. Register for college or adult-ed classes, or plan your overseas trip. Your in-laws may show up unexpectedly.

Tuesday, August 7 (Moon in Gemini) If you feel like you're running yourself ragged, take a few hours off and head over to your favorite bookstore. A good novel for a Gemini moon day: Greg Bear's *Darwin's Children* or F. Paul Wilson's *Hosts*. Both deal with what-if scenarios that will capture your imagination. Mars joins the moon in Gemini in your third house.

Wednesday, August 8 (Moon in Gemini) The Mars transit that began yesterday lasts until September 28; it brings activities related to siblings and other relatives, neighbors, and communication. Finish up that novel or screenplay!

Thursday, August 9 (Moon in Gemini to Cancer 1:37 a.m.) You feel more vulnerable emotionally, particularly where your home and family are concerned. An issue with a family member may reach a crescendo. Deal with it and move on.

Friday, August 10 (Moon in Cancer) Beautify your home this weekend by doing something as simple as painting your office or bedroom or something as complex as buying new furniture. It's a good time to clean out your closets, attic, and basement. You may want to pick up a book on feng shui to enhance particular energies in your home.

Saturday, August 11 (Moon in Cancer to Leo 6:42 a.m.) Here's that glorious Leo moon again, accentuating romance, pleasure, and creativity. If you're involved with someone, the relationship may reach a deeper level. If you're not involved, make yourself available.

Sunday, August 12 (Moon in Leo) The stars are stacked in your favor. Jupiter, Mars, and Mercury are forming harmonious angles to your sun, expanding your opportunities, and providing you with the energy and conscious intention to pursue these new venues. Even though Venus is still retrograde, you have enough positive energy to overcome any minor glitches with a partner.

Monday, August 13 (Moon in Leo to Virgo 2:04 p.m.) The moon joins Venus retrograde in your solar sixth house. This combination could make you more vulnerable emotionally. The best way to counter such feelings is to get involved in physical activity. Go to the gym. Go swimming. Go running with a friend or partner.

Tuesday, August 14 (Moon in Virgo) Already, it's a better day! Take advantage of all the fire energy in the zodiac. Pursue new dreams. Call friends you haven't connected with for a while, and keep your network of acquaintances intact. Your life is humming right along, following a blueprint that is faithful to your deepest beliefs.

Wednesday, August 15 (Moon in Virgo) You're in the mood for romance. If you're involved, you and your partner should consider getting away for a long weekend. It's time to renew your commitment to each other.

Thursday, August 16 (Moon in Virgo to Libra 12:05 a.m.) Your artistic sensibilities are particularly good. Use them to advance creative endeavors. You may have to mediate a dispute between two people you love. Sign those contracts that have been on your desk for some time.

Friday, August 17 (Moon in Libra) Your conscious mind turns toward legal matters. Don't procrastinate, Aries.

There's time to do it all if you just slow down, take a few deep breaths, and prioritize.

Saturday, August 18 (Moon in Libra to Scorpio 12:14 p.m.) On this intensely emotional day, it's to your benefit to think before you speak and to keep your own counsel. People around you may be unpredictable. That's their problem; don't let it become your problem.

Sunday, August 19 (Moon in Scorpio) Mercury moves into Virgo and your solar sixth house. For the next few weeks, you'll be a whiz with details and connect the dots in your work. You'll be after greater efficiency and practical results.

Monday, August 20 (Moon in Scorpio) As the summer moves quickly toward autumn, one more vacation looks very enticing. Even if you feel you can't take the time off, do it. You need to get away and out of your routine.

Tuesday, August 21 (Moon in Scorpio to Sagittarius 12:45 a.m.) Finally, a lunar energy that feels great for you. You may sign up for a course or take a workshop in a metaphysical topic that interests you. Your focus is on your worldview and your spirituality and ways in which you might incorporate both into your daily life. A Leo proves helpful. A great book for a Sagittarius moon day: Louise Hay's *You Can Heal Your Life.*

Wednesday, August 22 (Moon in Sagittarius) Can you take it right to the limit? You excel at pushing the envelope, so you'll do it, and probably come out on top! Just be careful that impatience or haste doesn't cause you to overlook something vital.

Thursday, August 23 (Moon in Sagittarius to Capricorn 11:20 a.m.) Stick to your guns. You may have a conflict with a boss or someone else whose authority over you can be intimidating. You know you're on the right track, so don't back down.

Friday, August 24 (Moon in Capricorn) You're in a good position now to begin achieving some of your long-range career goals. Don't lose sight of where you would like to be in five years. Use your trailblazing Aries energy to figure out how to achieve it.

Saturday, August 25 (Moon in Capricorn to Aquarius 6:35 p.m.) Pretty soon, your ruler, Mars, is going to slide into Cancer. This transit places emphasis on your home, so be sure that family issues and concerns are in order before August 28. That way, when the Mars transit arrives, you'll be able to make excellent use of that energy.

Sunday, August 26 (Moon in Aquarius) You meet with your support group. Whatever its central theme, you always gain from this group of people. Take what you learn out into the rest of your life. Belief is a force that can remove obstacles in your life.

Monday, August 27 (Moon in Aquarius to Pisces 10:35 p.m.) The next two days are preparation for when the moon is in your sign. Work on your beliefs about yourself, experiment with dream recall, or treat yourself to a past-life regression. Inner exploration is today's theme.

Tuesday, August 28 (Moon in Pisces) Early-childhood issues may surface. Resolve these issues so you can move forward more smoothly in your life. See a therapist so you have someone impartial with whom you can discuss whatever surfaces. A lunar eclipse in Pisces brings an emotional situation to light over the next six months. It could be related to something that happened to you a long time ago.

Wednesday, August 29 (Moon in Pisces) Dress as wildly as you want; be bold with colors and styles. The moon is in your sign, and you're feeling about as good as it gets. Your impatience may be at a high level, so try to move more slowly with others.

Thursday, August 30 (Moon in Pisces to Aries 12:25 a.m.) It's nice to complete a month with the moon in your sign. It provides you with the self-confidence and fortitude you need to enter a new month—and a new season. Give thanks for all that you have; then go out and celebrate with the one you love.

Friday, August 31 (Moon in Aries) As summer winds down, you're anticipating the fall, the change of seasons, and all the new opportunities this time of year brings with it. Don't take work home with you this weekend.

SEPTEMBER 2007

Saturday, September 1 (Moon in Aries to Taurus 1:36 a.m.) Earth moons may not be your favorites, but they serve a definite purpose. You are forced to be more practical and grounded, particularly in regard to money. Your sensuality may be humming right along, so be prepared!

Sunday, September 2 (Moon in Taurus) You may be challenged about a belief or value that you hold. Don't defend yourself; just ignore the attack and continue on your path. Be sure to balance your checkbook so that all those ATM withdrawals are accounted for! Saturn moves into Virgo, a major transit that lasts for two and a half years. Read on to find out what this means for you.

Monday, September 3 (Moon in Taurus to Gemini 3:31 a.m.) The moon joins Mars in Gemini in your solar third house. This may trigger a situation with a sibling or another relative who demands your attention. It's also a great day to work on any writing or communication projects that you have. Happy Labor Day!

Tuesday, September 4 (Moon in Gemini) Bookstores, TV, the Internet—any and all methods of obtaining information feature in your life. You may not be certain what you're looking for, but you'll recognize it when you find it. And when you do, a major piece of some very strange puzzle will fall into place.

Wednesday, September 5 (Moon in Gemini to Cancer 7:09 a.m.) Mercury moves into Libra and your solar seventh house. This transit favors communication with your partner or significant other and also favors legal contracts and documents.

Thursday, September 6 (Moon in Cancer) You feel nostalgic, perhaps for a former lover or partner. You may feel sad about your family or yearn for the good ol' days. Trust that these feelings will pass and try to be in the moment.

Friday, September 7 (Moon in Cancer to Leo 1:00 p.m.) You may not have your weekend planned out, but that's okay. Events will roll your way, and things will happen spontaneously. One thing is for certain—you're out for fun and enjoyment, and you'll get both in huge doses.

Saturday, September 8 (Moon in Leo) Venus moves direct finally! Your love life now straightens out, you find your comfort zone, and you generally feel better, particularly in your daily work routine.

Sunday, September 9 (Moon in Leo to Virgo 9:11 p.m.) The moon joins Saturn in Virgo in your sixth house this evening. The Saturn transit indicates that you will have heavier work responsibilities for the next few years. There could be delays with recognition for the work you do, but the payoff for you comes when Saturn moves into Libra in late 2009.

Monday, September 10 (Moon in Virgo) Remember that exercise routine you started last month? Time to return to it or to rework it. Schedule that dentist appointment you've put off. With Saturn in Virgo and your sixth house it's important that you safeguard your health.

Tuesday, September 11 (Moon in Virgo) As part of your new nutrition program, you're watching not only calories but carbs, sodium, and cholesterol. Vitamin supplements may be in order too. There's a solar eclipse in Virgo and your solar sixth house. This eclipse brings a work or health issue to light within the next six months.

Wednesday, September 12 (Moon in Virgo to Libra 7:32 a.m.) With all the emphasis on Virgo these days, this moon probably feels like a relief. Even though it opposes your sun, the element is compatible with your Aries sun. Take a closer look at an intimate relationship and decide how or if you can maintain the balance that's required.

Thursday, September 13 (Moon in Libra) You and a business partner reach an amicable agreement about an issue. Even if you have to compromise somewhat to reach this agreement, you feel positive about the outcome. The Libra moon urges you to be a team player.

Friday, September 14 (Moon in Libra to Scorpio 7:37 p.m.) And along comes the most emotionally intense moon in the zodiac. Well, you're forewarned. Now you can navigate these sometimes treacherous waters without fearing that you will lose yourself. You may be called upon to help out someone in need.

Saturday, September 15 (Moon in Scorpio) A good book for a Scorpio moon day: *Lab 257,* which concerns the government's secret germ laboratory on Plum Island. In fact, government conspiracies are an area you delve into. And there are plenty of resources to provide you with all the fodder you might need. Just check out the Internet.

Sunday, September 16 (Moon in Scorpio) The secret love of your childhood walks back into your life. You aren't sure how you feel about this person now. But it's certainly fun to remember your shared history. You realize just how different your perceptions of the past are.

Monday, September 17 (Moon in Scorpio to Sagittarius 8:21 a.m.) You have a handle on a certain situation. You're able to see the larger concept, the deeper truth, and you're able to make an informed decision. Never lose sight of the importance of the bigger picture.

Tuesday, September 18 (Moon in Sagittarius) No better time to get out of town and do something you'll enjoy. This trip could entail a spiritual or mythic quest, something from the deeper layers of your existence.

Wednesday, September 19 (Moon in Sagittarius to Capricorn 7:52 p.m.) One of your parents plays into the day's events. This person has advice you should listen to. You may not like the advice initially, but once you think about it, you realize it's sound.

Thursday, September 20 (Moon in Capricorn) Whatever you present is well received. Your boss and peers are impressed with your passion, your zeal, and your ability to launch new ideas. Your challenge is to finish what you start.

Friday, September 21 (Moon in Capricorn) This lunar transit forms a challenging angle to your sun, but it's like a booster rocket that helps you get things done. Work with the energy rather than resist it, and today will be a much smoother day!

Saturday, September 22 (Moon in Capricorn to Aquarius 4:18 a.m.) Okay, so it's been a challenging couple of days. Now you can kick back and relax a little. You've earned it. In fact, you're ready to hang loose with friends tonight, doing whatever you all enjoy as a group.

Sunday, September 23 (Moon in Aquarius) You're all intellect and action. This may seem like an oxymoron, but it isn't. You're able to think your way to a solution and then act on the situation to bring about that solution. Friends are helpful. Call on them for advice.

Monday, September 24 (Moon in Aquarius to Pisces 8:56 a.m.) This solitary day is good for your soul. And it starts early. In fact, you want to call in sick to work and spend the day writing, painting, photographing, dancing, composing music, whatever brings you creative joy.

Tuesday, September 25 (Moon in Pisces) When the moon joins Uranus in your twelfth house, your insights into your own unconscious are likely to be sudden and extremely helpful. A good book for today? *Jung: A Biography,* by Deirdre Bair.

Wednesday, September 26 (Moon in Pisces to Aries 10:23 a.m.) Put away the books and the solitude. Circulate, achieve, make new friends, find romance. Set your sights high and go for it, Aries!

Thursday, September 27 (Moon in Aries) Mercury moves into Scorpio. For the next few weeks, you'll be so empathic that it's important to associate only with positive, upbeat people. You're likely to keep secrets. You may find yourself entangled in metaphysical questions.

Friday, September 28 (Moon in Aries to Taurus 10:18 a.m.) Mars moves into Cancer and your fourth house. This transit lasts until the end of the year and is sure to stimulate enormous activity at home. You may feel protective of your family during this transit. Try not to smother your kids by being overprotective.

Saturday, September 29 (Moon in Taurus) If you're refurbishing your home, buy new furniture, paint, wallpaper, whatever you need. Get a couple of feng shui books and learn how to enhance the prosperity corner of your home or office.

Sunday, September 30 (Moon in Taurus to Gemini 10:35 a.m.) A neighbor requires attention or advice and you provide it. In return, the neighbor entrusts you with a secret.

OCTOBER 2007

Monday, October 1 (Moon in Gemini) Make the best use possible of the next ten days. On October 11, Mercury turns retrograde in your solar eighth house. This could present challenges in obtaining mortgages or loans. So if you're considering the purchase of a car or home, do it before then.

Tuesday, October 2 (Moon in Gemini to Cancer 12:58 p.m.) Necessity is the mother of invention—isn't that how the saying goes? Today, a necessity at home prompts you to react uncharacteristically. But it turns out to be exactly what's called for.

Wednesday, October 3 (Moon in Cancer) You may be feeling the effects of one of the eclipses today. With the moon in nurturing Cancer, you console or offer advice to a friend, employee, or coworker. Be careful that you don't become so immersed in this person's problems that you neglect self-nurturing.

Thursday, October 4 (Moon in Cancer to Leo 6:28 p.m.) As autumn tinges the air, you're in the mood for adventure, enjoyment, and romance. You and your significant other take in the sights at a new locale and discover just how much in common you have. You teach a child through example.

Friday, October 5 (Moon in Leo) With Saturn bearing down on you at work, you need these Leo moon days to kick back and rediscover the meaning of fun. Don't deny yourself enjoyment, Aries! Treat yourself to something that relates to your creativity.

Saturday, October 6 (Moon in Leo) How much are you willing to risk for romance or creativity, Aries? This is the central question of the day. You're the trailblazer of the zodiac. Where you go, others will follow.

Sunday, October 7 (Moon in Leo to Virgo 3:04 a.m.) Your intuition is speaking loud and clear, but you may not be listening. As a result, you encounter frustration and delays. Once you open up and heed your intuition, things smooth out considerably.

Monday, October 8 (Moon in Virgo) Your responsibilities at work have increased so much that you feel you should be working twelve hours a day. Resist the urge to take work home with you. This is Saturn speaking. However, be sure that the work you do is thorough and complete.

Tuesday, October 9 (Moon in Virgo to Libra 1:58 p.m.) Your cooperation is called for. Your business partner has ideas that you aren't crazy about. But listen with an open mind and then present your side. You may have to compromise, but the end result will be better.

Wednesday, October 10 (Moon in Libra) The balance you seek may elude you unless you can slow down and get a bird's-eye view of the situation. You may have to back off on a particular project or endeavor until the moon moves into your sign.

Thursday, October 11 (Moon in Libra) Mercury turns retrograde in your eighth house. This retrograde involves other people's resources and includes things like insurance, mortgages, loans, wills, and inheritances. Put off dealing with any of these areas until after November 1, when Mercury turns direct again.

Friday October 12 (Moon in Libra to Scorpio 2:14 a.m.) You're investigating something that has puzzled you. By following your intuitive guidance, you'll find what you're looking for much more quickly than if you rely just on left-brain logic. A Pisces or a Cancer may be helpful.

Saturday, October 13 (Moon in Scorpio) Your dreams may be particularly powerful and vivid. Keep your dream journal updated and practice dream recall. Gradually, the symbolism of your own unconscious will become clearer. In a sense, you're defining your personal myth.

Sunday, October 14 (Moon in Scorpio to Sagittarius 2:58 p.m.) You feel energized under the Sagittarius moon, just as you do under the Leo moon. Your sex appeal soars and your self-confidence attracts the people and opportunities that you need to solidify your beliefs.

Monday, October 15 (Moon in Sagittarius) Practice visualizing your goals and long-range dreams. See yourself doing whatever you hope to achieve. The more often you practice this and the more vividly you can imagine it, the greater your chances of attaining it. As a follow-up, page through Brian Green's masterpiece, *The Fabric of the Cosmos.*

Tuesday, October 16 (Moon in Sagittarius) Your spiritual quest may take you overseas to ancient sites that hold tantalizing mysteries: Stonehenge, Easter Island, the Galapagos. If strange memories or feelings surface, look for their source in past lives.

Wednesday, October 17 (Moon in Sagittarius to Capricorn 3:04 a.m.) The edgier you feel, the more important it is to ground your emotions in work that moves you toward a practical outcome. Your work is noticed by your boss, and there's talk about a promotion.

Thursday, October 18 (Moon in Capricorn) You have some unusual insights about your career. You may decide to take your energies in a new direction. A peer seeks your advice on a personal matter.

Friday, October 19 (Moon in Capricorn to Aquarius 12:52 p.m.) You meet up with old friends and spend time catching up on where your lives have gone since you last got together. It leaves you feeling nostalgic—yet also exhilarated.

Saturday, October 20 (Moon in Aquarius) You attend a workshop or seminar concerning a topic that intrigues you and provides you with insight about your own dreams and goals. You may dabble in astrology or some other form of divination today.

Sunday, October 21 (Moon in Aquarius to Pisces 7:03 p.m.) It's a day for you and a friend or partner to just enjoy yourseves quietly, exploring who you are and where you're going as individuals. What contributions can you make collectively and individually to the larger world?

Monday, October 22 (Moon in Pisces) A dream provides you with information or an idea that feeds right into your current creative projects. The information could be quite specific, so pay attention. Your intuition leads you in a new direction.

Tuesday, October 23 (Moon in Pisces to Aries 9:25 p.m.) Launch new projects and brainstorm with coworkers for ideas. If you've considered opening your own business, begin laying the foundation.

Wednesday, October 24 (Moon in Aries) Back to that business idea, Aries. Lay the groundwork, but don't sign any contracts until after November 1, when Mercury turns direct. Someone from your past may reenter your life today through e-mail, a call, or a letter.

Thursday, October 25 (Moon in Aries to Taurus 9:08 p.m.) This evening, you suddenly turn practical and stubborn. You surprise your family and friends, but you feel quite firmly about the opinion or stance you're defending. If you're expecting a check, it may not arrive until early November.

Friday, October 26 (Moon in Taurus) An earth-sign individual helps you with a personal matter. You may not like the way this person handles his or her own affairs, but the help you get about your concerns is sound. An unusual piece of jewelry or art catches your eye. It's pricey, though, and you should put off the purchase until the checks have cleared!

Saturday, October 27 (Moon in Taurus to Gemini 8:12 p.m.) You seem to spend a lot of time in your car, running errands, carpooling, or shopping. You dislike the disruption in your weekend festivities, but if you go with the flow, Aries, you'll be a lot happier.

Sunday, October 28 (Moon in Gemini) You may adopt a stray. And if it's not outright adoption, you make it clear to the animal that it has found a safe haven where three meals a day are served and there's a warm bed at night. You meet some resistance about this from a partner, but the animal wins over the reluctant human.

Monday, October 29 (Moon in Gemini to Cancer 8:50 p.m.) You and your kids are getting ready for Halloween. You buy costumes, decorate, and replenish the trick-or-treat supplies. If you don't have kids, you may act like a big kid for Halloween and toss your own party!

Tuesday, October 30 (Moon in Cancer) Living from a place of fear only serves to attract reasons to be afraid. When you wake this morning, repeat, "I am safe." If you feel inner resistance when you say the words, repeat them frequently throughout the day (and the next and the next) until the resistance is gone.

Wednesday, October 31 (Moon in Cancer) Where yesterday's mantra was "I am safe," today's is "I love and approve of myself." You're preparing yourself for when the moon moves into Leo tomorrow. By then, you'll be in the spotlight. Happy Halloween!

NOVEMBER 2007

Thursday, November 1 (Moon in Cancer to Leo 12:48 a.m.) Pack your bags, apply for a mortgage, get a loan. Mercury is now moving direct again. And with the moon in Leo, your love life suddenly picks up! In fact, November is a busy month in the zodiac with Venus, Mars, and Uranus changing signs or directions. Stay tuned!

Friday, November 2 (Moon in Leo) Your children—or someone else's kids—play active roles in your life. You may get a creative break that takes you to a completely new level. Listen to your hunches.

Saturday, November 3 (Moon in Leo to Virgo 8:45 a.m.) The moon joins Saturn in your sixth house (again!). You should have some idea of what this combination feels like. Delays and restrictions fall on one side of possible scenarios, and responsibility and efficiency fall on the other. Try to strike a balance between the two that you can live with.

Sunday, November 4—Daylight Saving Time Ends (Moon in Virgo) Start scheduling your week and prioritizing what you need to accomplish. You're going to be picky, and it's best if you keep your criticism to yourself rather than projecting it on others.

Monday, November 5 (Moon in Virgo to Libra 6:47 p.m.) You have to mediate for friends or with a partner. It's not over a major issue, but it is important that all parties understand the ground rules. Communicate succinctly and clearly.

Tuesday, November 6 (Moon in Libra) You're moving ahead on a contract negotiation, and things are looking very encouraging. Be sure that you have delineated what you expect and don't settle for anything less.

Wednesday, November 7 (Moon in Libra) A great book for a Libra moon day? *Life of Pi* by Yann Martel. In the meantime, nurture your patience. You'll need it with a romantic or business partner.

Thursday, November 8 (Moon in Libra to Scorpio 7:19 a.m.) Venus moves into Libra, an excellent transit for your love life! Even though Venus now forms a challenging angle to your sun, your relationships will still benefit. This transit lasts until early December.

Friday, November 9 (Moon in Scorpio) It may be a day of unexpected beginnings and endings. But take heart,

Aries. Your life actually is unfolding exactly in sync with the way your deepest beliefs have designed it. If you dislike what you're experiencing, change your beliefs.

Saturday, November 10 (Moon in Scorpio to Sagittarius 7:59 p.m.) It's usually a relief for you when the moon moves from a water sign into a fire sign. You suddenly come alive and feel as if you're waking from a deep sleep. Your mood attracts attention from someone special.

Sunday, November 11 (Moon in Sagittarius) Pretty soon, Mars in Cancer turns retrograde in your fourth house. Prepare for it by making sure that your family concerns are in order. In other words, start making plans for Thanksgiving. You may want to do the same thing for Christmas since Mars will be retrograde until New Year's Eve.

Monday, November 12 (Moon in Sagittarius) You're in the groove, Aries. Regardless of which groove it is, you're exactly where you should be. Is it serendipity or synchronicity? Either way, you're in charge.

Tuesday, November 13 (Moon in Sagittarius to Capricorn 8:01 a.m.) A short business trip may be in order. Pack light, but be prepared for virtually anything, from casual to formal evening wear. A Virgo sheds light on a puzzling situation you encounter on the trip.

Wednesday, November 14 (Moon in Capricorn) Sometimes, this moon can feel like an irritating itch to you, Aries. You aren't sure what's causing the itch; all you want to do is scratch it. But if you can't find the source of your discomfort, you won't be able to alleviate it. It may involve someone who is close to you professionally.

Thursday, November 15 (Moon in Capricorn to Aquarius 6:31 p.m.) Mars turns retrograde in Cancer. Since this movement happens in your solar fourth house, you should be careful about accidents at home. Don't be in such a rush that you become careless, especially if you're involved in any home-improvement jobs.

Friday, November 16 (Moon in Aquarius) You're preparing for the Thanksgiving holidays. Whether you're going away or having people over, make sure that all the details are attended to and that your plans are in place soon. Whatever you're doing, try not to create more stress for yourself.

Saturday, November 17 (Moon in Aquarius) Your friends are important to you. You may be acting as someone else's support system. These events somehow revolve around your dreams and wishes.

Sunday, November 18 (Moon in Aquarius to Pisces 2:15 a.m.) Even if you don't feel like it, head to the gym or a yoga or aerobics class. You need to distract yourself from a constant inner dialogue. You may visit someone in a hospital or nursing home this afternoon.

Monday, November 19 (Moon in Pisces) During meditation or through a dream, you discover information or stumble upon an insight that illuminates a concern you have. Never underestimate the power of your subconscious mind.

Tuesday, November 20 (Moon in Pisces to Aries 6:25 a.m.) Your Thanksgiving preparations are in high gear and may be fluctuating by the hour. That's okay. Thanks to the moon in your sign, you're in a high power mode today. You can roll with all the punches.

Wednesday, November 21 (Moon in Aries) With Venus in Libra and the moon in your own sign, you're feeling romantic, even passionate. Despite a few minor glitches in communication, your partner is impressed with your indomitable spirit.

Thursday, November 22 (Moon in Aries to Taurus 7:19 a.m.) You dig in your heels today and won't budge an inch. This may be a good thing, but don't overdo it. Even if you're right, the other person may find your attitude overbearing. Besides, it's Thanksgiving!

Friday, November 23 (Moon in Taurus) Watch your finances. There may be a discrepancy between your balance and the bank's. If things have been tense or uncomfortable at home, just step back and detach emotionally. Part of the problem may be that you feel volatile.

Saturday, November 24 (Moon in Taurus to Gemini 6:29 a.m.) You've earned some time off. If you can shuffle your work responsibilities around right now, by all means do so. What's really important is that you live every day as though it's your last.

Sunday, November 25 (Moon in Gemini) If you're still enjoying the company of family and friends for the Thanksgiving holidays, gather everyone around and head out to do something fun. Be sure to solicit opinions from the kids in your group about what constitutes fun.

Monday, November 26 (Moon in Gemini to Cancer 6:07 a.m.) The moon joins retrograde Mars in your fourth house. You could be suffering from indigestion. Try papaya enzymes to settle your stomach. It might be time to alter your diet somewhat. Vegetarian, anyone?

Tuesday, November 27 (Moon in Cancer) Relax, Aries. Pretty soon, your home will be your own again. Rather than doing all the cleanup yourself, hire a cleaning service. Put off major house renovations until spring. After all, the holidays are just around the corner, and you'll be spending plenty.

Wednesday, November 28 (Moon in Cancer to Leo 8:23 a.m.) Finally, another fire sign moon. Get out and enjoy yourself with friends or family.

Thursday, November 29 (Moon in Leo) A child teaches you something about humility and gratitude. Synchronicities abound. You're feeling more sensitive and attuned to your family and kids, and they notice and appreciate it.

Friday, November 30 (Moon in Leo to Virgo 2:45 p.m.) Your critical eye is turned on. You notice imperfections. Keep your criticisms to yourself. You won't win any friends by being critical.

DECEMBER 2007

Saturday, December 1 (Moon in Virgo) Mercury moves into Sagittarius and your ninth house. This transit, which lasts until December 20, favors writing, publishing, and higher education. Your thoughts are on foreign places.

Sunday, December 2 (Moon in Virgo) Your perfectionist tendencies may annoy people who are close to you. Turn your focus to health issues or projects at work that you need to tackle this week. Exercise is an excellent outlet for the energies of the Virgo moon.

Monday, December 3 (Moon in Virgo to Libra 1:02 a.m.) Light is shed on a relationship issue. Whatever you learn helps you navigate a personal or professional relationship more smoothly. You may have to be more of a team player.

Tuesday, December 4 (Moon in Libra) You're in the mood for holiday shopping; you're on a search for a gift for your partner or significant other. You've got your special account to draw from, and it looks as if a piece of art is the hands-down winner!

Wednesday, December 5 (Moon in Libra to Scorpio 1:32 p.m.) Venus moves into Scorpio and your solar eighth house. This transit lasts until the end of December. If you become romantically involved, the relationship is sure to be emotionally and sexually intense.

Thursday, December 6 (Moon in Scorpio) The moon joins Venus in your eighth house. Your intuition is remarkable. Listen to it and you'll be in the right place at the right time. A Pisces or a Taurus figures into the day's events.

Friday, December 7 (Moon in Scorpio) Look for end-of-the-year tax cuts. Consult with your accountant. It's possible that a big-ticket item could provide the exact tax benefit you need. Are your insurance payments up-to-date? How about your will?

Saturday, December 8 (Moon in Scorpio to Sagittarius 2:12 a.m.) This should be a stimulating day. You're on a roll with education, publishing, an overseas trip, and spirituality. It all depends on your particular slant in life and where you are in the scheme of your life.

Sunday, December 9 (Moon in Sagittarius) An idea is only that until you do something with it. The big question for you is how far can you take your idea? Do you have the support group to help you? The finances? Is the market large enough to accommodate your idea?

Monday, December 10 (Moon in Sagittarius to Capricorn 1:51 p.m.) The holiday spirit is definitely in the air, even at work. You can tap into this generosity of spirit to further your own agenda. Be careful that you don't step on any toes.

Tuesday, December 11 (Moon in Capricorn) Your professional planning and strategy begin to pay off. You're due a raise or promotion, and it looks as if you could get it early next year, if not by the end of this year. Don't spend the money yet, Aries!

Wednesday, December 12 (Moon in Capricorn) You're torn between career and family obligations. You may have to balance the two somehow. Perhaps a friend or relative can help you out. Accept aid when it's offered.

Thursday, December 13 (Moon in Capricorn to Aquarius 12:02 a.m.) Saturn and retrograde Mars are traveling in a nice angle to each other, and they bring some unusual events into your home and creative life. Your friends or support group may provide the unusual events.

Friday, December 14 (Moon in Aquarius) Today requires an adjustment in your thinking concerning friends or family issues. Nothing serious, Aries. It's just time to slow down and develop a bit of introspection so that you can successfully navigate the busy holidays.

Saturday, December 15 (Moon in Aquarius to Pisces 8:15 a.m.) When the moon joins Uranus in Pisces, you can count on unusual emotional responses. It could be that people around you are acting erratically as well. Don't obsess about it. Just move on.

Sunday, December 16 (Moon in Pisces) Venus and Uranus are winking at each other across the heavens! If you meet a special someone, it could be a highly unusual and idiosyncratic relationship. You'll enjoy the adventure and the romance, Aries. But don't be hasty about commitment.

Monday, December 17 (Moon in Pisces to Aries 1:53 p.m.) Now that the moon is moving into your sign again, life evens out somewhat. You're in such a high and frivolous mood that you and friends and family hit the mall for holiday shopping. Even inclement weather can't dampen your spirits.

Tuesday, December 18 (Moon in Aries) Get all your shopping done. By tomorrow, you won't be feeling quite as frivolous. You and your partner head out on the town this evening. Jupiter moves into Capricorn and will be there for the next year. This transit is excellent for an expansion in your career.

Wednesday, December 19 (Moon in Aries to Taurus 4:38 p.m.) Saturn in Virgo turns retrograde in your sixth house. This could mean more responsibility at work through the end of the year. Responsibility doesn't bother you, not as long as you get credit for what you do.

Thursday, December 20 (Moon in Taurus) Mercury joins Jupiter in Capricorn. You've got great ideas about how to expand your career. You'll begin to implement these ideas early next year. In the meantime, write down all your thoughts and plans.

Friday, December 21 (Moon in Taurus to Gemini 5:14 p.m.) If you've taken time off for the holiday, then today will be especially enjoyable. Friends drop by; family members arrive. Your holidays are in full swing!

Saturday, December 22 (Moon in Gemini) E-mails and phone calls concern a relative or neighbor who needs support and help. You and others in your area rally to the cause. The spirit of the holidays, after all, isn't just about gifts. It's about loving and helping one another.

Sunday, December 23 (Moon in Gemini to Cancer 5:19 p.m.) Your mother or another nurturing female figures into the day's events. Perhaps it's your mom's birthday! If so, make sure she feels loved and appreciated.

Monday, December 24 (Moon in Cancer) How appropriate that on Christmas Eve, the moon is in home-loving Cancer. You feel nostalgic, grateful, and protective of your loved ones. You may also feel torn between your obligations to your career and your family. For today and tomorrow, leave your work at the office.

Tuesday, December 25 (Moon in Cancer to Leo 6:53 p.m.) Romance should be great. Both you and your partner are in buoyant moods, and your romantic feelings are helped along by Venus and Neptune as they move at harmonious angles through the heavens. At the end of the day, the memories you take away from this Christmas can get you through many cold nights!

Wednesday, December 26 (Moon in Leo) You shine among your family and friends. Your generosity is rewarded by their loyalty and love. Even if you're still feeling some career angst, know that Jupiter is prepared to help expand your opportunities!

Thursday, December 27 (Moon in Leo to Virgo 11:45 p.m.) Late tonight, you wake in a near panic, thinking about the little things that have to be done tomorrow. It's just the Virgo moon whispering to you. Ignore it for now. You'll have plenty of time to tidy up loose ends.

Friday, December 28 (Moon in Virgo) Start planning today for New Year's Eve. If you don't want to have the party at your place (and you may not), rent a clubhouse or another space for the evening. It might be less stressful!

Saturday, December 29 (Moon in Virgo) List your goals for the next year. You're in a frame of mind where you can think clearly about this. While you're at it, create a five-year plan for yourself. These goals should be personal as well as professional.

Sunday, December 30 (Moon in Virgo to Libra 8:38 a.m.) Venus moves into Sagittarius and your solar ninth house. This transit favors romance overseas or with someone you met through publishing, higher education, or spiritual practice. Your deeper beliefs enter a period of greater smoothness, and you can begin to incorporate them into the rest of your life.

Monday, December 31 (Moon in Libra) Balance and cooperation may be called for this evening. It looks like a very nice day and night to spend with your spouse or significant other.

HAPPY NEW YEAR!

JANUARY 2008

Tuesday January 1 (Moon in Libra to Scorpio 8:33 p.m.) New Year's Day begins on a romantic note, with the moon in your seventh house of partnership. But as the day moves forward, emotions become more intense. You may be looking for the absolute bottom line concerning an issue or concern. Practice patience, Aries.

Wednesday, January 2 (Moon in Scorpio) It's a good time to check on your insurance policies and to make sure accounts are current. Someone close to you could need help in this area too. Something nags at you for most of the day, but it's like an itch you can't scratch. Wait until the moon is in Sagittarius to figure out what's bugging you.

Thursday, January 3 (Moon in Scorpio) With Mercury in Capricorn at the beginning of the year, you may be traveling for business between January 1 and 7. Contract negotiations are also possible. Allow your hunches to guide you in this regard.

Friday, January 4 (Moon in Scorpio to Sagittarius 9:14 a.m.) Oh, how you love the Sagittarius moon! It stimulates your mind and prompts you to think about your personal philosophy and beliefs. Today, in fact, you may be revamping your educational goals. You could be toying with the idea of studying overseas.

Saturday, January 5 (Moon in Sagittarius) You have the larger picture, and it helps you to connect the dots concerning an issue or situation. Don't rush to make any decisions, Aries. Bide your time and let things unfold. Then decide what to do.

Sunday, January 6 (Moon in Sagittarius to Capricorn 8:43 p.m.) As the moon joins Jupiter and Pluto in your tenth house this evening, it's time to lay out your career plans and make your goals. Try a weekly goal. Then a monthly goal. Then get really ambitious and go wild: six-month goals.

Monday, January 7 (Moon in Capricorn) Mercury moves into Aquarius. You and friends commiserate about career and professional matters. Your mind is particularly sharp and you're able to visualize exactly what you would like for yourself in terms of a career.

Tuesday, January 8 (Moon in Capricorn) With the moon moving through your career house, your thoughts are focused on professional matters. A boss or coworker notices how hard you've been working and the attention pays off down the line.

Wednesday, January 9 (Moon in Capricorn to Aquarius 6:13 a.m.) The moon joins Mercury in Aquarius in your eleventh house. You have your choice of social activities. Regardless of what you do or where you go, friends figure in the day's equation in a major way. You may be rethinking your goals.

Thursday, January 10 (Moon in Aquarius) Your support of a friend is remembered long after today. You're loyal when it counts, Aries. Your friends and family know that. On other fronts, you may be confused about a relationship; talking it over with a close friend is the best way to define the problem.

Friday, January 11 (Moon in Aquarius to Pisces 1:44 p.m.) You aren't fond of the Pisces moon. It seems to leave you feeling ambivalent and undecided. Besides, it's in your twelfth house with Uranus; the combination could bring about unusual emotional reactions.

Saturday, January 12 (Moon in Pisces) You visit a friend or family member in the hospital or sick at home. Bring a gift. It doesn't have to be anything expensive. Even a bouquet of flowers will be appreciated.

Sunday, January 13 (Moon in Pisces to Aries 7:24 p.m.) With the moon entering your sign early this evening, you're on a roll. Tackle projects and issues about which you have procrastinated. If you're involved with someone, plan for a romantic evening.

Monday, January 14 (Moon in Aries) You're in your element. Bosses, coworkers, and partners pay attention to you today. Your sex appeal and self-confidence are at an all-time high. Use them to your advantage, but without hurting anyone else!

Tuesday, January 15 (Moon in Aries to Taurus 11:13 p.m.) Your focus is on what makes you feel emotionally secure. Is it money or thrills, chills, and constant excitement? Maybe a stable home life? It's important for you to figure this out, Aries.

Wednesday, January 16 (Moon in Taurus) With both Mars and Venus in Sagittarius, your romantic life may be taking an upward swing with a foreigner. Or is this person's belief system foreign to you? Whatever it is, romance and love look awfully appealing right now.

Thursday, January 17 (Moon in Taurus) You're noticeably more stubborn. And that's fine. It's exactly what's needed for the situation. Just be careful that you're not so stubborn you spite yourself! You're enthusiastic about a new project, and that may require some stubbornness to win support.

Friday, January 18 (Moon in Taurus to Gemini 1:30 a.m.) If travel is on your mind, blame the Gemini moon! It has entered your third house of travel and communication. Expect to be on the road more than usual, perhaps carpooling or driving your kids to after-school activities. Be sure to save time for yourself later in the day.

Saturday, January 19 (Moon in Gemini) The last week of the month is going to be hectic. Three planets are going to change signs or directions, so you can expect more activities related to your career, social life, and romance. The dates to watch for are January 24, 28, and 30.

Sunday, January 20 (Moon in Gemini to Cancer 3:06 a.m.) Get together with your family today—blood, adopted, extended, it doesn't matter. It's a fine time to cement bonds, to apologize and forgive. Release the past and move on. You aren't the type to hold grudges.

Monday, January 21 (Moon in Cancer) Your mother or another nurturing female in your life has advice you need to hear. Whether you follow it is up to you. But it's important that you listen. You may feel some conflict between home and professional obligations.

Tuesday, January 22 (Moon in Cancer to Leo 5:22 a.m.) Now here's a moon you love. Romance heats up and everything you do for fun and pleasure is splashy, large, excessive. In fact, a certain someone flatters you, and you eat the attention up.

Wednesday, January 23 (Moon in Leo) With the moon in emotional Leo, you feel the need for more commitment from the one you love. You usually tend to be quite independent, but your need for emotional intimacy overpowers everything else.

Thursday, January 24 (Moon in Leo to Virgo 9:49 a.m.) Venus enters Capricorn and your tenth house. This transit favors success and ease in professional matters. It's also possible that a flirtation with a boss or peer heats up and becomes something more.

Friday, January 25 (Moon in Virgo) A major change happens as Pluto enters Capricorn. This transit lasts into late 2024, so it behooves you to see where Capricorn is in your birth chart. Expect gradual but profound change in that area of your natal chart. If you have Aries rising, as well as an Aries sun, Pluto will enter your tenth house of careers, spelling big changes.

Saturday, January 26 (Moon in Virgo to Libra 5:36 p.m.) This afternoon, the moon enters Libra and your seventh house. Your focus turns to your closest partnerships, both personal and professional. Be sure you give your partner the attention he or she deserves. Now isn't the time to cut corners on business contracts.

Sunday, January 27 (Moon in Libra) If you have a contract pending, insist on signing. Tomorrow, Mercury turns retrograde, and you don't want to sign then. In fact, you should prepare yourself with friends and groups because that retrograde will be in Aquarius, your eleventh house of friends!

Monday, January 28 (Moon in Libra) If you haven't backed up your computer files, be sure to do so early. Over the next few weeks, do it daily. Mercury retrograde often plays havoc with computers and other communication devices.

Tuesday, January 29 (Moon in Libra to Scorpio 4:35 a.m.) You aren't especially fond of the Scorpio moon. Too much deep stuff. Too much emotion. But this transit can turn you into an effective detective and researcher. That research may concern the resources and finances you share with someone else.

Wednesday, January 30 (Moon in Scorpio) Mars turns direct, which is good news for you, Aries, since it rules your sign. You now have the get up and go to do whatever you need to do, and then some! Try to exercise patience for people who don't move or think as quickly as you do.

Thursday, January 31 (Moon in Scorpio to Sagittarius 5:08 p.m.) Your travel bug is back with a vengeance. But since Mercury is retrograde, confine yourself to virtual traveling. Get on the Internet and check out the latest winter deals.

FEBRUARY 2008

Friday, February 1 (Moon in Sagittarius) As one of the bleakest months of winter begins, you feel as if you're basking on a Caribbean beach. Expect an appliance to go on the fritz or your computer to get a virus or your travel plans to get messed up. Not to worry. That's par for Mercury retrograde. By February 18, you'll be on course again.

Saturday, February 2 (Moon in Sagittarius) If there's a know-it-all in your midst, don't bother arguing or debating with this person. Neither of you will change the other's views. If it's such a pressing issue for you, wait until the moon is in your sign and you've got all the facts to back up your argument.

Sunday, February 3 (Moon in Sagittarius to Capricorn 4:52 a.m.) The moon joins Pluto and Jupiter in your tenth house. You have the emotional resources to tackle a professional issue or situation. Lay out your strategy today and implement it tomorrow.

Monday, February 4 (Moon in Capricorn) Even though the Capricorn moon can feel uncomfortable for you, it helps you to focus and home in on what you need to do to accomplish a goal. A boss or peer has advice you need to hear about how to get ahead in the game.

Tuesday, February 5 (Moon in Capricorn to Aquarius 2:10 p.m.) With the moon moving into compatible Aquarius, your social life picks up steam. You may meet with your support group this evening to brainstorm. There's someone in your group whose true nature you don't see clearly.

Wednesday, February 6 (Moon in Aquarius) Over the next six months, the solar eclipse in Aquarius could trigger events that allow you to see a friendship in a clearer light. It may also help you to revise a goal or dream that you have. Check your natal chart to see if you have any planets at 17 degrees in an air or a fire sign. If you do, the eclipse may have a big impact on you.

Thursday, February 7 (Moon in Aquarius to Pisces 8:47 p.m.) The moon's entry into Pisces and your twelfth house may leave you feeling dreamy and indecisive. Your dreams are especially vivid, so glean the information you need from them.

Friday, February 8 (Moon in Pisces) Past-life memories could surface. They may rouse dreams that you remember when you're doing something routine. Explore these memories. Try to figure out what connection they have to your present life.

Saturday, February 9 (Moon in Pisces) If you're faced with making a decision, try putting it off until the moon is in your sign. Then there won't be any conflict between your head and your heart. For today, do something fun and imaginative.

Sunday, February 10 (Moon in Pisces to Aries 1:18 a.m.) The moon is in your sign. Make decisions you've put off and get started on that home-improvement project you've been intending to do. Whatever you do should go well. You have the impetus and drive to make things happen.

Monday, February 11 (Moon in Aries) Take your charisma and go to bat for someone around you who needs help. You can raise awareness and support by doing little more than just asking. Is a flirtation at work becoming more serious?

Tuesday, February 12 (Moon in Aries to Taurus 4:35 a.m.) With the moon entering your second house of finances and Venus in Capricorn moving through your tenth house of careers, there may be talk about a raise or promotion. The big question for you, Aries, is whether you're tired of the job.

Wednesday, February 13 (Moon in Taurus) Time to check your accounts, Aries. That means balancing your checkbook and taking a hard, honest look at how you spend, earn, and save money. Are your values and the way you earn your living in sync?

Thursday, February 14 (Moon in Taurus to Gemini 7:20 a.m.) Happy Valentine's Day! Set aside time for the one you love. Plan something romantic! Gather your information about a pressing issue. Try the Internet's resources first.

Friday, February 15 (Moon in Gemini) You have a lot on your mind and a lot to say. Get everything out into the open. Be honest, but calm. Have your facts straight. Don't dwell on the past. Once you've said your piece, move forward.

Saturday, February 16 (Moon in Gemini to Cancer 10:30 a.m.) As the moon enters your fourth house this morning, your attention turns to home and hearth. You may have friends or relatives over for dinner this evening. Or your kids may have plans that necessitate a ride!

Sunday, February 17 (Moon in Cancer) Venus enters Aquarius and your eleventh house. This terrific transit favors romance with a friend or with someone you meet through friends. Wait until after Mercury turns direct tomorrow.

Monday, February 18 (Moon in Cancer to Leo 1:52 p.m.) Mercury turns direct, which is cause for celebration for everyone! Tomorrow, make the reservations for the trip you've been wanting to take. Sign back on to your e-mail account. Get connected.

Tuesday, February 19 (Moon in Leo) People are watching you. It's hard not to notice you, Aries! Your self-confidence is soaring. A special someone may extend an invitation for dinner. Are you ready for romance?

Wednesday, February 20 (Moon in Leo to Virgo 7:07 p.m.) The lunar eclipse at 10 degrees Virgo is in your sixth house of daily health and work. Expect an emotional issue to surface concerning health or work. You could feel somewhat crazed. Actually, if you can afford the time, take the day off.

Thursday, February 21 (Moon in Virgo) You're quite the perfectionist. Good thing. Your desk is piled high with things that needed your attention yesterday. Work your way through the pile slowly, meticulously, and you'll get to the bottom by the end of the day.

Friday, February 22 (Moon in Virgo) You're more discerning when it comes to work. Be wise and delegate some responsibility. Be sure that the people you pick to do the job adhere to your standards. You're on a roll. You just don't know it yet.

Saturday, February 23 (Moon in Virgo to Libra 2:45 a.m.) The Libra moon can be both beautiful and problematic for you. It urges you to cooperate with others, when you may feel like going your own way. This moon also makes it necessary to focus on intimate relationships. However, it heightens your artistic appreciation for beauty; how can that be a bad thing?

Sunday, February 24 (Moon in Libra) You and your partner are feeling romantic and may decide to head out of town to someplace you've never been before. A little exploration. Travel is a good way to get to know the one you love.

Monday, February 25 (Moon in Libra to Scorpio 1:06 a.m.) You find your thoughts turning to the big questions: What's your purpose in life? What happens when you die? Sign up for a seminar on a topic that interests you and takes you in a different direction.

Tuesday, February 26 (Moon in Scorpio) Time to see your accountant and look for write-offs before tax day. While you're at it, get your papers in order.

Wednesday, February 27 (Moon in Scorpio) Your emotions are intense and deep. Play your hand, but keep your strategy to yourself. Other people would like to hear your secrets, but you're better off keeping them to yourself.

Thursday, February 28 (Moon in Scorpio to Sagittarius 1:23 a.m.) You wake up in a gregarious mood and can't wait to get down to business. You have a handle on a problem or an issue that has been bothering you; you know how to resolve it.

Friday, February 29 (Moon in Sagittarius) Your in-laws make a surprise visit. Be nice, Aries. Take everyone out to dinner. Show your appreciation for your family, even if they aren't blood relatives!

MARCH 2008

Saturday, March 1 (Moon in Sagittarius to Capricorn 1:33 p.m.) You and a boss or a professional peer get together for some kind of social activity. With both Mercury and Mars moving direct, you're in the mood to discuss, party, and to win over those who may be skeptical about your ideas and plans.

Sunday, March 2 (Moon in Capricorn) Everything in your public life is expanding. New opportunities arrive in your e-mail almost daily. The toughest thing, Aries, will be deciding which direction you want to go professionally.

Monday, March 3 (Moon in Capricorn to Aquarius 11:25 p.m.) The moon enters compatible Aquarius, so it isn't surprising that you and friends get together after work. These individuals have ideas and passions similar to your own. Brainstorm. Be sure someone in the group takes notes.

Tuesday, March 4 (Moon in Aquarius) Mars enters Cancer and your fourth house. This transit spurs lots of activity related to your family and personal life over the next two months. You may set up a home office, do renovations on your home, or even move, if you've been making preparations in that direction.

Wednesday, March 5 (Moon in Aquarius) The gathering tonight is at your place. Nothing fancy. But have some extra food and drinks on hand. On the work front, friends are in your corner today; some of these people are like family to you. Be sure to show your appreciation.

Thursday, March 6 (Moon in Aquarius to Pisces 5:54 a.m.) The moon enters your twelfth house early this morning. You may be feeling nostalgic for the past, especially about your childhood or a relationship concerning a parent. Try to write about your feelings and hunches.

Friday, March 7 (Moon in Pisces) Compassion and idealism are your hallmarks. And emotions show too. Other people notice the difference in you and comment on it. Your dream life is especially vivid, so be sure to keep a journal next to your bed to record your dream excursions.

Saturday, March 8 (Moon in Pisces to Aries 9:24 a.m.) There's a perceptible shift in your mood. The dreamy ambivalence of the last few days is replaced with resolute action. People around you think you've got the answers. Even if you don't see yourself as an authority, give the best guidance and advice that you can.

Sunday, March 9—Daylight Saving Time Begins (Moon in Aries) You're a bundle of such incredible energy that you're able to sweep up everyone around you and enlist their help. Whether it's a home-improvement project, a family vacation, or a work-related endeavor, your enthusiasm is infectious.

Monday, March 10 (Moon in Aries to Taurus 12:15 p.m.) Someone close to you challenges your values. Are you ready to defend what you believe? Can you do it without anger? Aim for passion, not empty rhetoric.

Tuesday, March 11 (Moon in Taurus) Pretty things catch your attention today: jewelry, art, expensive stuff. Indulge yourself, but only if you can afford to. Determine what makes you feel emotionally secure and then strive to create those conditions in your life.

Wednesday, March 12 (Moon in Taurus to Gemini 1:55 p.m.) Venus enters Pisces and your twelfth house. This transit, which lasts until April 6, opens up the possibility of a secret romance. You aren't exactly the secretive type, so if you consent to secrecy, it won't last once Venus moves into your sign on April 6.

Thursday, March 13 (Moon in Gemini) You have more contact than usual with siblings and neighbors. Maybe it's due to the touch of spring in the air or to that secret love affair. Have an urge to tell all, Aries? Keep things to yourself.

Friday, March 14 (Moon in Gemini to Cancer 4:38 p.m.) Mercury joins Venus and Uranus in your twelfth house. This combination eases communication between you and your partner. If you're a writer, you can count on smooth sailing for the next several weeks. You'll be able to find the ideas, characters, and story lines you need.

Saturday, March 15 (Moon in Cancer) It's a home day, Aries. Whether you're single or married, a parent or not, you putter around the house, putting things in order. If you're a parent, plan something fun for your kid this weekend.

Sunday, March 16 (Moon in Cancer to Leo 9:04 p.m.) You're primed for pleasure and showmanship. Others look up to you as a paragon of whatever they are trying to achieve. Someone comes to you for guidance. Be sure to listen rather than talk about yourself!

Monday, March 17 (Moon in Leo) With three planets in your twelfth house and the moon in your fifth, your secret romance is really heating up. You, however, want to show off your new love; this could be a big problem in early April.

Tuesday, March 18 (Moon in Leo) You get together with friends this evening. Don't get all bent out of shape if people fail to acknowledge you in the way you think you deserve. The Leo moon can bring your ego into focus. Your need for applause will have passed by tomorrow.

Wednesday, March 19 (Moon in Leo to Virgo 3:25 a.m.) The things that need your attention require a knowledge and recognition of details. If health matters prevail, be sure you have all the facts before making a decision. It could be something as simple as whether you should join a particular gym.

Thursday, March 20 (Moon in Virgo) Make appointments with your doctor, dentist, or trainer. You may want to alter your exercise routine to accommodate the warm weather. Why not start walking a mile a day and watch the pounds melt away?

Friday, March 21 (Moon in Virgo to Libra 11:45 a.m.) You and your partner spend a romantic evening together. It doesn't matter where you go as long as you're together. Your artistic abilities shine in the most beautiful ways.

Saturday, March 22 (Moon in Libra) If you're a reader, find a book that will fire up your idealism. You and friends get together this evening for the opening night of a long-awaited movie.

Sunday, March 23 (Moon in Libra to Scorpio 10:07 p.m.) With your ruler, Mars, still transiting your fourth house, your home life is chaotic. But it's the kind of chaos on which you thrive, Aries. Let it feed your artistic and creative side.

Monday, March 24 (Moon in Scorpio) You're an emotional powerhouse. If being so makes you uncomfortable, just try to get through the day without taking anything personally. Follow your instincts. Your intuition is heightened, particularly when it comes to relationships and other people's motives.

Tuesday, March 25 (Moon in Scorpio) Something requires intensive research and detective work. If you're working on a long-term project, collect facts, figures, and statistics that you'll need to convince someone else about how good this idea really is.

Wednesday, March 26 (Moon in Scorpio to Sagittarius 10:12 a.m.) A comfortable day. You feel good when the moon is in a fellow fire sign: Leo or Sagittarius. With today's lunar transit, your itch to travel is too great to ignore. Go on the Internet to take a virtual tour of some far-flung corners of the globe.

Thursday, March 27 (Moon in Sagittarius) You grasp the larger picture. You may not love everything you see, but you have the power to change what you don't like. Get busy, Aries. Your work is cut out for you.

Friday, March 28 (Moon in Sagittarius to Capricorn 10:44 p.m.) Career and professional matters take center stage. A boss assigns you a special project. He or she knows that you can do it in half the time it would take someone else. Your challenge is to stay the course without getting bored!

Saturday, March 29 (Moon in Capricorn) You get help from Venus, Mercury, and Uranus, all in compatible water signs. In fact, whatever you need is at your fingertips. All you have to do is look within to find the answers. Someone with an unusual personality or belief system may be helpful.

Sunday, March 30 (Moon in Capricorn) Jupiter in your tenth house of careers is expanding your professional opportunities. You meet someone necessary to your career expansion. Are you ready to rise to the challenge?

Monday, March 31 (Moon in Capricorn to Aquarius 9:35 a.m.) As the moon enters Aquarius, your network of acquaintances plays an important role in the day's events. Get advice from a trusted friend before you make a pressing decision.

APRIL 2008

Tuesday, April 1 (Moon in Aquarius) Whenever the moon joins Neptune in your eleventh house, your idealism cranks up a notch or two. You may be able to put your idealism into action. Whether it's through volunteer work or simply doing a favor for a friend, you understand the phrase "walking the walk."

Wednesday, April 2 (Moon in Aquarius to Pisces 4:56 a.m.) A busy day in the heavens. Mercury enters Taurus and your second house, and Pluto turns retrograde in Capricorn. For the next several weeks, your daily life and conscious thoughts will be focused on money. Expect events that bring this issue to the forefront. The Pluto retrograde signals a slow unfolding of professional events that cause you to reevaluate your career goals.

Thursday, April 3 (Moon in Pisces) If yesterday was hectic for you, today should unfold at a leisurely pace. In fact, it may be so leisurely that you don't feel compelled to do much of anything. At the very least, go for a walk or head to the gym. Then do some creative work that gets your imagination moving.

Friday, April 4 (Moon in Pisces to Aries 8:28 p.m.) Does it get much better than this? When the moon is in your sign, everything in your life functions smoothly. Gone is that struggle between your head and your heart. You act with resolve.

Saturday, April 5 (Moon in Aries) The new moon is in your sign, a wonderful harbinger for opportunities, relationships, and events flowing into your life. This new moon happens only once a year, so take advantage of it by launching ideas and projects with care and forethought.

Sunday, April 6 (Moon in Aries to Taurus 9:20 p.m.) The romantic chapter of your life this year begins. Venus joins Mercury in your sign. Following so closely on the heels of the new moon in your sign, this terrific transit should bring love right to your doorstep. If you're involved already, the relationship heats up.

Monday, April 7 (Moon in Taurus) You're so upbeat and optimistic that you're tempted to buy something you know you can't afford. Resist the temptation and balance your bank accounts first. If there's money for this big-ticket item, go online and find out if you can get it less expensively elsewhere.

Tuesday, April 8 (Moon in Taurus to Gemini 9:27 p.m.) Oh, how you're talking. And you have plenty to say. Whether you're defending your position on an issue or simply explaining what you think about something, you do it in a convincing manner.

Wednesday, April 9 (Moon in Gemini) You and a neighbor hang out. You've been tapped by your neighbors to head up some sort of community project. Everyone knows you're great at getting projects off the ground. Only you know that you may get bored halfway through it.

Thursday, April 10 (Moon in Gemini to Cancer 10:43 p.m.) With Venus still in your sign and the moon entering your fourth house, your love life might take some unprecedented turns. Despite a little friction, you're able to iron out the issues that concern you.

Friday, April 11 (Moon in Cancer) If you haven't already finished your tax return, get busy. You've got four days to do what needs to be done. On other fronts, an issue at home needs your attention. Your son or daughter may need support now.

Saturday, April 12 (Moon in Cancer) It's spring, and you're in the mood for home renovations! Whether you're repainting a room, putting down new carpeting, or just moving furniture around, get everyone involved. Let the kids decide on color schemes for their own rooms. Tonight, have friends or relatives over for a leisurely barbecue.

Sunday, April 13 (Moon in Cancer to Leo 2:29 a.m.) There are levels to showmanship; a fellow fire sign exhibits unappealing behavior. Rather than criticizing, keep your own counsel and make sure you limit your future contact with this individual.

Monday, April 14 (Moon in Leo) Romance is in the air and the person who has caught your interest may be a bit older than you. You don't really care about age differences as long as the other person is as honest and forthright as you are.

Tuesday, April 15 (Moon in Leo to Virgo 9:07 a.m.) Tax day. If you haven't mailed off your return yet, be sure to do it early in the day and avoid the crush at the post office. With Venus in your sign until the end of the month, you should be in pretty good shape with taxes—and just about everything else.

Wednesday, April 16 (Moon in Virgo) Work is filled with small, vital details. Connect the dots, Aries, and watch the big picture emerge. A boss or coworker notices how hard you're working on a particular project. It may not result in a raise just yet, but it gets you noticed!

Thursday, April 17 (Moon in Virgo to Libra 6:11 p.m.) It's a perfect evening to do something with your partner. Even if you just stay home and chill, romance is in the air. Be careful that you don't become excessive. Watch what you eat and drink. Mercury enters Taurus and your second house, so you compare and contrast your partner's values with your own.

Friday, April 18 (Moon in Libra) If you've been negotiating a contract, sign before Mercury turns retrograde on May 26. Read the fine print, ask for the best deal you believe you can get, and schedule the actual signing before that landmark date in May. Listen to input from trusted friends and family members.

Saturday, April 19 (Moon in Libra) Get ready for tomorrow's full moon in Scorpio. Something related to work or health will reach fruition. If you've been following a strict diet and exercise regimen, tomorrow you step on the scales and realize you've reached your desired weight!

Sunday, April 20 (Moon in Libra to Scorpio 5:02 a.m.) Saturn, which is in a great angle to tonight's full moon, could bring about a deeper commitment in a relationship or a work offer you can't refuse. It may also help you solidify a creative project.

Monday, April 21 (Moon in Scorpio) Work could be a bit intense. A coworker has answers that would help you make a decision, but he or she is not forthcoming with the information. Bide your time, Aries. You won't get the answers by arguing.

Tuesday, April 22 (Moon in Scorpio to Sagittarius 5:08 p.m.) If you're a writer or in the publishing business, you get positive news. You also may be planning a trip overseas. If so, try not to travel between May 26 and June 19, when Mercury is retrograde.

Wednesday, April 23 (Moon in Sagittarius) You have an opportunity today to sign up for a workshop or seminar on a topic that fascinates you. Don't allow a lack of self-confidence to hold you back. Granted, self-confidence usually isn't an issue for you, but it could be.

Thursday, April 24 (Moon in Sagittarius) If you're college bound in the fall or in your first year of college, be sure that you give more thought to a major. It's important that you work at something you love rather than just putting in time at a job. You're an innovator, Aries. You can find a niche no one else has explored.

Friday, April 25 (Moon in Sagittarius to Capricorn 5:48 p.m.) Once again, the moon joins Jupiter and Pluto in Capricorn and your tenth house. You could feel emotionally vulnerable. Don't let it hold you back. Rely on your razor-sharp instincts. They won't steer you wrong.

Saturday, April 26 (Moon in Capricorn) You and friends or coworkers get together to brainstorm for ideas and strategies related to your profession. Perhaps you and your group have some hot new product idea that you want to pitch. Get your act together and do your pitching before May 26!

Sunday, April 27 (Moon in Capricorn to Aquarius 5:28 p.m.) By this afternoon, you're in rare form. Friends are dropping by, or you're on the phone making plans for tonight or next weekend. Try not to run yourself ragged between now and the end of the month.

Monday, April 28 (Moon in Aquarius) Vitamins and nutrition are on your mind. Hit the bookstore for the newest tomes on how to live forever. Fired up, you also stock up on everything the books you've bought recommend.

Tuesday, April 29 (Moon in Aquarius) Whenever the moon joins Neptune in your eleventh house, your idealism and compassion deepen. You do something for someone else without any thought of compensation.

Wednesday, April 30 (Moon in Aquarius to Pisces 2:11 a.m.) Venus enters Taurus and your second house. This transit should be a nice bonus for your income. Until May 26, invest with wisdom and forethought, and watch your portfolio grow.

MAY 2008

Thursday, May 1 (Moon in Pisces) With the moon and Venus now forming a terrific angle to each other, today could mark a breakthrough in a creative project. The dreams or impressions you receive during meditation could provide answers and guidance.

Friday, May 2 (Moon in Pisces to Aries 6:51 a.m.) Mercury enters Gemini and your third house, and Saturn turns direct in Virgo and your sixth house. The first transit stimulates travel in your daily life and any kind of communication. The second transit releases energy you can put to use in your daily work routine.

Saturday, May 3 (Moon in Aries) You're in very good shape. With the moon in your sign, you're able to move like the wind, zipping through projects and tasks that would take a mere mortal days to complete.

Sunday, May 4 (Moon in Aries to Taurus 7:58 a.m.) The moon joins Venus in your second house of money. Your intuition about finances and investments is sharp. Listen to your intuition, gather your facts, and then make your choices.

Monday, May 5 (Moon in Taurus) Your ruler, Mars, enters Leo and your fifth house. This transit, lasting until July 1, certainly spices up your love life. If you're not involved, you will be soon. The relationship may not be that of soul mates, but you won't ever be bored! Tonight's a new moon. In the next two weeks, expect new opportunities with finances. A raise, perhaps?

Tuesday, May 6 (Moon in Taurus to Gemini 7:18 a.m.) The moon links up with Mercury in Gemini and your third house. What a combo. Expect lots of discussion and other types of communication. If you're planning on signing a contract, do it before May 26, when Mercury turns retrograde in Gemini.

Wednesday, May 7 (Moon in Gemini) You get together with neighbors or relatives. Discussions ensue about family-related matters or about issues concerning your neighborhood. You don't want to offend anyone, but it's hardly your way to keep quiet when you have something to say.

Thursday, May 8 (Moon in Gemini to Cancer 7:03 a.m.) Let's face it. You're not one of those individuals whose emotions bubble indefinitely beneath the surface. Everything for you is more immediate, and when you feel it, you blurt out those feelings. With the Cancer moon, everything becomes so personal you can't process rapidly enough to blurt. So you become introverted. Just remember, there are no accidents. All is as it should be.

Friday, May 9 (Moon in Cancer) Jupiter turns retrograde in Capricorn. It simply means the planet's wonderful qualities go into a dormant state. You have several months to think about your professional direction. If you don't like where you're headed, change course.

Saturday, May 10 (Moon in Cancer to Leo 9:11 a.m.) Your day gets off to a great romantic start. Your partner and you may decide to head out of town for the weekend. If you're in a festive mood, you may want to get together with friends. Either way, the point is to spend time together.

Sunday, May 11 (Moon in Leo) Your daily life is so hectic that it's wise to put on the brakes and just chill. Granted, you have a tough time allowing yourself to relax, but your body is screaming for a rest. Grab a good book.

Monday, May 12 (Moon in Leo to Virgo 2:49 p.m.) By this afternoon, you're in a pickle with details. Things you have glossed over the last few days haunt you. Deal with the mess, delegate responsibility, and by tomorrow, you should be in the clear.

Tuesday, May 13 (Moon in Virgo) Time to schedule things like dentist appointments, Aries. Best to take care of it while Saturn—which rules teeth and bones—is in your sixth house of health and work. With your ruler, Mars, in compatible Leo, your love life should be heating up. If it's not, then reevaluate your romantic needs!

Wednesday, May 14 (Moon in Virgo to Libra 11:48 p.m.) Do something for someone else. Do it with an open heart and without thought of compensation. On other fronts, negotiate and sign contracts. Mercury turns retrograde on May 26, so tie up details before then.

Thursday, May 15 (Moon in Libra) There could be tension between your needs and those of a partner. You feel conflicted. Best to be as cooperative as possible; try to find the middle ground. Once Venus moves into compatible Gemini on May 24, things should be on an even keel.

Friday, May 16 (Moon in Libra) Your partner needs your support. There isn't any huge issue involved. It's just that you haven't been around much lately. Time to renew bonds, Aries. Strive for fairness and balance.

Saturday, May 17 (Moon in Libra to Scorpio 11:00 a.m.) Are your insurance payments up-to-date? What about your quarterly taxes? Tend to these kinds of details, and save yourself a headache later. A friend or family member may need your help.

Sunday, May 18 (Moon in Scorpio) Think about the bottom line. You're the consummate researcher or investigator; you won't rest until you find whatever you're looking for. You may need to adjust your attitude in a relationship. There are other ways of doing things, Aries. Be open to them.

Monday, May 19 (Moon in Scorpio to Sagittarius 11:20 p.m.) The day may feel a bit uncomfortable until the moon enters Sagittarius this evening. Then you put on your party shoes and head out. You have a grasp of the big picture; use it to your advantage. Be careful, Aries, that you don't step on anyone else's toes!

Tuesday, May 20 (Moon in Sagittarius) It's a power day. No question about it. The people around you feel your presence before you even open your mouth. And because you're so sure you're right, you may blurt out something that you'll regret when the moon enters Capricorn the day after tomorrow. Think before you speak.

Wednesday, May 21 (Moon in Sagittarius) Your spiritual outlook gets a boost. It may be nothing more than an odd synchronicity that catches your attention or perhaps something you read in a book or hear from someone. Whatever it is coincides with a hunch you have, affirming its validity.

Thursday, May 22 (Moon in Sagittarius to Capricorn 11:56 a.m.) Pay attention to professional concerns. Your goals or strategies look solid, but when Mercury turns retrograde on May 26, you may reevaluate your beliefs and position.

Friday, May 23 (Moon in Capricorn) The moon joins Jupiter and Pluto in your tenth house, a powerful combination of planets. Use the energy to advance a professional issue, concern, or goal. You'll come out way ahead of your competitors. Get in touch with your parents. Let them know how much you appreciate all their efforts through the years. Gratitude is always a perfect potion for the soul!

Saturday, May 24 (Moon in Capricorn to Aquarius 11:52 p.m.) Venus enters Gemini and your third house. A flirtation or friendship with a neighbor or someone you meet through a brother or sister could start heating up. Are you in the mood for romance or commitment, Aries?

Sunday, May 25 (Moon in Aquarius) With the moon in your eleventh house, friendships come into play. You and a group of like-minded individuals get together for a mutual interest or passion. Remember that good friends are worth their weight in gold.

Monday, May 26 (Moon in Aquarius) Mercury turns retrograde in Gemini, and Neptune turns retrograde in Aquarius. The first could put a damper on your communications for the next three weeks. Don't sign any contracts. The second retrograde unfolds with more subtlety, but may encourage you to look within for answers.

Tuesday, May 27 (Moon in Aquarius to Pisces 9:39 a.m.) You may have unusual emotional reactions to personal issues. It's easier to grasp the intuitive truth of a situation than it is to verbalize what you feel. A dream you have tonight could bring insight to a situation or relationship. Have your notebook at your bedside!

Wednesday, May 28 (Moon in Pisces) The moon links up with Uranus in your twelfth house. This combination always has an air of unpredictability to it, particularly in terms of your emotional responses. Your intuition is right on. Listen to it.

Thursday, May 29 (Moon in Pisces to Aries 3:53 p.m.) By this afternoon, the energy shift is palpable. Suddenly, your moody indecisiveness is gone, your physical stamina increases, and you're on a roll. For the evening, plan something special with friends or a partner.

Friday, May 30 (Moon in Aries) Think about your heart's desire and decide how to make this real. You'll have to come up with a plan, Aries. Anything about which you are passionate can be achieved.

Saturday, May 31 (Moon in Aries to Taurus 6:19 p.m.) With Mercury still retrograde, your plans for the weekend may change unexpectedly. Don't fret. Go with the flow; be comfortable with what is.

JUNE 2008

Sunday, June 1 (Moon in Taurus) Here you are, concerned about money. Don't be. Your earning capacity is excellent, and even if your bank account doesn't quite meet your expectations, it's a good time to think abundance, Aries.

Monday, June 2 (Moon in Taurus to Gemini 6:07 p.m.) As the moon links up with retrograde Mercury, you find yourself revisiting issues and feelings you thought had been resolved. Old friends or former lovers or spouses may pop into your life again.

Tuesday, June 3 (Moon in Gemini) It's a new-moon day in Gemini, your third house. Get in touch with relatives, friends, or neighbors. Over the next few days, a new project concerning communication may come up. Seize the opportunity. Since Venus is also in Gemini, the new opportunity could involve romance!

Wednesday, June 4 (Moon in Gemini to Cancer 5:17 p.m.) With Mars lighting up your fifth house of romance and Venus still in your third house, that new romance could be with someone in your neighborhood. Maybe even a next-door neighbor? Whoever it is, don't make commitments you can't keep.

Thursday, June 5 (Moon in Cancer) They say that home is where the heart is. This adage certainly fits you. You may delve into genealogy, searching for information. The question that initiates this search comes to you in an unusual way.

Friday, June 6 (Moon in Cancer to Leo 6:01 p.m.) The beauty of the moon in Leo is that it bolsters your natural confidence and boldness. You aren't impatient and edgy, and people notice. A friend confides a secret. A new romance is in the offing, Aries. Can you slow down to enjoy it?

Saturday, June 7 (Moon in Leo) Get out and enjoy yourself. With the moon in gregarious Leo, you're in a party mood and the more the merrier. If you're not involved, get out and party. If you have a partner, check with him or her first to be sure a crowd is the way to go. It may be that your honey wants to spend time just with you.

Sunday, June 8 (Moon in Leo to Virgo 10:02 p.m.) Even though it's Sunday, you might want to tie up a project at work or to revise something you're working on. With Mercury still retrograde, revise and reevaluate.

Monday, June 9 (Moon in Virgo) Your ruler, Mars, continues its transit through Leo and your fifth house. It's a terrific transit for romance. But it calls for patience and thoughtful responses to questions. So think before you blurt out something, Aries.

Tuesday, June 10 (Moon in Virgo) Meticulous planning goes a long way. Make a list of priorities, and work your way through the list. It may not be the way you like to do things. But it's necessary. You get help from a Taurus or a Capricorn who can help you chart a course and stick to it.

Wednesday, June 11 (Moon in Virgo to Libra 5:56 a.m.) Mediation, cooperation, team work come into play. The emphasis is on relationships, both personal and professional, and how well you can balance your life.

Thursday, June 12 (Moon in Libra) If you're negotiating a contract, keep fine-tuning, but don't sign until after Mercury turns direct on June 19. The same goes with your travel plans. Be a virtual traveler, but don't make your final plans until Mercury turns direct.

Friday, June 13 (Moon in Libra to Scorpio 4:54 p.m.) If you're in the midst of separating your assets from someone else's, take your time. There's no rush here, Aries, even if you think there is. You will get a much fairer deal if you wait until after June 19.

Saturday, June 14 (Moon in Scorpio) Your emotions are intense, and your intuition is powerful. The challenge is to use both attributes for achievement and something positive rather than to make yourself miserable.

Sunday, June 15 (Moon in Scorpio) Someone near you needs help and emotional support. Even if you're busy or stressed yourself, extend a helping hand. Sometimes, the best thing to do is the obvious thing. Make sure your insurance payments are current.

Monday, June 16 (Moon in Scorpio to Sagittarius 5:20 a.m.) Getting itchy to travel, Aries? No wonder. The moon enters nomadic Sagittarius, your ninth house of long-distance travel.

Tuesday, June 17 (Moon in Sagittarius) You've got the larger picture concerning an event or situation, but may not know how to connect the dots to arrive at where you want to be. Make notes, try to work it out on paper, and then engage a trusted friend in some creative brainstorming.

Wednesday, June 18 (Moon in Sagittarius to Capricorn 5:52 p.m.) Venus enters Cancer and your fourth house. This transit, lasting until July 12, should bring romance back into your home life. Even if you aren't living with anyone or involved in a committed relationship, Venus's transit through Cancer brings beauty and harmony into your home. Tonight's full moon in Sagittarius promises to be quite romantic!

Thursday, June 19 (Moon in Capricorn) Mercury turns direct. It's a powerful time to communicate with people you haven't seen or have neglected in the past several weeks. Get in touch. Start up your e-mail loop again.

Friday, June 20 (Moon in Capricorn) The moon joins Jupiter and Pluto in your tenth house. This combination happens once a month, and it would be to your advantage to start keeping a journal of what happens on these days. Is your professional life different in some way? What kinds of experiences do you have? How are your interactions with others, particularly with people in authority over you? You're on a search for patterns, Aries.

Saturday, June 21 (Moon in Capricorn to Aquarius 5:34 a.m.) This air-sign moon is certainly more to your liking. It attracts unusual people. Or is it just one very intriguing individual? At some point in the day, you get together with a theater group, a writing group, or an adventure-travel group.

Sunday, June 22 (Moon in Aquarius) Anytime the moon teams up with elusive Neptune, the results can be quite revealing. Today is no exception. You clean out your closets, garage, or attic, and give everything to a charitable organization. Or you have a garage sale and turn the money over to charity.

Monday, June 23 (Moon in Aquarius to Pisces 3:33 p.m.) By this afternoon, you're ready for some solitude. A long hike in the woods, a workout at the gym, or even a strenuous swim will do you wonders. It's important that you have an outlet for stress.

Tuesday, June 24 (Moon in Pisces) It's a good day for dream work. Before you fall asleep, give yourself suggestions that you want answers to or insights into a particular situation or issue. Keep your pad and pen handy. Once you start exploring your inner world, it becomes addictive!

Wednesday, June 25 (Moon in Pisces to Aries 10:50 p.m.) The moon moves into your sign late this evening. To honor this, list what you would like to accomplish during the next two days. Then lay down a strategy for doing this. You are at your most powerful.

Thursday, June 26 (Moon in Aries) Uranus turns retrograde in Pisces and remains that way until November 24. Its effects unfold slowly, but some of the possibilities are sudden insights into your own motivations, unexpected events concerning institutions like hospitals and nursing homes, and vivid dream work.

Friday, June 27 (Moon in Aries) With the moon still in your sign, your sexuality and confidence are at a peak. You are noticed by someone who has attracted your attention these past few months, and the chemistry is mutual. Is this just a flirtation or the real thing?

Saturday, June 28 (Moon in Aries to Taurus 2:51 a.m.) Mars is still in compatible Leo, heating up your love life. Take advantage of it while it lasts. On July 1, it moves into Virgo, and you may not be as pleased with that transit. On the other hand, Mars in Virgo will enable you to get more done.

Sunday, June 29 (Moon in Taurus) With the moon now in Taurus and your second house, you feel stubborn about something you value. It's exactly what the situation calls for. Don't apologize for how you feel.

Monday, June 30 (Moon in Taurus to Gemini 4:04 a.m.) The month ends with the moon's passage into compatible Gemini. And suddenly, you're everyone's best friend. Be careful. You could be tapped to head up a community project.

JULY 2008

Tuesday, July 1 (Moon in Gemini) Mars enters Virgo. For the next six weeks or so, you'll have your hands full at work. Whether it's meeting deadlines or simply tending to daily work, you may feel you don't have time for anything else.

Wednesday, July 2 (Moon in Gemini to Cancer 3:54 a.m.) It's summer, and you stick close to home. Put in for vacation time if you haven't done so already. In a few weeks, your yen for travel will be so powerful you won't be able to resist taking off. The new moon may prompt you to start a home-improvement project.

Thursday, July 3 (Moon in Cancer) The moon joins Venus in Cancer in your fourth house. This pair brings an intuitive softness to your love life. It's possible that your partner or you may experience some sort of past-life recall related to your relationship.

Friday, July 4 (Moon in Cancer to Leo 4:16 a.m.) The moon enters your fifth house. There are many possible manifestations of this energy, and it won't be the same every month. For today, though, you find the perfect venue for pleasure. It may be something as simple as visiting a theme park with your kids or settling in with a good book.

Saturday, July 5 (Moon in Leo) You're in the mood for romance and pleasure. This may involve a trip with a partner to someplace you've never been before, working on your manuscript or screenplay, or even staying in bed with your honey all day! It all depends on your priorities and needs.

Sunday, July 6 (Moon in Leo to Virgo 7:04 a.m.) The moon joins Mars in Virgo in your sixth house. Buckle into your job by paying attention to every detail that crosses your desk. You may have to delegate responsibility temporarily to others until you can wade through the labyrinth to find what you need.

Monday, July 7 (Moon in Virgo) It's time to do something for a person in your office who may be unappreciated. You know the type of person: the one who tackles difficult tasks without complaints or who gets the job done silently. These are the unrecognized heroes of your daily workday.

Tuesday, July 8 (Moon in Virgo to Libra 1:32 p.m.) Review contract negotiations and sign on the dotted line. Be sure that you have been fair to yourself as well as to others in this negotiation. If you're shopping for something special for your partner, be generous but don't spend more than you can afford.

Wednesday, July 9 (Moon in Libra) With the new moon only a week in the past, partnerships are still where the action is. Whether it's a new romance or a new chapter for an old romance, your emotional life is in good shape. Your optimism and sense of well-being should be strong. You may need to carry that feeling through the next few days.

Thursday, July 10 (Moon in Libra to Scorpio 11:35 p.m.) Mercury enters Cancer and your fourth house. This two-week transit triggers lots of communication at home and within your family. You may do more traveling in the next few weeks and find yourself on the road more than usual.

Friday, July 11 (Moon in Scorpio) If you're in the midst of a separation or divorce, be sure that you have all your facts before you ask for your fair share. This may take some research and investigative work on your part, but down the road, you'll be glad you took the time.

Saturday, July 12 (Moon in Scorpio) Venus enters Leo and your fifth house of love and romance. The next three weeks are fantastic for romance, creative projects, and anything to do with children. In fact, this is the prime time all year for meeting someone who brings harmony and love to your life.

Sunday, July 13 (Moon in Scorpio to Sagittarius 11:50 a.m.) With Venus in a fellow fire sign and the moon moving into another fire sign, you're in rare form. Your enthusiasm and self-confidence are infectious; people seem to flock to you. You're calling the shots, Aries. Make sure your judgment is sound.

Monday, July 14 (Moon in Sagittarius) Publishing, the law, and higher education are possibilities for the day's focus. Your business or products may find a new niche in an overseas market, or you may be planning a trip overseas to direct that expansion. Either way, business is looking up.

Tuesday, July 15 (Moon in Sagittarius) It's one of those days when the moon joins Jupiter and Pluto in Capricorn, in your house of careers. You're a powerhouse; you won't make a wrong move as long as you listen to your intuition.

Wednesday, July 16 (Moon in Sagittarius to Capricorn 12:20 a.m.) It's a career power day, Aries. Making all the right moves will pay off down the line. With Mars in meticulous Virgo, you won't be able to take any shortcuts, but that's exactly what the situation calls for.

Thursday, July 17 (Moon in Capricorn) You feel somewhat vulnerable in terms of your career, but you really shouldn't. You're in good shape professionally, and your love life is picking up. With Venus in fellow fire sign Leo, your sex appeal is soaring.

Friday, July 18 (Moon in Capricorn to Aquarius 11:41 a.m.) Friends and friendships are highlighted. If someone in your circle needs emotional support, you're the one to give it. You have a real gift for boosting people when they're down. Your enthusiasm for life is infectious; that's just what this person needs.

Saturday, July 19 (Moon in Aquarius) There's a lot going on. Your energy may feel scattered; it's likely you're being pulled in a dozen different directions. Best to slow down and regroup. You'll get more done that way.

Sunday, July 20 (Moon in Aquarius to Pisces 9:09 p.m.) As the moon enters your twelfth house, you could feel the need to be alone. You tend to be a solitary, independent person, but this is a different sort of feeling altogether. It's as if your energy turns inward, seeking solutions and insight from dreams or meditations.

Monday, July 21 (Moon in Pisces) Your dream recall is vivid. Be sure to give yourself a suggestion before falling asleep to remember any dreams that pertain to pressing issues in your life. In your waking life, you have some unusual emotional reactions to events in your love life.

Tuesday, July 22 (Moon in Pisces) In about four days, Mercury will join Venus in Leo, your fifth house. Get ready. You'll be encouraging heart-to-heart talks with a romantic partner, and he or she may not be in the mood. Set the stage.

Wednesday, July 23 (Moon in Pisces to Aries 4:23 a.m.) With the moon in your sign, you're on a roll and ready to take on everything you encounter. Your physical energy is especially good; whatever doubts you've had lately about life, love, and the cosmos have magically disappeared.

Thursday, July 24 (Moon in Aries) You're a powerhouse, and people around you may not be able to keep up. You need to burn off some of that excessive energy. Go hiking. Take a long swim. Throw a party. Go shopping. Whatever you do, activity is called for.

Friday, July 25 (Moon in Aries to Taurus 9:15 a.m.) You feel grounded, practical. You feel so practical, in fact, that you may do stuff like clean out your closets, attic, or basement. Practice a bit of feng shui in the area of your life that you would like to improve.

Saturday, July 26 (Moon in Taurus) Mercury enters Leo and joins Venus in your fifth house. This powerful combination can open up channels of communication with the one you love! It can also benefit you in creative projects. Your muse is ready to serve, Aries!

Sunday, July 27 (Moon in Taurus to Gemini 11:56 a.m.) You're in a playful mood, and someone interested in you notices. This person may be someone you already know. Your brother or sister stops by for a visit or gets in touch by phone or e-mail. The news is positive.

Monday, July 28 (Moon in Gemini) Your mind hums right along, filled with a million ideas. The trick is to bring it all down to earth and pour it into a creative endeavor. Or you need to communicate it somehow.

Tuesday, July 29 (Moon in Gemini to Cancer 1:12 p.m.) Granted, the Cancer moon is not one of your favorites. It's wise to use this energy for researching your ancestral past or to deal more effectively and compassionately with your parents and family. Also, this moon comes with a healthy dollop of intuition. Listen to yours.

Wednesday, July 30 (Moon in Cancer) You stick close to home. You may be expecting news about a parent or other family member. Be sure your cell phone is charged up and in working order. Follow your hunches and impulses.

Thursday, July 31 (Moon in Cancer to Leo 2:22 p.m.) By this afternoon, the moon has joined Venus in Leo. This should spice up your love life. With Saturn in picky Virgo, honor the planet in some way. Complete a project or meet a responsibility, and things will improve immeasurably.

AUGUST 2008

Friday, August 1 (Moon in Leo) The solar eclipse at 10 degrees Leo and your fifth house causes external events that permit you to see a love relationship or a creative project in a new light. The impact of solar eclipses usually lasts for at least six months, until the next solar eclipse. If you have a copy of your birth chart, see if you have any planets at 10 degrees Leo or 10 degrees in any of the other fixed signs—Scorpio and Taurus.

Saturday, August 2 (Moon in Leo to Virgo 4:59 p.m.) Back to earth! The Virgo moon asks for exactness, perfection, and an attention to details. A relationship may feel a bit strange and unsettling. But it's a passing thing. Best to roll with events and make the best of what exists.

Sunday, August 3 (Moon in Virgo) In a few days, both Mercury and Venus will enter Virgo, so think of this moon as the precursor to all that grounded energy. If you're pickier than usual about having things in your life just so, you're on track. A Capricorn or Taurus individual plays a part in today's events.

Monday, August 4 (Moon in Virgo to Libra 10:28 p.m.) Relationships are the focus. You're called upon to be a team player, or you may get caught in the middle of a dispute. Either way, your people skills come into play. Don't take sides if you're in the middle of someone else's discussion. Just mediate.

Tuesday, August 5 (Moon in Libra) Venus enters Virgo and joins Mars in your sixth house. Until August 30, an office flirtation heats up. Things at work hum along smoothly, with you delegating tasks when the situation calls for it. Be sure that if your love life is soaring, you don't neglect your responsibilities at work or vice versa. Balance and precision are called for.

Wednesday, August 6 (Moon in Libra) Your business or romantic partner has something to discuss with you. Get certain issues out into the open. Once Mercury turns retrograde in late September, conditions won't be as conducive to mutual understanding.

Thursday, August 7 (Moon in Libra to Scorpio 7:27 a.m.) As the moon enters intense and passionate Scorpio, you're able to intuit other people's motives and agendas. You may be overconcerned with things like insurance, loans, and mortgages.

Friday, August 8 (Moon in Scorpio) Something odd grabs your attention. It could be a synchronicity that causes you to think more deeply about cosmic questions. You may sign up for a workshop on an esoteric topic that fascinates you.

Saturday, August 9 (Moon in Scorpio to Sagittarius 7:11 p.m.) This evening, the moon enters fellow fire sign Sagittarius, and you feel the shift immediately. Use this energy to grasp the bigger picture concerning a relationship or issue that concerns you. But don't make any impulsive decisions.

Sunday, August 10 (Moon in Sagittarius) Mercury enters Virgo and joins Venus and Mars in your sixth house. This lineup of planets certainly brings the pressure to bear on your daily work life. Expect lots of activity, discussion, and energy concerning work-related projects and relationships.

Monday, August 11 (Moon in Sagittarius) If you're preparing to head to college or return to college in the fall, you receive information related to your higher education. Or if you're still in high school, you may be preparing for SATs and making your way through summer reading lists.

Tuesday, August 12 (Moon in Sagittarius to Capricorn 7:43 a.m.) Regardless of what kind of job or career you have, you may be having second thoughts about all of it. Plan for whatever job skills you feel you may need for a new career path. Research on the Internet. Use local resources available to you.

Wednesday, August 13 (Moon in Capricorn) You're so focused that you can easily come up with a long-range strategy for achieving your professional goals. Start with a short time frame—three months. Then expand your vision to six months or a year. Keep tabs on your daily progress.

Thursday, August 14 (Moon in Capricorn to Aquarius 6:57 p.m.) Off you go with friends tonight. You meet either with your support group or trusted friends you have known for years. Time to brainstorm, touch base, and come up with new creative ideas.

Friday, August 15 (Moon in Aquarius) You're in a visionary frame of mind. Try to apply your cutting-edge ideas to your line of work or to a creative project. How can you make these ideas comprehensible and practical for other people?

Saturday, August 16 (Moon in Aquarius) The lunar eclipse at 24 degrees Aquarius impacts your eleventh house. An emotional issue surfaces related to your friendships or your wishes and dreams. You may experience some tension or unpleasantness with your kids or your creative projects. Don't worry. By tomorrow, it won't seem so bad.

Sunday, August 17 (Moon in Aquarius to Pisces 3:47 a.m.) Get ready for the new moon in Virgo on August 30. Give some thought to what you would like to achieve in September, and figure out how you can best reach your goal. The beauty of the Pisces moon is that it provides the intuitive tools for you to do this.

Monday, August 18 (Moon in Pisces) Today's hunch, if you follow it, may turn into tomorrow's achievement. Be alert for strong emotions concerning events and relationships. Everything is leading you toward a particular experience.

Tuesday, August 19 (Moon in Pisces to Aries 10:11 a.m.) Mars enters Libra and your seventh house. Until October 3, a lot of your energy is focused on personal relationships and trying to find balance within them. You and your romantic partner may experience contentions, but patience and tolerance go a long way toward resolving differences.

Wednesday, August 20 (Moon in Aries) With the moon in your sign opposed to your ruler, Mars, no telling what kind of surprises today might bring. You may find yourself locked in a conflict with a partner—or swept up in an affair. Your inner and outer selves are in sync with each other.

Thursday, August 21 (Moon in Aries to Taurus 2:38 p.m.) With Mercury and Venus still in earth-sign Virgo and the moon entering an earth sign, you're feeling very grounded and practical. Your communication and love life even show as much! Sweet nothings whispered in your ear aren't enough; you want concrete evidence of your partner's intentions.

Friday, August 22 (Moon in Taurus) Think of it this way. The more you save, the more you will have down the road. However, if you save because you believe there isn't enough abundance to go around, it won't matter how much you save. Change your belief.

Saturday, August 23 (Moon in Taurus to Gemini 5:49 p.m.) This air-sign moon is compatible with your sun sign. It makes you more willing to discuss your feelings with family and friends and to communicate generally about what's on your mind.

Sunday, August 24 (Moon in Gemini) If yesterday was about communication, today is about travel—running around as opposed to pleasurable travel. But you have the energy to do it all and actually end up enjoying the contact with people you meet along the way.

Monday, August 25 (Moon in Gemini to Cancer 8:19 p.m.) You're working your way to the second new moon of the month. It will be at 8 degrees Virgo, your sixth house. This new moon brings opportunities related to your daily health and work; you could feel the effects already.

Tuesday, August 26 (Moon in Cancer) If you're a student and headed back to school soon, you may stick around the house. There's a certain pleasure for you in puttering and fixing up things you've neglected this summer. You may even get out some family photo albums and reminisce.

Wednesday, August 27 (Moon in Cancer to Leo 10:51 p.m.) Today is just fine for you. The only possible glitch is that your partner may be trying to restrict you in some way. Get over it and move on. You're your own boss.

Thursday, August 28 (Moon in Leo) Mercury enters Libra, joining Mars in your seventh house. Negotiate and sign contracts. Discuss personal issues with your partner. Communication is a priority.

Friday, August 29 (Moon in Leo) Get ready for the new moon tomorrow. Give some thought to what you would like to see unfold in your daily work and health. If you don't already have an exercise routine, start one so you'll be primed and ready for the new moon.

Saturday, August 30 (Moon in Leo to Virgo 2:19 a.m.) You not only have a new moon in Virgo, but Venus enters Libra, joining both Mercury and Mars in your seventh house. This is an impressive lineup that certainly puts romance and love foremost in your life. If you're not involved, you probably will be before Venus and Mars move on—before September 23 and October 3, respectively.

Sunday, August 31 (Moon in Virgo) Even though the earth-sign moon probably isn't your favorite, you're energized where your daily work and health are concerned. Make dental and doctor's appointments if you've postponed them.

SEPTEMBER 2008

Monday, September 1 (Moon in Virgo to Libra 7:45 a.m.) The moon enters Libra and your seventh house, so the day's emphasis is on relationships. Cooperation will take you much farther than confrontation. Your spouse or partner needs more personal attention.

Tuesday, September 2 (Moon in Libra) Your artistic abilities surface. You feel the creative need to dive into a project that you may have put on the back burner. Time to pull out the manuscript, screenplay, or portfolio and get to work! With Saturn moving direct in your sixth house, you may suddenly find you have more responsibility at work.

Wednesday, September 3 (Moon in Libra to Scorpio 4:03 p.m.) Keep working to manifest the goal that you identified on the night of the full moon. With the moon in Scorpio, you have the intense emotions and willpower to break through any obstacles you face. The challenge is to use this energy without hurting anyone else.

Thursday, September 4 (Moon in Scorpio) If you have guests coming in for Labor Day weekend, you may want to take some time just for yourself before company arrives. If you're going away for the weekend, have everything lined up before you leave.

Friday, September 5 (Moon in Scorpio) The moon is waxing, and as it grows toward the full moon on September 15, your opportunities in terms of mortgages and loans increase. You may decide to take out additional life or health insurance.

Saturday, September 6 (Moon in Scorpio to Sagittarius 3:12 a.m.) With the moon entering Sagittarius, your optimism and confidence are back on track. You have an opportunity for an international trip. Or you may check out spots that interest you on the Internet.

Sunday, September 7 (Moon in Sagittarius) Jupiter turns direct in Capricorn and your tenth house. Expect your career to expand in positive ways before the end of the year. In fact, an opportunity that has long-range repercussions may drop in your lap.

Monday, September 8 (Moon in Sagittarius to Capricorn 3:46 p.m.) Pluto turns direct in Capricorn and your tenth house. With two planets turning direct in the career sector of your chart, you're in a beneficial position to achieve your goals. Prepare for the new moon in Pisces that's coming up on September 15.

Tuesday, September 9 (Moon in Capricorn) Your ability to focus is strong. Make a list of your professional priorities over the course of the next month. Create a strategy that allows you to achieve these goals. Then go out three months, six months, or a full year. Even though you usually aren't the type to plan, you can make significant strides by doing so.

Wednesday, September 10 (Moon in Capricorn) Your father, a boss, or some other authority figure has important insights for you. You may feel like this person is interfering in your business, but it's best to listen. A Virgo or a Taurus plays into events as well.

Thursday, September 11 (Moon in Capricorn to Aquarius 3:20 a.m.) On September 24, Mercury makes its final retrograde for the year, in Libra and your seventh house. If you're in contract negotiations, be sure to wrap up everything before then. Otherwise, wait until after October 15, when Mercury will be moving direct.

Friday, September 12 (Moon in Aquarius) If you're chafing under the restrictions or delays imposed by Saturn in your sixth house, the Aquarius moon offers welcome relief. Friends and groups of like-minded individuals offer a reprieve from the daily grind.

Saturday, September 13 (Moon in Aquarius to Pisces 12:05 p.m.) The moon joins Uranus in Pisces in your twelfth house. Every month, this powerful combination leads to sudden insights into your own unconscious. Your dream recall is vivid during this lunar period. If you haven't started keeping a dream journal, it's never too late to start.

Sunday, September 14 (Moon in Pisces) You have unusual emotional reactions to situations and relationships. If there are people in your personal environment who grate on you for some reason, keep your feelings to yourself. Once the moon goes into your sign, say your piece, but without anger.

Monday, September 15 (Moon in Pisces to Aries 5:39 p.m.) The full moon in Pisces lights up your twelfth house. Expect some motive, information, or situation that has been hidden from you to surface. It would be a great day for a past-life regression.

Tuesday, September 16 (Moon in Aries) Every month when the moon enters your sun sign, it's a high-power day and this one is no exception. But because Mercury, Venus, and Mars are in Libra, opposite the moon, you may feel conflicted concerning your needs and those of a partner. Honest discussion and cooperation mitigate the conditions.

Wednesday, September 17 (Moon in Aries to Taurus 8:57 p.m.) This earth-sign moon forms a harmonious angle with Jupiter and Pluto in Capricorn, in your tenth house. Use the energy to ground your professional endeavors. As an Aries, you're great at launching ideas and projects; these three earth-sign planets help you to stay the course.

Thursday, September 18 (Moon in Taurus) Your values concerning money and your earning ability come into play. If you feel you're underpaid, decide how much you need to live the way you want and initiate a plan for achieving that. Perhaps, Aries, you would be happier working for yourself in a home-based business.

Friday, September 19 (Moon in Taurus to Gemini 11:17 p.m.) It's a relief when the moon enters a compatible sign like Gemini. Your mind races along at the speed of light; your communication skills accelerate. Jot down a list of things that you need to tackle.

Saturday, September 20 (Moon in Gemini) You're tapped to head up a community project of some kind. Even if the idea excites you, be sure that you'll see it through to completion. Your intentions are sincere, but you may find your time is pinched farther down the line.

Sunday, September 21 (Moon in Gemini) Memos, meetings, books, ideas, and contracts are the day's highlights. On September 24, Mercury turns retrograde in Libra. So finish negotiating any contracts and sign on the dotted line before then.

Monday, September 22 (Moon in Gemini to Cancer 1:49 a.m.) With the moon opposed to Jupiter and Pluto in Capricorn, your emotions may get blown out of proportion over something small and insignificant. Don't take things so personally.

Tuesday, September 23 (Moon in Cancer) Venus moves into Scorpio, the most intense and secretive sign in the zodiac. Keep your company's finances to yourself. Someone is meddling in personal information that is none of his business. However, Venus brings a break in financial matters. Your spouse or partner could see a raise before October 18.

Wednesday, September 24 (Moon in Cancer to Leo 5:14 a.m.) Mercury turns retrograde in Libra and your seventh house. Before October 15, when Mercury turns direct, you and your partner may not be communicating well. You both know what you want to express, but the other person just doesn't seem to be hearing you correctly.

Thursday, September 25 (Moon in Leo) The moon enters compatible fire-sign Leo, boosting your love life and creativity—despite Mercury's retrograde. So even though there may be some drudgery at work, you have plenty to anticipate.

Friday, September 26 (Moon in Leo to Virgo 9:53 a.m.) When the moon links up with Saturn in Virgo every month, there can be a sudden drop in your optimism and self-confidence. Don't fret. Saturn demands that we live up to our responsibilities, and the moon in Virgo makes you obsessive about details. Go with the flow, Aries. You'll be happier.

Saturday, September 27 (Moon in Virgo) In two days, there will be a new moon in Libra. It provides you with an opportunity to turn over a new leaf in your relationships. Until then, keep your nose to the proverbial grindstone and make the best of things.

Sunday, September 28 (Moon in Virgo to Libra 4:06 p.m.) The focus this afternoon is on cooperation, teamwork, and relationships in general. Since Mars is in Libra, you've got the enthusiasm to do whatever is necessary to make your personal relationships work.

Monday, September 29 (Moon in Libra) The new moon in Libra asks that you take the time for the people you love. Peace and harmony are always preferable to hostility and mean-spirited discussions. Try to create peace in your life and personal relationships for the next month.

Tuesday, September 30 (Moon in Libra) Tomorrow, the moon joins Venus in Scorpio in your eighth house. You're dealing with bottom-line issues concerning finances you share with someone else. There's a good deal of passion involved. Put it to positive use.

Wednesday, October 1 (Moon in Libra to Scorpio 12:27 a.m.) It's October but may feel like the depths of winter. Chill out, Aries. Get out and do something fun with your partner this weekend. Then come back renewed on Monday, ready to take on the world.

Thursday, October 2 (Moon in Scorpio) A secret may surface this weekend and have to be dealt with. Even though you aren't the secretive type, Aries, someone close to you may be. Once you have the information or insight that you need, you'll be able to move forward.

Friday, October 3 (Moon in Scorpio to Sagittarius 11:15 a.m.) Your ruler, Mars, enters Scorpio, a sign that it corules. Suddenly, your joint finances are highlighted in a major way. If you're thinking about refinancing your home, do the research first. Get quotes from different lenders. Don't do anything about it until after Mercury turns direct on October 15.

Saturday, October 4 (Moon in Sagittarius) Party time! That's one of the ways the Sagittarius moon makes you feel. It can also urge you to explore the larger picture of a situation, event, or relationship. However you use the energy, resist the temptation to boast that you have all the answers.

Sunday, October 5 (Moon in Sagittarius to Capricorn 11:49 p.m.) A boss or other authority figure asks for your help or advice on a professional matter. You aren't sure you have the right answer or insights. Rather than making something up on the spot, take the time to research the situation.

Monday, October 6 (Moon in Capricorn) This earth-sign moon makes a beneficial angle to Uranus in Pisces in your twelfth house. Whatever you need can be found within. It's just a matter of sifting through your own unconscious to find it.

Tuesday, October 7 (Moon in Capricorn) You have to adjust your attitude concerning a professional matter. Either your perception of the situation is too narrow or there are other factors involved that you aren't aware of. A Taurus lends a helping hand.

Wednesday, October 8 (Moon in Capricorn to Aquarius 12:03 p.m.) The moon joins Neptune in Aquarius in your eleventh house. Each month when this happens, you may experience confusion about a friendship or a group to which you belong. Extend help to someone who needs it.

Thursday, October 9 (Moon in Aquarius) You get together with like-minded friends. The thread that binds you together may be artistic, political, even spiritual. You come away from this gathering with a renewed belief in the power of the human spirit.

Friday, October 10 (Moon in Aquarius to Pisces 9:31 p.m.) If the Mercury retrograde has been driving you crazy with computer crashes, electronic glitches, and communication breakdowns, take heart. On October 15, Mercury turns direct. Until then, you just have to try to stay on top of things.

Saturday, October 11 (Moon in Pisces) Your imagination tends to be quite strong when the moon is in Pisces. With Uranus also there, your insight can be abrupt, startling, even brilliant. Take advantage of this combination by spending some time alone.

Sunday, October 12 (Moon in Pisces) Miscommunication and changes in your schedule remind you that Mercury is still retrograde. If you're having trouble with appliances and electronic equipment, don't rush out and replace big-ticket items. In three days, Mercury will turn direct.

Monday, October 13 (Moon in Pisces to Aries 3:07 a.m.) You need today's boost! With the moon in your sign, get out and do something physically active. Then pamper yourself with something special: a cold glass of juice with an energy boost, a visit to your local bookstore, or even something as simple as a long, hot bath.

Tuesday, October 14 (Moon in Aries) You're in charge, and everyone around you knows it. Your energy is sometimes a challenge to other people because you're so sure of yourself and your choices. You're out to get the job done. This full moon in your sign may be deliciously romantic.

Wednesday, October 15 (Moon in Aries to Taurus 5:31 a.m.) Mercury turns direct. Wait until tomorrow to iron out differences with your partner. In the meantime, the moon enters stabilizing Taurus. Balance your checkbook and make sure all your finances are in order.

Thursday, October 16 (Moon in Taurus) In two days, Venus moves into Sagittarius and your ninth house. That's a beautiful transit for long-distance travel. So if you've had the travel bug lately, get on your computer and start checking out airfares and locations.

Friday, October 17 (Moon in Taurus to Gemini 6:26 a.m.) Communication is foremost. You may spend a lot of time today exchanging e-mails with friends or relatives. Your general pace picks up, with a lot of running around for errands or carpooling.

Saturday, October 18 (Moon in Gemini) Venus enters Sagittarius. Your love life may pick up in a major way, especially if the person who interests you lives in or comes from another country. This transit, which lasts until November 23, also favors anything to do with higher education, the law, and your personal worldview.

Sunday, October 19 (Moon in Gemini to Cancer 7:41 a.m.) Your ruler, Mars, continues its transit through Scorpio and forms a beneficial angle to the Cancer moon. With both planets in water signs, you may be feeling more emotional today and tomorrow, and perhaps even nostalgic for a relationship or the good old days.

Monday, October 20 (Moon in Cancer) Mom or her equivalent in your life gets in touch or drops by. Whether your relationship with her is good or strained, attempt to cement the bonds.

Tuesday, October 21 (Moon in Cancer to Leo 10:36 a.m.) This morning, the moon enters another fire sign. These fire-sign-moon days are undoubtedly your favorite. You're able to zip through your work without sacrificing details and have plenty of energy left over to play this evening. And play you will, with a new romantic partner.

Wednesday, October 22 (Moon in Leo) With Mercury moving direct, you may want to revisit a creative project you put on a back burner. Carve out the time you need for this project. If you have to, explain to your family why you need the time and ask for their consideration.

Thursday, October 23 (Moon in Leo to Virgo 3:41 p.m.) The Virgo moon, linking up with Saturn in your sixth house, loves to drive you crazy! The combination boosts Jupiter's energy in Capricorn, so professional issues and situations surface. Are you ready for a new chapter in your career, Aries? It's closer than you think.

Friday, October 24 (Moon in Virgo) It's an odd day, with a mixture of energies that may leave you with feelings you don't understand. You're intuitively connected to the people around you, but uncertain of your own motives in a relationship or work situation.

Saturday, October 25 (Moon in Virgo to Libra 10:48 p.m.) A contract negotiation or signing happens right on schedule. However, if you signed the contract while Mercury was retrograde, you may discover details that escaped you. Is it too late to renegotiate?

Sunday, October 26 (Moon in Libra) Relationships, cooperation, and fairness—keep those three words in mind. Whether you're dealing with a business or romantic partner, honesty is called for, but bluntness should be avoided.

Monday, October 27 (Moon in Libra) Tomorrow night there's a new moon in Scorpio, your eighth house. Prepare a list of things you would like to achieve and figure out a way to achieve them. If, for instance, you want to refinance your house, start your comparison shopping for mortgage interest rates.

Tuesday, October 28 (Moon in Libra to Scorpio 7:48 a.m.) The new moon is here. This is always a time of renewal. New opportunities, new relationships, and new experiences arrive. You gain insight into an esoteric area that interests you.

Wednesday, October 29 (Moon in Scorpio) You and your family start your Halloween preparations: pumpkin carving, costume decisions, who's going where and at what time. You thrive on this sort of chaos.

Thursday, October 30 (Moon in Scorpio to Sagittarius 6:41 p.m.) The moon joins Venus in Sagittarius, in your ninth house. If you're overseas, romance is following you like a shadow. Another possible manifestation of this combined energy is publishing. Send off your manuscript.

Friday, October 31 (Moon in Sagittarius) Happy Halloween! Rather than just using tonight for trick or treating, you can talk with your kids about the history of Halloween. You may learn something in the process!

NOVEMBER 2008

Saturday, November 1 (Moon in Sagittarius) As you head into the month, the moon in Sagittarius may bring news concerning a trip you're planning or related to school plans. You may not have the full scoop on friends or the intentions of a group to which you belong.

Sunday, November 2—Daylight Saving Time Ends (Moon in Sagittarius to Capricorn 6:13 a.m.) Election day is coming up. Regardless of your politics, be sure you vote.

If you don't vote, you don't have the right to complain when the results are in. You, like the rest of the country, are up against authority.

Monday, November 3 (Moon in Capricorn) Every planet except Uranus is moving direct. This gives you the opportunity to draw on each planet's energy to achieve a particular thing.

Tuesday, November 4 (Moon in Capricorn to Aquarius 7:02 p.m.) Mercury teams up with Scorpio and your eighth house. Your love life and your sex life pick up appreciably. Your conscious mind is as intense as it gets, and you're looking for the absolute bottom line.

Wednesday, November 5 (Moon in Aquarius) The Aquarius moon always lifts your spirit and fills your head with ideas. You and friends share a camaraderie that is rare, and when you get together, you honor the best in one another.

Thursday, November 6 (Moon in Aquarius) You aren't afraid to take risks. Today, that risk involves a dream or wish you have. Follow your creative impulses and see where things lead. The results may surprise you!

Friday, November 7 (Moon in Aquarius to Pisces 5:44 a.m.) Think of the Pisces moon as a chance to clean out closets, garages, and attics. This symbolic act indicates you're making room in your life for new opportunities, relationships, goals, and experiences. Your imagination is especially strong. Use it to visualize the change you desire in your life.

Saturday, November 8 (Moon in Pisces) Since tomorrow will be a power day, prepare by deciding your priorities for the next two days. To keep things simpler, decide on professional and personal priorities. If you don't already keep track of your dreams, you should start. Your unconscious is receptive.

Sunday, November 9 (Moon in Pisces to Aries 12:27 p.m.) Your love life picks up momentum. Your restlessness to travel should be acknowledged. Either start planning your trip or pack your bag and leave ASAP!

Monday, November 10 (Moon in Aries) Feeling pressed for time? You really aren't. It's just your perception of events that makes it seem that way. It's a message, Aries, that you need to pause once in a while to reflect on where you're going and where you've been.

Tuesday, November 11 (Moon in Aries to Taurus 3:06 p.m.) This afternoon, you and an earth-sign individual review your agenda for the next few weeks. It may be that in your exuberance, you've taken on more than you can handle realistically. Cut back on your commitments.

Wednesday, November 12 (Moon in Taurus) Lots of grounding is happening for you. Venus joins Jupiter in Capricorn in your tenth house. Expect easy sailing and lots of expansion in terms of your career. There could even be a romance starting with a peer or even a boss.

Thursday, November 13 (Moon in Taurus to Gemini 3:13 p.m.) The full moon in Gemini sheds light on relationships with relatives and your community. There can be tension associated with any full moon. Be careful that you don't run yourself ragged with a lot of errands and general travel.

Friday, November 14 (Moon in Gemini) Family discussions ensue. It may be connected to a family outing, vacation, or reunion. If everyone has a different idea about what to do or when to leave, make the decision the democratic way: vote. The majority rules.

Saturday, November 15 (Moon in Gemini to Cancer 2:53 p.m.) As the days close in on Thanksgiving, you may be feeling nostalgic for childhood or for years that you remember fondly. Fight the nostalgia blues by decorating your home or office with festive colors to celebrate the holidays.

Sunday, November 16 (Moon in Cancer) Your ruler, Mars, enters Sagittarius for a transit that lasts until December 27. This period should be quite exciting for you. Every facet of your life picks up steam. If you're traveling, do so in a measured way and don't take unnecessary risks.

Monday, November 17 (Moon in Cancer to Leo 4:08 p.m.) With both the moon and your ruler in fire signs, your physical energy is excellent, and your self-confidence soars. You're quite attractive to the opposite sex and may feel like taking risks in your love life.

Tuesday, November 18 (Moon in Leo) You're in a creative mood, and you have so many options. Focus on one thing and dive in, Aries. If you're trying to complete something you started a while back, stay at it as long as it takes.

Wednesday, November 19 (Moon in Leo to Virgo 8:13 p.m.) It's all a matter of perspective. Remind yourself of that when things at work get on your nerves. You may want to leave early, in fact, and take your work home with you.

Thursday, November 20 (Moon in Virgo) Early holiday shopping is on your list. You may be buying for coworkers or employees. Try not to play favorites. You don't want anyone's feelings to get hurt.

Friday, November 21 (Moon in Virgo) A bit of forethought and consideration goes a long way toward mitigating a disagreement with someone. You're able to see the details and may think you're right. The other person can see the big picture and thinks he or she is right. Put your heads together and discover what's really right!

Saturday, November 22 (Moon in Virgo to Libra 3:20 a.m.) You're heading into Thanksgiving week with a lot on your plate. You need the time off, so don't hesitate to take it. A short trip overseas or even to some nice spot in the next state may be just the ticket.

Sunday, November 23 (Moon in Libra) Mercury joins Mars in Sagittarius until December 12. This powerful combination, combined with the moon in Libra, allows you to see relationships on a broad canvas. You're more open to discussing philosophy and spiritual issues and attempt to understand how these issues fit into your life. Your partner may be overwhelmed by all this openness!

Monday, November 24 (Moon in Libra to Scorpio 12:54 p.m.) The moon is alone in Scorpio and your eighth house. Your thoughts may turn to dark topics. Sometimes, it's worth exploring the subterranean universe of desires and weird imaginings. But if you can put this energy to work in research or use it to investigate something, you'll be happier.

Tuesday, November 25 (Moon in Scorpio) Insurance, shared bank accounts, and jointly held property play roles. If you're in the midst of a divorce negotiation, think about what you believe is fair for you. While you're mulling that over, be grateful for all you have. Happy Thanksgiving!

Wednesday, November 26 (Moon in Scorpio) After retrograding back into Sagittarius, Pluto reenters Capricorn and your tenth house. Your profession and career are about to undergo a slow but profound change. Jupiter's expansiveness helps the process along by opening doors you have never imagined.

Thursday, November 27 (Moon in Scorpio to Sagittarius 12:14 a.m.) The new moon in Sagittarius brings in fresh opportunities in education, publishing, and overseas travel. Your worldview benefits from these experiences and helps you to understand how you fit in the larger scheme of things.

Friday, November 28 (Moon in Sagittarius) Your epiphanies continue. Although you don't have the edge on truth, a few people around you may believe that you think you do. Convert people by listening to what they have to say.

Saturday, November 29 (Moon in Sagittarius to Capricorn 12:48 p.m.) As you head into the busy holiday season, you may need to take a few minutes to arrange your priorities for the month. This includes giving thoughtful consideration about gifts for the special people in your life.

Sunday, November 30 (Moon in Capricorn) Every planet is moving direct. This allows you to move forward on an even keel, and to use your talents and abilities as best you can.

DECEMBER 2008

Monday, December 1 (Moon in Capricorn) If the weather is disagreeable where you live, figure out how you can take a business trip to someplace that's warmer or colder. It depends on what you're looking for. If you're self-employed, perhaps this trip could be for research!

Tuesday, December 2 (Moon in Capricorn to Aquarius 1:45 a.m.) With Venus still in your tenth house and the moon moving into Aquarius and your eleventh house, you should get help from friends on a professional project. Don't hesitate to delegate, if you have to.

Wednesday, December 3 (Moon in Aquarius) Jupiter and Saturn form a harmonious angle to each other, bringing structure and backbone to your professional endeavors. This angle favors health and fitness matters. If you don't have a regular exercise routine, start one. An aerobics class might be the way to go.

Thursday, December 4 (Moon in Aquarius to Pisces 1:24 p.m.) You're preparing for the new moon in Aries, which is coming up in a couple days. Spend some time practicing some feng shui in your house. A trusted friend or family member has information or insights that will help.

Friday, December 5 (Moon in Pisces) You uncover information about yourself or someone close to you that may be upsetting. Take it in stride, mull things over, and decide what to do about it. On other fronts, one of your family members or a close friend provides emotional stability.

Saturday, December 6 (Moon in Pisces to Aries 9:45 p.m.) Your intuition is strong and becomes progressively more so as the moon enters your sign. By late this evening, you're in a very good place within yourself. You are completely certain of what to do and when to do it.

Sunday, December 7 (Moon in Aries) Venus enters Aquarius and your eleventh house and remains there through the end of the year. This transit could spark a romance with a friend or someone you meet through one of the groups with whom you associate. If the relationship begins under a moon in your sign, it should be filled with passion and excitement.

Monday, December 8 (Moon in Aries) It's a power day. You call the shots, and everyone else falls into line behind you. It's time to pitch a project, idea, or agenda.

Tuesday, December 9 (Moon in Aries to Taurus 1:53 a.m.) You have an impulse to buy something expensive, either as a gift for someone else or for yourself. Regardless of whom the gift is for, it's wise to take stock of your finances to see if you can really afford it. If you can't, that's fine. You'll find a backup!

Wednesday, December 10 (Moon in Taurus) An unexpected check arrives. It could be repayment on a loan you made to a friend or family member, or perhaps a royalty check or an early Christmas gift. You may decide to send out holiday e-cards this year and conserve on paper and postage.

Thursday, December 11 (Moon in Taurus to Gemini 2:34 a.m.) You and your sister or brother or a neighborhood friend hit the mall. If the chain stores strike you as too much of the same, look for small, independent shops with unique gifts. A child or family member may get too curious about all the stuff you've brought home. Hide it!

Friday, December 12 (Moon in Gemini) With Mercury in your tenth house through the end of the year, you have the gift of gab you need to solidify your professional position and to convince skeptics you're the person to head up a new committee or job. The full moon in your third house indicates that something you've been working on in your community reaches fruition.

Saturday, December 13 (Moon in Gemini to Cancer 1:41 a.m.) Even if your mind isn't on work, use this window of opportunity to move your agenda ahead. You're also in a good place for planning your strategy. Plan long-range. Be visionary.

Sunday, December 14 (Moon in Cancer) Family and your personal past are part of the day's emotions and events. That's not surprising, considering the proximity of the holidays. Touch base with people in your past. If there are long-standing disagreements, resolve them. Forgive and forget and move on.

Monday, December 15 (Moon in Cancer to Leo 1:23 a.m.) Romance drifts in the air. Whether you choose to act is entirely up to you. Ask yourself whether you're interested in a flirtation or commitment. Then, depending on what you think this relationship could be, make your decision.

Tuesday, December 16 (Moon in Leo) You're being noticed wherever you go. Even strangers can tell there's something special going on in your life. Perhaps you and your partner have decided to start a family or to go into business together. Whatever is making you glow, revel in it, Aries.

Wednesday, December 17 (Moon in Leo to Virgo 3:36 a.m.) You and a coworker are preparing for an office party and may be doing some last-minute shopping. You attend to the details. Let your fellow shopper initiate the action.

Thursday, December 18 (Moon in Virgo) The moon joins Saturn in Virgo, in your sixth house. Your work probably revolves around the holidays. You may be doing more last-minute gift buying or shifting the holiday schedule around. If you're going out of town, recheck your schedule.

Friday, December 19 (Moon in Virgo to Libra 9:23 a.m.) The emphasis is on your partnerships. Whether you're dealing with a romantic or a business partner, a sibling or a friend, you're called upon to cooperate, be attentive, and to listen to what others have to say.

Saturday, December 20 (Moon in Libra) The festivities are beginning! Whether people are coming to your place or you're going out of town, everyone is in a glorious mood. You're coming up on a new moon in Gemini on December 27, so you may be feeling its impact already. New friends, more contact with siblings, and involvement in your community are the highlights.

Sunday, December 21 (Moon in Libra to Scorpio 6:37 p.m.) Passions surface. Positive or negative, things are intense, edgy. Try to keep your cool, Aries. In the long run, what you don't say may be far more important than what you do say.

Monday, December 22 (Moon in Scorpio) With Mars in Sagittarius, Venus in Aquarius, Mercury in Capricorn, and the moon in Scorpio, all four elements are represented among the inner, more personal planets. This makes for a balanced day. You're able to act decisively, plan, intuit, and visualize.

Tuesday, December 23 (Moon in Scorpio) If anyone in your family or among your close friends is a Capricorn born today, throw the person a great party. Even if no one in your group was born today, have a pre-Christmas party that people will be talking about for months to come. Record the event with digital photos so you can e-mail the memories to people after the holidays.

Wednesday, December 24 (Moon in Scorpio to Sagittarius 6:14 a.m.) Let bygones be bygones. They say that the holidays can be stressful. Buck that trend, Aries. You have a grasp of the dynamics of your family and close friends.

Thursday, December 25 (Moon in Sagittarius) Merry Christmas. However you celebrate, your mood is excellent; your confidence and optimism are steady. You and a family member or friend may brainstorm ideas related to publishing or higher education.

Friday, December 26 (Moon in Sagittarius to Capricorn 6:57 p.m.) The moon joins Jupiter and Pluto in Capricorn, your tenth house. You probably aren't thinking much about your career or work. But in some way, shape, or form, an expansion is happening with your professional opportunities. It's as if your image of yourself is undergoing a steady transformation.

Saturday, December 27 (Moon in Capricorn) Mars joins the lineup in Capricorn. Despite the fact that it's Saturday, the pressure of four planets in your career house is bound to spur you to action. You may want to update your e-mail list or contact your network of professional contacts to wish everyone happy holidays. Take a step related to your career.

Sunday, December 28 (Moon in Capricorn) Yesterday's action shows results. Take advantage of the season's generous spirit to advance your pet project. Take calculated risks.

Monday, December 29 (Moon in Capricorn to Aquarius 7:44 a.m.) There's something fitting about the year ending with the moon in Aquarius. Your thoughts and concerns turn to those in the world who lack the basics: food, medical care, education, and civil rights. What can your group of friends and contacts do to ease other people's pain?

Tuesday, December 30 (Moon in Aquarius) You're preparing for tomorrow night's festivities. While you're at it, make up a list of goals. Be sure they're realistic so that you don't get discouraged. If, for instance, you want to lose twenty pounds, create goals that are incremental: five pounds in a month, ten pounds in two months.

Wednesday, December 31 (Moon in Aquarius) Saturn, the planet that governs the laws of physical existence, turns retrograde. It's not the greatest way to head into 2009. However, if you use its energy in the most positive way, you can look within to find the structures you need in your life.

HAPPY NEW YEAR!

SYDNEY OMARR

Born on August 5, 1926, in Philadelphia, Pennsylvania, Sydney Omarr was the only person ever given full-time duty in the U.S. Army as an astrologer. He is regarded as the most erudite astrologer of our time and the best known, through his syndicated column and his radio and television programs (he was Merv Griffin's "resident astrologer"). Omarr has been called the most "knowledgeable astrologer since Evangeline Adams." His forecasts of Nixon's downfall, the end of World War II in mid-August of 1945, the assassination of John F. Kennedy, Roosevelt's election to a fourth term and his death in office . . . these and many others are on the record and quoted enough to be considered "legendary."

ABOUT THE SERIES

This is one of a series of twelve *Sydney Omarr® Day-by-Day Astrological Guides* for the signs of 2008. For questions and comments about the book, go to www.tjmacgregor.com.